Mastering Chef Provisioning

Learn Chef Provisioning like a boss and finally own your infrastructure

Earl Waud

BIRMINGHAM - MUMBAI

Mastering Chef Provisioning

First published: June 2016

Production reference: 1230616

Published by Packt Publishing Ltd.
Livery Place
35 Livery Street
Birmingham B3 2PB, UK.

ISBN 978-1-78588-891-5

www.packtpub.com

Credits

Author
Earl Waud

Reviewer
Federico Gimenez

Commissioning Editor
Sarah Crofton

Acquisition Editor
Rahul Nair

Content Development Editor
Mamata Walker

Technical Editor
Pramod Kumavat

Copy Editor
Dipti Mankame

Project Coordinator
Kinjal Bari

Proofreader
Safis Editing

Indexer
Monica Ajmera Mehta

Graphics
Kirk D'Penha

Production Coordinator
Shantanu N. Zagade

Cover Work
Shantanu N. Zagade

Foreword

First and foremost, if you have this book in your hands, congratulations! You are part of the top talent pool in the IT industry, focusing on systems management and provisioning at scale using powerful automation tools.

I have been in the industry for more than 12 years, implementing and leading next generation platform architecture and engineering efforts in world-class enterprise data centers hosting tens of thousands of servers. Throughout my professional journey, I've had a chance to be part of many paradigm shifts, including virtualization, the cloud era, software-defined data centers, and the latest but not the least, infrastructure as a code.

It was during one of these paradigm shifts when I met the author of this book, Earl Waud. Shortly after meeting, and after spilling a cup of coffee on his notebook, we became very close both professionally and as friends.

Earl has always impressed me with how he cares about people, how he values relationships, while still being very professional, methodical, and self-driven to achieve any goal. Additionally, Earl is not short of innovations, driving them all the way from the back of a napkin into highly available multi-data center production deployments that successfully address today's biggest IT challenges. When you combine these traits with his tremendous experience, it becomes a very effective recipe for success both personally and professionally. *Mastering Chef Provisioning* is the latest example of that success.

In today's IT world, we are experiencing another paradigm shift. In order to support ever-evolving business needs, traditional IT must adopt critical skillsets around infrastructure automation and orchestration. Although there are numerous automation tools available, many professionals have chosen to use Chef because it is one of the most effective platforms to successfully implement provisioning system automation and orchestration.

One of the fundamentally critical and most repeated functions of IT in mission-critical environments is provisioning compute systems. Because of this, provisioning is one of the major targets of automation in IT. In *Mastering Chef Provisioning* by Earl Waud, the author clearly depicts how you can strategize, design, and implement provisioning automation with Chef across all major hosting platforms anywhere from your own data center all the way out to Amazon Web Services Public Cloud. With the skillset that you will gain from this book, you will be able to implement your own custom provisioning automation to deliver systems rapidly and accurately for all your business needs.

Considering that we are in the middle of another paradigm shift, *Mastering Chef Provisioning* is one of the most important references that you can have in your library. As a matter of fact, I have already begun using it as a guideline to aid our provisioning automation efforts in delivering thousands of systems in a very short period of time.

I am very confident that you will enjoy this book, and by mastering the techniques within its pages, you will learn how to provision systems effectively with Chef, saving you tremendous amounts of time in your day-to-day operations and reaffirming your position as part of top talent pool in the IT industry.

I would like to conclude by saying thank you to the author of this book, Earl Waud, for leading the way by setting an example for the rest of the world, both at a professional level and a personal level. "We always win!" my friend.

Mert Cubukcuoglu
Senior Manager, Intuit Inc.

About the Author

Earl Waud is a virtualization development professional with more than 10 years of focused industry experience, creating innovative solutions for hypervisor provisioning, management, and automation. He is an expert in aligning engineering strategy with organizational vision and goals, and delivering highly scalable and user friendly virtualization environments.

With more than 20 years of experience developing customer-facing and corporate IT software solutions, he has a proven track record of delivering high-caliber and on-time technology solutions that significantly impact business results.

Earl lives in San Diego, California. He is blessed with a beautiful wife, Patti, and three amazing daughters, Alexis, Daniella, and Madison.

Currently, Earl is a senior software engineer with Intuit Inc., a company that creates business and financial management solutions that simplify the business of life for small businesses, consumers, and accounting professionals.

Earl can be found online at `http://sandiegoearl.com`.

Acknowledgments

Creating this book was a much larger undertaking than I imagined, and as a result, I owe a debt of gratitude to many.

Thank you to my Heavenly Father. Thank you for my days and for my many blessings. Thank you for this book. Thank you for the opportunity to learn and grow as I created its content. Thank you for allowing me to get it right. And thank you for blessing all who read it so that they can find the solutions they need. I love Thee very much. Thank you.

Thank you to my amazing wife Patti. Thank you, honey, for your patience with me and for being okay with all the time I had to invest to create this book. You carried a lot of the weight of our household, so I could research, write, and revise the information within these pages, and without your support, this book would not exist. Thank you for your confidence in me, which helped me get through some moments of self-doubt. And thank you for loving me. I love you very much. Thank you.

Thank you to my daughter Madison. Thank you, Madison, for your light and for your faith in me. Thank you for seeing me the way that you do. Thank you for being willing to give up a lot of our father-daughter time over the past few months. I know how precious that time is, and I hope we can catch up on some of it before you go off to college. I love you very much. Thank you.

Thank you to my daughter Alexis. Thank you, Lexi, for believing in me. And thank you for the confidence and pride you have for me. Thank you for having faith in my ability to be a writer. I love you very much. Thank you.

Thank you to my daughter Daniella. Thank you, Dani, for your energy and unique perspective. Thank you for your support and your belief in me and my ability to write this book. I love you very much. Thank you.

Thank you to my friend Mert Cubukcuoglu. Thank you, Mert, for your friendship and trust. Thank you for your confidence in me and my ability to write a book about Chef provisioning. And thank you for writing the book's Foreword. Thank you.

Thank you to my friends at work. Thank you Ray Eivaz, Barry Ruffner, Wayne Chatham, Achal Shah, Amy Tam, Angela Bouchard, Mai Lubega, Thy Guintivano, Mike Sharp, and the many others at Intuit that I work with every day. Thank you for your excitement about and interest in my book. Thank you for expressing your belief that I could do it. And thank you for your eagerness to read it when it comes out. Thank you Jay Grissom for being one for the first to preorder your copy. Thank you Michel Cole for being the first to request that I write a second book. Thank you.

Thank you to my friend Tom "Big Al" Schreiter. Thank you, Tom, for suggesting that I start writing books and for being such a great example by taking your own advice and creating a fantastic set of training books. And thank you for your excitement about my book. Thank you.

Thank you to my reviewer Federico Gimenez. Thank you, Federico, for poring over the chapters of this book and making sure I've presented the most accurate content and examples possible. Thank you.

Thank you to my Packt Publishing team. Thank you Mamata Walkar, Rahul Nair, Pramod Kumavat, Sachin Karnani, and Kinjal Bari. Without you, this book would never have happened. Thanks for allowing me to officially become an author and for making sure that my book is a good as it can be. Thank you.

"I can no other answer make, but, thanks, and thanks."

– William Shakespeare

About the Reviewer

Federico Gimenez works currently as a software quality engineer for Canonical in the Snappy team. He has an extensive background supporting agile teams in all the product delivery steps, focusing on applying software engineering solutions to multidisciplinary problems. For the past 7 years, he has also contributed to several open source projects, including Docker, Kubernetes, OpenStack, Ceph, and Debian.

www.PacktPub.com

eBooks, discount offers, and more

Did you know that Packt offers eBook versions of every book published, with PDF and ePub files available? You can upgrade to the eBook version at `www.PacktPub.com` and as a print book customer, you are entitled to a discount on the eBook copy. Get in touch with us at `customercare@packtpub.com` for more details.

At `www.PacktPub.com`, you can also read a collection of free technical articles, sign up for a range of free newsletters and receive exclusive discounts and offers on Packt books and eBooks.

`https://www2.packtpub.com/books/subscription/packtlib`

Do you need instant solutions to your IT questions? PacktLib is Packt's online digital book library. Here, you can search, access, and read Packt's entire library of books.

Why subscribe?

- Fully searchable across every book published by Packt
- Copy and paste, print, and bookmark content
- On demand and accessible via a web browser

Table of Contents

Preface

Today, the DevOps Engineer is responsible for delivering infrastructure that is rock solid and consistently configured every time. What's more, these superheroes need to supply the infrastructure rapidly and at scale, often to the tune of dozens or even hundreds of identically configured systems.

The days of doing this superhero work manually are long gone. Now the only question is "which superpower will best serve our heroes in their time of greatest need?" The answer is the power that can transform their infrastructure into code so that it can be managed the same way as any other source code-based project. Chef is that superpower.

And *Mastering Chef Provisioning* is your secret decoder ring for learning how to use that power to provision containers, servers, and networking devices across the universe of hosting targets, including your local workstation, the traditional data center, and in the clouds.

In this book, you will learn the secrets of how to automate and document every aspect of your infrastructure. You will find the best practices for describing your infrastructure as code. You will learn to automate the provisioning of everything from the smallest container deployed to your local workstation to the biggest distributed application clusters deployed to the cloud, all in a single bound.

This book will help you, the DevOps superhero, to create a perfect model system where everything is represented as code beneath your fingertips. You will be able to make the best possible use of your resources, avoid redundancy, and always be ready to scale — faster than a speeding bullet. And you don't have to leave your home planet, get bitten by a radioactive spider, or fall in a vat of toxic waste to do it.

But as the great Stan Lee wrote, "*With great power …*".

What this book covers

Chapter 1, Setting Up a Development Environment on Your Workstation, reviews Chef basics and covers the installation of our Chef workstation and an on-premise Chef Server.

Chapter 2, Knife Tooling and Plugins, shows how to get all the help you need with knife, explores using both common and uncommon knife subcommands, and teaches you how to create your own custom knife plugins.

Chapter 3, Leveraging Roles, Environments, and Policies, examines Chef roles, environments, and organizations, covers the attribute precedence hierarchy, and investigates the exciting new Chef policy feature.

Chapter 4, Custom Resources, introduces the custom resource, explores how the custom resource has improved upon LWRPs and HWRPs, and shows how to create and use your own custom resources.

Chapter 5, Provisioning in the Traditional Data Center, presents provisioning in the traditional data center, covering provisioning to VMware vSphere, OpenStack, VMware's desktop hypervisors, and common network devices, and teaches how to deploy your own development OpenStack environment.

Chapter 6, Provisioning in the Cloud, presents provisioning in the cloud, covering provisioning to Amazon AWS, Microsoft Azure, Google Compute Platform, and Linode, and shows how to provision containers in Docker.

Chapter 7, Test-Driven Development, teaches how to use several of the tools available to implement a test-driven development cycle for infrastructure code development, including RuboCop, Foodcritic, ChefSpec, and Test Kitchen.

Chapter 8, Using Chef Provisioning, reveals how to use the ChefDK feature known as Chef provisioning, providing examples for Vagrant, AWS, and Docker.

What you need for this book

The examples in this book were written with the ChefDK version 0.12.0. Examples were tested primarily on Mac OS X and Ubuntu workstations, although all examples should work equally well on other flavors of Linux as well as on Microsoft Windows.

Who this book is for

This book is for software engineers, system administrators, and DevOps Engineers who need to quickly deliver reliably consistent infrastructure at scale. You are expected to have intermediate experience with Chef and Ruby and will be reading this book to advance your knowledge and take your skillset to the next level.

Conventions

In this book, you will find a number of text styles that distinguish between different kinds of information. Here are some examples of these styles and an explanation of their meaning.

Code words in text, database table names, folder names, filenames, file extensions, pathnames, dummy URLs, and user input are shown as follows: "What this error message is probably indicating is that there is no valid host entry in the /etc/hosts file."

A block of code is set as follows:

```
# add a rule for ssh
neutron security-group-rule-create $ID \
  --direction ingress --ethertype IPv4 \
  --protocol tcp --port-range-min 22 --port-range-max 22 \
  --remote-ip-prefix 0.0.0.0/0
```

When we wish to draw your attention to a particular part of a code block, the relevant lines or items are set in bold:

```
# add a rule for ssh
neutron security-group-rule-create $ID \
  --direction ingress --ethertype IPv4 \
  --protocol tcp --port-range-min 22 --port-range-max 22 \
  --remote-ip-prefix 0.0.0.0/0
```

Any command-line input or output is written as follows:

```
$ sudo knife openstack image list
Name                      ID                                     Snapshot
cirros-0.3.4-x86_64-uec   84dff654-7f0d-45c8-a20b-b08c0ef39fd1   no
```

New terms and **important words** are shown in bold. Words that you see on the screen, for example, in menus or dialog boxes, appear in the text like this: "Click on the **Continue** button to advance the installation."

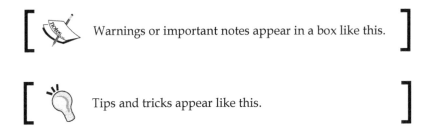

Warnings or important notes appear in a box like this.

Tips and tricks appear like this.

Reader feedback

Feedback from our readers is always welcome. Let us know what you think about this book—what you liked or disliked. Reader feedback is important for us as it helps us develop titles that you will really get the most out of.

To send us general feedback, simply e-mail feedback@packtpub.com, and mention the book's title in the subject of your message.

If there is a topic that you have expertise in and you are interested in either writing or contributing to a book, see our author guide at www.packtpub.com/authors.

Customer support

Now that you are the proud owner of a Packt book, we have a number of things to help you to get the most from your purchase.

Downloading the example code

You can download the example code files for this book from your account at http://www.packtpub.com. If you purchased this book elsewhere, you can visit http://www.packtpub.com/support and register to have the files e-mailed directly to you.

You can download the code files by following these steps:

1. Log in or register to our website using your e-mail address and password.
2. Hover the mouse pointer on the **SUPPORT** tab at the top.
3. Click on **Code Downloads & Errata**.

4. Enter the name of the book in the **Search** box.

5. Select the book for which you're looking to download the code files.

6. Choose from the drop-down menu where you purchased this book from.

7. Click on **Code Download**.

You can also download the code files by clicking on the **Code Files** button on the book's webpage at the Packt Publishing website. This page can be accessed by entering the book's name in the **Search** box. Please note that you need to be logged in to your Packt account.

Once the file is downloaded, please make sure that you unzip or extract the folder using the latest version of:

- WinRAR / 7-Zip for Windows
- Zipeg / iZip / UnRarX for Mac
- 7-Zip / PeaZip for Linux

The code bundle for the book is also hosted on GitHub at `https://github.com/PacktPublishing/Mastering-Chef-Provisioning`. We also have other code bundles from our rich catalog of books and videos available at `https://github.com/PacktPublishing/`. Check them out!

Errata

Although we have taken every care to ensure the accuracy of our content, mistakes do happen. If you find a mistake in one of our books—maybe a mistake in the text or the code—we would be grateful if you could report this to us. By doing so, you can save other readers from frustration and help us improve subsequent versions of this book. If you find any errata, please report them by visiting `http://www.packtpub.com/submit-errata`, selecting your book, clicking on the **Errata Submission Form** link, and entering the details of your errata. Once your errata are verified, your submission will be accepted and the errata will be uploaded to our website or added to any list of existing errata under the Errata section of that title.

To view the previously submitted errata, go to `https://www.packtpub.com/books/content/support` and enter the name of the book in the search field. The required information will appear under the **Errata** section.

Piracy

Piracy of copyrighted material on the Internet is an ongoing problem across all media. At Packt, we take the protection of our copyright and licenses very seriously. If you come across any illegal copies of our works in any form on the Internet, please provide us with the location address or website name immediately so that we can pursue a remedy.

Please contact us at `copyright@packtpub.com` with a link to the suspected pirated material.

We appreciate your help in protecting our authors and our ability to bring you valuable content.

Questions

If you have a problem with any aspect of this book, you can contact us at `questions@packtpub.com`, and we will do our best to address the problem.

1

Setting Up a Development Environment on Your Workstation

In today's fast-paced IT world, it is a requirement to deliver infrastructure at warp speed. There's really only one way to achieve this requirement, and that is through automation.

One of the best paths to infrastructure automation is via Chef. Using Chef, you can turn your infrastructure into code. With infrastructure as code, you can automate the way you build, deploy, and manage all of it. Using Chef, your infrastructure becomes very consistent, very duplicable, and version-controlled. Using Chef, you can easily test your infrastructure setup and configuration. With Chef, you can become an IT superhero!

In this chapter, we're going to detail the setup and configuration of a complete development system or workstation. The main focus will be centered on deploying the **Chef Development Kit** (**ChefDK**) and preparing the various components of a development environment. The chapter also includes suggestions for additional tools to round out the DevOps toolbox. However, before we dive into ChefDK, we will fly through a high-level review of the what-and-how of Chef so that we are all on the same page.

> *"If you wish to make an apple pie truly from scratch, you must first invent the universe."* – Carl Sagan

Here is what you will find in this chapter:

- Filling in the gaps in your Chef knowledge base
- Exploring ChefDK
- Installing ChefDK
- Setting up a standard Chef repo
- What else do you need?
- Using chef-apply

Re-introducing Chef

If you are reading this book, then you've probably been working with Chef for some time now, and you know the many benefits it brings. You may also know that, in the past, it was a somewhat daunting task to set up a new Chef workstation. You had to download and install Chef, then download and install a variety of community tools, and make sure that all the versions were compatible and configured correctly.

Today, a lot of the work is done for you via the ChefDK. Once you install it, you have a basic workstation setup and are ready to create, modify, and test Chef code.

What version of the Chef tools do I use?

To make it easy to follow along with the contents, let's go over the versions of the tools that will be used throughout this book.

In March 2016, chef.io announced the release of ChefDK 0.12.0, which includes Chef client 12.8.1. As this is the latest version at the time of writing, I will be using it as the version for this book. All of the examples shown will be based on this version of the ChefDK and Chef client. This is very exciting because a lot of really exciting changes are in this release, including Policies and the transition from Resource Providers to Custom Resources.

Currently, there are ChefDK installers available for Mac OS, Windows OS, and Linux OS (RHEL, Debian, and Ubuntu). In the examples within this book, the workstation used will be Mac OS X, so the ChefDK version will be the Mac OS version.

With the many choices available to use for your Chef Server mode, including Hosted Chef Server, Private Chef Server, Open Source Chef Server, and Chef-Solo, it would be difficult to show examples for each mode. Therefore, the majority of examples you'll see in this book will be based on using the Hosted Chef Server mode. Later in this chapter, I will briefly review the installation and setup of a Private Chef Server onto an Ubuntu server, for readers who want to use Chef Server on-premise.

Which OS do I use for my workstation? Everyone has their own, nearly religious, choice for the best workstation platform. However, it would make this book way too long to provide examples for the major OSes alone. Therefore, to keep the focus on Chef content and not on the differences between workstation implementations, I will be using a Mac OS X (Yosemite version 10.10) workstation for the examples. I may at times show additional examples on a Windows or Ubuntu workstation where the differences are significant and worth the extra detail. And for the nodes used in the examples, a variety of OSes will be represented in the hope of having some overlap with the reader's real environment.

References

- IT infrastructure automation begins at `https://www.chef.io/`
- Additional opportunities to learn Chef can be found at `https://learn.chef.io/`

Filling in the gaps in your Chef knowledge base

First things first. Let's have a quick, high-level review of Chef. A Chef 101 class, if you will. The plan here is to make sure that all readers are on the same page with me so that the rest of the book will be easier to follow and benefit from. If you are already a Chef ninja, you can probably skip right on past this section and start exploring the ChefDK in the next section. Otherwise, let's audit our 101 class now.

Major pieces of a Chef puzzle

Chef is a ruby framework, and its main purpose is to facilitate the automation, reuse, and documentation of server configurations. Chef allows you to treat server configuration just like any other type of software code.

There are three major components of this framework for almost all corporate-level Chef deployments—the workstation, the Chef Server, and the nodes. Let's talk a little about each of these components:

- **Workstations**: The Chef workstation is, as the name would suggest, where the real "work" is done. This is where developers will create their infrastructure code. It's also where they will test their creations. The workstation is where developers will interact with their source code control systems. It is where genius is born. It is where the "desired state" of nodes is defined via code.

- **Chef servers**: The Chef server is a database-backed web API server with a browsable user interface. It is like the matrix housing the hive mind of the Chef universe. The "work" created in the workstation is uploaded into the Chef server so that it can be used to automate the configuration of the many nodes. It stands ready to provide the desired state information to the Chef client on a node so that it can bring that node into alignment or convergence with the desired state of configuration.

- **Nodes**: Nodes are the ultimate targets of the "work" that's been created on the workstation and uploaded to the Chef server. A node is where the automation occurs via the Chef client. Nodes are transformed into the desired state configuration. Commonly, nodes are servers, either virtual or physical, but a node can be anything that needs to be configured, such as a Docker container, or a network device such as a switch or router. Every node has a unique name, such as the FQDN of a server.

The Chef client

The Chef client is the tool that is deployed to all nodes and used to configure or reconfigure the node to its desired state. The Chef client is what executes the automation. It is the magician that, through the magic of Chef, transforms an ordinary server into the desired state node that the developer defined back on his workstation.

The Ohai Chef tool

Ohai is the tool that gathers information about a node. Information such as platform details, operating system data, and processor information is made available to the Chef client so that the latter can have the know-how to bring the node to the desired state. Ohai is executed at the beginning of a Chef client run to gather the state of the node. At the end of a Chef client run, all of the data gathered by Ohai (usually) is shared as node data with the Chef server, and the shared data is available for searches done against the Chef server. Ohai can be extended via plugins, and we'll take a look at that in a later chapter.

Recipes and cookbooks

Recipes are the building blocks used to define the desired states. Recipes are files of ruby code that define the commands to be run on nodes. They are like blueprints used to "build" a node. Recipes are collections of Chef resources. We will explain more about Chef resources shortly.

Cookbooks are collections of related recipes, templates, files, and custom resources. They provide organization and versioning for recipes. Each unique version of a cookbook represents unique sets of functionality, such as bug fixes or added features.

Cookbooks define a scenario, such as everything needed to install and configure apt-docker or Sublime text, and they contain all the elements needed to support the defined scenario.

Recipes and cookbooks provide modularity and let you easily reuse code.

Chef run lists

A "run list" is, as the name would suggest, a list of, and the sequence for, the recipes, cookbooks, and policies (spoiler alert!) to be applied to a node. A run list contains all of the information required to configure a node to a desired state. That is, a Chef run list describes the desired final state of the node. It is important to note that, if the node's state already matches what the resources in the run list describe, then no action will be taken to change the node's state.

Chef roles

Roles are functional groupings of recipes and cookbooks used to describe the full blueprint needed for a node to become everything it is intended to be. Roles are reusable configurations, and they can be applied to multiple nodes to make functionally identical servers, such as a farm of web servers.

Chef resources

Chef resources are statements of configuration policy. They are defined in recipes and take actions through the Chef client to put the node into the desired state. Chef resources have some types: Package, Template, Service, and so on. They have a name and parameters. Also, Chef resources can send notifications to other resources.

Chef resources define what we want to happen to a node. They don't say how to do it. The how to do it is left to the providers which are platform-specific. That is to say, the way you install a package will be different depending on the OS, and the provider determines the correct way to do it—the "how". The Chef resource simply defines the "what," such as "install ntp".

- **Package**: This contains software or applications, such as apache, ntp, and cron, and the action to be performed on that software or application, such as "install".
- **Template**: These are files with place-holders for attributes that are transformed into configuration files for package installation and execution.
- **Service**: This is the installed executable of the package and the actions that the executable can perform, such as start, stop, or restart. Service also defines whether the software or application is launched at node startup.

More things to consider

Apart from the three types of Chef resources we saw earlier, let's look at some other important aspects of recipes and cookbooks.

- **Attributes**: These are variables used in recipes and templates. Generally speaking, a recipe will represent the pattern used in configuration. The attributes provide the specific details for the recipes. For example, the recipe will say "configure the port" and the attribute will say "which port?". Attributes can be provided in a large variety of places, such as cookbooks, roles, and environments. As such, there is a necessity for an order of precedence. There is a complete description of attribute precedence on the chef.io site. You can find it at `https://docs.chef.io/attributes.html`.

- **Order matters**: When creating recipes, the resources need to be listed in order. First, the package, then the template, and finally the service; when creating run lists, the order of policies, roles, cookbooks, and recipes is the order in which they are evaluated. Any recipe that appears in a run list (or as a dependency of a policy, role, or cookbook) more than once will only be evaluated the first time.

- **Convergence and idempotence**: A Chef client run converges the node into the desired state. What this means is that only things that do not equal the desired state on the node are modified during the Chef client run. If, for example, the recipe says that the desired state of the node is to have the ntp demon running, the `ntp` package is already installed on the node, and the ntp demon is already running, then Chef client will take no action to install or start ntp.

Chef resources are idempotent. That is, applying them more than once results in the same outcome every time. If no inputs related to the resource have changed, then applying that resource won't change anything after the first application. In fact, if none of the inputs have changed, the corresponding commands don't even get run.

This is actually one of the most important concepts and features of Chef.

Data bags

Data bags are containers for information that is not tied to a specific node. Data bags are the global variables of a Chef server. They can be used in recipes and can be searched like node data via the Chef server. One common use case for data bags is for user and group information. Items in a data bag can be encrypted. This allows secret information to be stored in them, for example, passwords.

Environments

Environments allow you to define specific cookbook versions that are applied to a given set of nodes. They permit you to model the stages of your infrastructure workflow, that is, Development, Test, Stage, and Production. By identifying specific nodes as Development, and other nodes as Production, for example, you can apply different versions of your cookbooks to the nodes based on their environment membership.

The Chef supermarket

The supermarket is a site that provides shared cookbooks. There is a public supermarket that contains community-created and -maintained cookbooks. This site is hosted by Chef and is available at `https://supermarket.chef.io`. In addition to the public supermarket, anyone can create and manage a private supermarket that can host cookbooks intended for the private consumption of you and your organization.

 It is always best practice to do a thorough code review of any cookbooks obtained from the public community supermarket before using them in your production environments.

Chef Development Kit

The ChefDK contains everything you need to start working with Chef on a workstation. It provides all the tools that a developer needs to create and modify cookbooks and upload them to a Chef server. We are going to go into a lot of detail regarding the ChefDK later in this chapter.

You can jump ahead to the ChefDK sections now, or you can read on and learn how to set up your very own private Chef server.

Setting up an on-premise (private) Chef Server

Many companies will have strong reasons to keep their infrastructure configuration data within the firewalls of their datacenters, and Chef server has a mode for that. It's called on-premise or private Chef server.

There are some real benefits to using an in-house solution, including control. With a private installation, you have full control of your system, and for some that reason is enough. But there are additional considerations such as performance. Since a private Chef server will likely be physically closer to the node's network, Chef client runs will be faster. For example, if Chef is used in a load-based on-demand server deployment solution, then the extra speed the private Chef server can provide when converging your new Nodes can make all the difference in meeting the load demand in time.

With all the reasons to use an on-premise Chef server, there is a downside: you are responsible for the deployment, configuration, and maintenance of your Chef servers.

To get you started, let's take a look at the deployment and initial configuration of a standalone private Chef server now. We'll go through the steps to get a new Chef server set up on an Ubuntu 14.04 server.

The first step is downloading the required Chef server installer version. Visit the Chef server page at this link `https://downloads.chef.io/chef-server/` to find and download the version you will use for your installation.

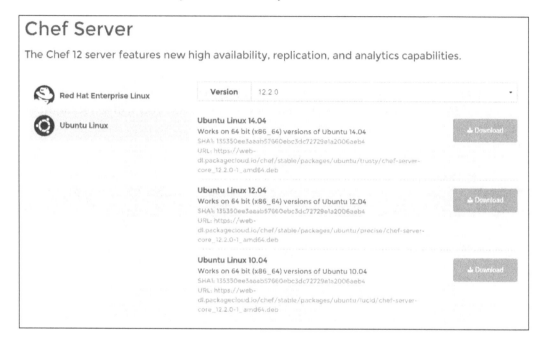

Next, you will want to transfer the downloaded installer package to your soon to be Chef server.

Once the installer is available on your server, you will want to install the package. The command to do this is:

```
sudo dpkg -i chef-server-core_12.2.0-1_amd64.deb
```

Once the Chef server package has been installed onto your server, the first thing to do is start the Chef server services. The command to do this is:

```
sudo chef-server-ctl reconfigure
```

The Chef server startup does a lot of work and as such you will see a lot of activity displayed as the setup progresses. When the startup command finally finishes successfully (a few minutes later; you might want to get a cup of coffee), the result will be a running Chef server.

Do you get an error in the nginx.rb file during the reconfigure?

The private Chef server has a dependency on the nginx cookbook, and in some cases you may experience an error when this dependency is resolved. The error may look something like this:

"common_name nil currently does not overwrite the value of common_ name."

What this error message is probably indicating is that there is no valid host entry in the /etc/hosts file. You should check that file, and if there isn't a valid entry, create one.

Are we there yet? Well, we do have a Chef server up-and-running, but it is not much good to us yet. If you browse to your new Chef server, you will see something like this:

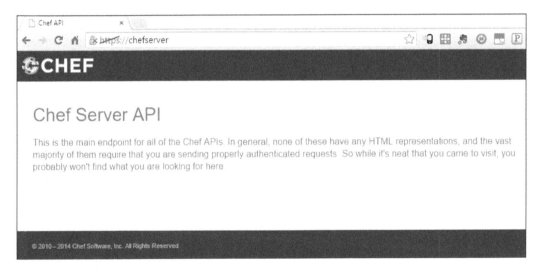

That is a good start, but there is still work to be done. Next up is creating your first Chef user on the Chef server with the user-create command. That user will be the initial Chef admin for the server. The format of the user-create command is:

```
sudo chef-server-ctl user-create user_name first_name last_name email
password --filename FILE_NAME
```

Here is an example of what that command might look like:

```
sudo chef-server-ctl user-create earlwaud Earl Waud earl@sandiegoearl.com
MyPassword99 --filename /home/earlwaud/earlwaud.pem
```

Here is what it looks like when you issue the command on your Chef server (along with the `user-show` command):

```
root@chefserver: ~                                                    —   □   ×

root@chefserver:~# chef-server-ctl user-create earlwaud Earl Waud earl@sandiegoearl.com MyPa
ssword99 --filename /home/earlwaud/earlwaud.pem
root@chefserver:~# chef-server-ctl user-show earlwaud
display_name: Earl Waud
email:        earl@sandiegoearl.com
first_name:   Earl
last_name:    Waud
middle_name:
public_key:   -----BEGIN PUBLIC KEY-----
MIIBIjANBgkqhkiG9w0BAQEFAAOCAQ8AMIIBCgKCAQEAyrZO8nqs8akRfkbWVIpR
KjLVixsIzLrlA2rYXK0T5BILy09A+CSCTJFX3ZEnIy2bohtFdG1M8T/wuxSqMwKv
u3APqMa8O5ZHQ1gf05RP3rAMC25Wju0IWfTtmiY1LnKPeISjyvKpxo0/17Lc68Xq
SJa7RBQEq3zz5QYrAe01FK2cX7+ybXXOw+DCs9kRgQVUZCh1tLlHqkEIoqgZ5GDQ
7CHoIVk+2w7x0D7QbzJBQHS+P3oi/Qj3Gluf4XNr8+OUjxzD6vZsN4HoNaWibFLb
N8qpqDo8r2QrqHfhKwzgT+HJg+QW9CMAqBjp5+mRuIN63J6IWp9fJsVoNYbm47Ad
mwIDAQAB
-----END PUBLIC KEY-----


username:     earlwaud
root@chefserver:~# █
```

The filename parameter used in the `user-create` command provides the location at which to store the user's private key. The contents of this key file should be securely stored so that they can be provided to the user whose account has been created.

The next step is to create the first organization in your Chef server. The format of that command is as follows:

```
sudo chef-server-ctl org-create short_name "full_organization_name"
--association_user user_name --filename ORGANIZATION-validator.pem
```

Here is the command I used to create the organization on my example Chef server:

```
sudo chef-server-ctl org-create sdearl "San Diego Earl" --association_
user earlwaud --filename /home/earlwaud/sdearl-validator.pem
```

You can see that, in the example, the key file was saved at `/home/earlwaud/sdearl-validator.pem`.

If the filename parameter is not provided in the `org-create` command, the validator key will be displayed to `stdout`.

Either way, it is vital that the key information be captured and securely stored since it is not saved in the Chef server database and cannot be recovered if lost. The only option available when an organization's private key is completely lost is to reset the validation key.

Next, we need to install a package that will allow management of the Chef server via a web interface. The package is named `opscode-manage`. The command to install the package is:

```
sudo chef-server-ctl install opscode-manage
```

Now we need to restart the Chef server services by issuing the `reconfigure` command again:

```
sudo chef-server-ctl reconfigure
```

And finally, we need to start the opscode-manage services. This is done by issuing the command:

```
sudo opscode-manage-ctl reconfigure
```

If everything went as planned, you should now be able to browse to the new Chef server, and log in with your newly created admin user. Of course, there is still more work to do, such as integrating your new Chef server with your corporate domain to allow domain user access control. Still, this is a good start, right?

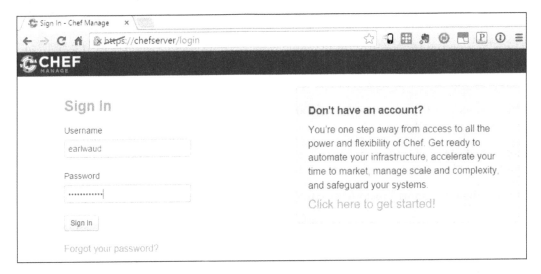

References

- Explore the Chef community Supermarket at this link:
  `https://supermarket.chef.io`

- Download Chef server from `https://downloads.chef.io/chef-server/`

- Learn more about installing Chef server at `https://docs.chef.io/release/server_12-2/install_server.html`

- Learn more about attributes and attribute precedence at `https://docs.chef.io/attributes.html`

- Read more about the "common name" error at `https://github.com/chef-cookbooks/chef-server/issues/108`

Exploring the Chef Development Kit

The Chef Development Kit, or ChefDK, is the omnibus installer used to set up a Chef development environment on a workstation. It includes the Chef client itself, an early version of the new Chef tool, an embedded version of Ruby, RubyGems, OpenSSL, and command-line utilities such as Knife, Ohai, and Chef Zero. It also includes community tools, such as Test Kitchen, Foodcritic, Berkshelf, Chef Vault, Rubocop, and ChefSpec.

Included in the ChefDK installer is the new Chef command-line tool. It is the new go-to way to generate cookbooks, recipes, templates, custom resources, and more. It also downloads RubyGems for the chef-client environment, and it will verify the ChefDK installation and configuration.

The Chef client is a key component of everything Chef. The Chef client is not only used on nodes for converging configuration data, but it is also used on workstations and the Chef server.

The Chef Knife

Knife is a command-line tool that supplies the interface between your chef-repo and your Chef server. It allows developers to upload their work on the workstation to the Chef server, from where it can be distributed to the nodes during their Chef client runs. Knife also allows you to obtain cookbooks from the supermarket, and it provides a mechanism to bootstrap nodes.

Community tools

Some of the most commonly used community tools are installed as part of the ChefDK. Test Kitchen is installed, so you can test the results of your recipes and cookbook development on deployed test nodes. Berkshelf is installed to manage your cookbooks and their dependencies. Foodcritic is included in the ChefDK installation. Foodcritic will help you check your cookbooks for common errors and omissions.

Another valuable community tool installed with the ChefDK is Rubocop. You can use it to give you cookbooks some "style" and make sure that you're following the same conventions used by other developers in your organization. There is also ChefSpec, which is based on the ruby tool RSpec. ChefSpec will allow you to unit-test your cookbooks and recipes. We will have to exercise a lot of these community tools in later chapters, so please stay tuned.

References

- Learn more about the Chef Development Kit at `https://docs.chef.io/chef_dk.html`

- Learn more about Berkshelf in this video-recorded interview at `https://www.chef.io/blog/chefconf-talks/the-berkshelf-way-jamie-winsor/`

- Learn more about Foodcritic at this link `http://www.foodcritic.io/`

- Learn about the Knife command line tool at this link: `https://docs.chef.io/knife.html`

- And download an excellent printable Knife reference guide at this link `https://github.com/chef/quick-reference/blob/master/qr_knife_web.png`

Installing Chef Development Kit

In this section, you will learn how easy it is to get your workstation up and running using the Chef Development Kit. First, you will download ChefDK. Next, you will install ChefDK; and finally, you will validate the installation with some quick version checks.

Downloading ChefDK

You are going to download Chef Development Kit by opening your favorite browser and visiting the Chef.io ChefDK downloads page found at this URL: `https://downloads.chef.io/chef-dk/`.

1. Select the platform you are going to install the Chef Development Kit on and then click on the download button that corresponds to the OS Version you are using. In my case, I am selecting the Mac OS X 10.10 version of the ChefDK installer.

2. As expected, clicking on the download button will transfer the ChefDK installer to your local workstation.

3. Expand the `Downloads` folder and click on the ChefDK disk image file to mount the image on your desktop.

Installing ChefDK

To initiate the installer for the Chef Development Kit, double-click on the mounted ChefDK image icon.

1. The ChefDK image will open, exposing the chefdk package. Double-click on the package icon to begin the installation process.

2. You will see the Chef Development Kit installer introduction screen. Click on the **Continue** button to advance the installation.

3. You will be presented with license information for the Chef Development Kit, which is the commonly used Apache License. I would suggest that you read through the entire license document and perhaps even consult with your lawyer to make sure that you are able to accept this license agreement. Then, click on the **Continue** button to advance the installation.

4. Once you've carefully read and understood the license agreement, click on the **Agree** button to advance the installation.

5. At this point, you can begin to customize the installation. The options available here are to install for all users or only the currently logged in user. In the example, I am installing for all users of this computer (even though I am the only user).

6. Next, you can choose the install location. For consistency with regard to the examples in this book, I have left the install location at the default. Click on the **Install** button when you are ready to begin the actual installation.

7. As always, you will have to provide credentials to allow the system to install new software. Enter your username and password and click on the **Install Software** button to continue.

The installer will now go about its business of installing the super fantastic Chef Development Kit, including the corresponding versions of community tools such as Test Kitchen, Food Critic, and Rubocup.

Finally, you will get the installation summary screen congratulating you on your successful installation and keen DevOps Kung-Fu.

The captain has turned off the seat-belt sign, so it is now OK to unmount the ChefDK image, and move about the installation.

Installing ChefDK on Ubuntu

It is even easier to install the ChefDK on an Ubuntu system. Once you have downloaded the installer, you simply issue a dpkg command as follows:

```
sudo dpkg -i ~/Downloads/chefdk_0.12.0-1_amd64.deb
```

That's it. You should see the "Thank you for installing Chef Development Kit" message.

Verifying ChefDK

The ChefDK installer is a superhero for DevOps aficionados, saving them time and energy by installing the major necessities for a Chef workstation. Still, let's double-check the work done by the installer to make sure that we are really ready to go.

First, let's just try a simple command to see if things look right. Open a terminal window and issue the command chef --help. If the install was successful, you should see information about using Chef.

Next, let's use the new Chef tool to do a deeper validation of the install. Issue the following command in your terminal session:

```
chef verify
```

You should see the Chef tool validate each of the major packages installed during the ChefDK installation. Note that, depending on the state of your (OS X) workstation at the time you run this command, you may receive an error message regarding the need to install the command-line tools for gcc. It may look something like this:

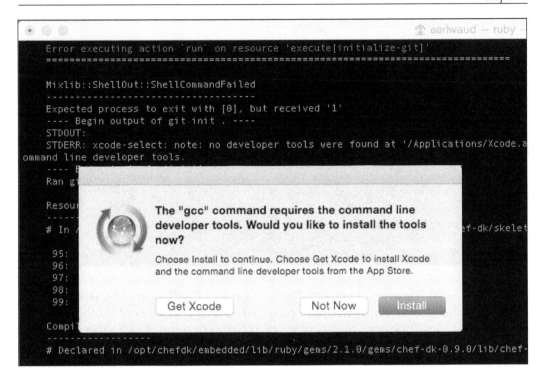

If you get a message such as the preceding one, go ahead and install the command-line tools and then run the `chef verify` command again. This time, you should get a clean run of the command, and the output should be very similar to that shown in the preceding screenshot.

Now, at this point, things are looking pretty good, and you should be feeling fine. So, let's do one last validation check just to be 100% certain. Let's check the versions of some of the expected tools installed via the ChefDK installer.

Issue the following commands:

```
chef --version
ohai --version
foodcritic --version
rubocop --version
rspec --version
```

Your results should look something like this:

```
Last login: Sun Oct 25 13:43:09 on ttys000
Earls-Mac:~ earlwaud$ chef --version
Chef Development Kit Version: 0.9.0
chef-client version: 12.5.1
berks version: 4.0.1
kitchen version: 1.4.2
Earls-Mac:~ earlwaud$ ohai --version
Ohai: 8.7.0
Earls-Mac:~ earlwaud$ foodcritic --version
foodcritic 5.0.0
Earls-Mac:~ earlwaud$ rubocop --version
0.32.1
Earls-Mac:~ earlwaud$ rspec --version
-bash: rspec: command not found
Earls-Mac:~ earlwaud$
```

Hey wait… what happened to rspec? The Version 0.12 ChefDK installer does not seem to have successfully installed rspec, which is a requirement for the Chef-specific tool ChefSpec. That's not good. What went wrong? Everything seemed to have been installed based on the verify command we just used. What gives?

Well, rspec is installed, there is just one more step that we need to do. By the way, I think this is something that should be done by the ChefDK installer, but for whatever reason it's not, and it falls on our shoulders to handle it.

So what do we have to do? We need to set up the environment used in our terminal window for our Chef workstation development. How do we do that?

Fortunately, Chef has a command for that. It is the `chef shell-init` command. You can run this command interactively every time you open a new terminal window, or you can update your profile so that it is run automatically. I would recommend updating your profile, but let me show you both ways so you can make the call.

To make the interactive change, you would issue a command in the following format:

```
eval "$(chef shell-init SHELL_NAME)"
```

The actual call will be the following for the bash shell:

```
eval "$(chef shell-init bash)"
```

If you want to make the change more permanent, then you need to issue a command in the following format:

```
echo 'eval "$(chef shell-init SHELL_NAME)"' >> ~/.YOUR_SHELL_RC_FILE
```

If you are using Mac, the commands will be:

```
echo 'eval "$(chef shell-init bash)"' >> ~/.bash_profile
source ~/.bash_profile
```

If you are using Ubuntu, the commands will be:

```
echo 'eval "$(chef shell-init bash)"' >> ~/.bashrc
source ~/.bashrc
```

This `echo` command will add the eval command to your bash startup so that each run of your bash session will already have the desired environment ready to go for your Chef development work.

It should look something like this:

By the way, when you install the ChefDK onto a Windows system, the installation creates a Chef Development Kit icon on your desktop. When you execute from icon, a Chef-specific PowerShell session is launched. It will automatically run the chef `shell-init` command and set up the full environment needed for Chef. So there is no need to do this last step on a Windows workstation.

>
> **Chef Development Kit on a Windows workstation**
> When you launch Chef Development Kit from your Windows workstation, remember to right-click the icon and choose "Run as administrator." This allows PowerShell to use the correct permissions to set up the Chef environment.

```
                                       Administrator: ChefDK (EarlWaud)
PowerShell 4.0 (Microsoft Windows NT 6.3.9600.0)
Ohai, welcome to ChefDK!

PS C:\Windows\system32> rspec --version
3.3.2
PS C:\Windows\system32> _
```

Well, there you have it: the successful installation of the ChefDK. Your workstation is ready to do some real Chef work now. You should feel pretty awesome!

References

- Visit this link to download the installer for the ChefDK or Chef server at `https://www.chef.io/chef/get-chef/`.
- Here is Chef.io's information on installing the Chef Development Kit: `https://docs.chef.io/install_dk.html`. The Chef DK change log can be found at `https://github.com/chef/chef-dk/blob/master/CHANGELOG.md`.

Setting up a standard Chef repo

Ever Chef workstation has at least one Chef repository. The Chef repo is where all working copies of the cookbooks, recipes, templates, and so on live. It is where you do your development work. It is from where you check your work into your source code repository, and it is from where you upload your work to the Chef server.

Let's take a look at how to set up a new empty Chef repo on your new ChefDK-installed workstation.

Using the Chef tool for Chef repo

Another benefit of the new Chef command-line tool is that it will create a standard chef repo for you. You no longer need to download or clone a starter repo from GitHub. You can use the `chef generate` command to create your new repo. Let's take a look at the `chef generate repo` command's help:

chef generate repo -help

Based on the description of the default values for the chef generate repo command, we can simply issue the following command on our workstation:

chef generate repo ~/chef-repo

That was easy! So what do we get? Well, let's have a look:

```
tree -a chef-repo
chef-repo
├── .chef-repo.txt
├── .git
│   ├── HEAD
│   ├── branches
│   ├── config
│   ├── description
│   ├── hooks
│   │   ├── applypatch-msg.sample
│   │   ├── commit-msg.sample
│   │   ├── post-update.sample
│   │   ├── pre-applypatch.sample
│   │   ├── pre-commit.sample
│   │   ├── pre-push.sample
│   │   ├── pre-rebase.sample
│   │   ├── prepare-commit-msg.sample
│   │   └── update.sample
│   ├── info
│   │   └── exclude
│   ├── objects
│   │   ├── info
│   │   └── pack
│   └── refs
│       ├── heads
│       └── tags
├── .gitignore
```

```
├── LICENSE
├── README.md
├── chefignore
├── cookbooks
│   ├── README.md
│   └── example
│       ├── README.md
│       ├── attributes
│       │   └── default.rb
│       ├── metadata.rb
│       └── recipes
│           └── default.rb
├── data_bags
│   ├── README.md
│   └── example
│       └── example_item.json
├── environments
│   ├── README.md
│   └── example.json
└── roles
    ├── README.md
    └── example.json
```

This list of files looks pretty good but, as you may have noted, an essential folder is missing: the `.chef` folder, which needs to contain the private key files and the `knife.rb` file, used to communicate with the Chef server. Let's take a look at creating or obtaining these files. One way is to use the starter kit. It is an OK way if this is a new Chef server. But, if it's not, be sure to read the following Starter Kit info; it could save your job!

The repo starter kit

You still need the `.chef` files for your new workstation to securely communicate with your Chef server. These files are your user private key file, the organization's validator private key file, and the `knife.rb` file. These files need to be placed in a `.chef` folder in your chef-repo.

When setting up a new organization in your Chef server, there is an easy way to get the files: with the repo starter kit.

Warning!!! Only download the starter kit if you are the Chef server admin and are the first (or only) person setting up your repo for a brand new organization. Currently, the act of downloading the starter kit will reset both your user private key and the organization validator key.

Let me say this again. Downloading the Starter Kit will reset the private key values for both your user and your organization.

Downloading the starter kit on a mature organization will essentially break the Internet.

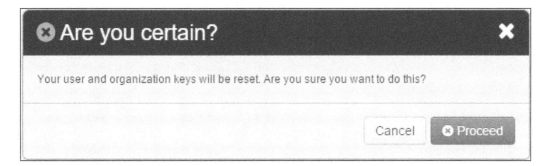

With this warning, if you are still going to use the starter kit, proceed at your own risk.

To get the starter kit, you will want to browse to your Chef server and log in. Once there, click on **Administration** and then select your Organization. Now click on **Starter Kit** and you will see the **Download Starter Kit** button. When you click the button, you will get the warning shown earlier. Click on the **Proceed** button to transfer a zip archive to your workstation, then unzip it into your chef-repo folder, and you're done.

Files for your .chef folder – a safer way

Really, the only files you need from the starter kit are the .chef folder files:

- The organization's validator private key file
- Your user private key file
- A knife.rb file

The organization's key file can be provided by an administrator of the Chef server. The organization's validator key is generated when the organization is created. When the command-line tool is used to create the org, the location of the validator key file may be provided in the command. Otherwise, it will be displayed to stdout. The Chef server admin will have captured the validator key info and will be able to provide it to you now.

The user private key is much like the organization's private key in that it is created when the user is created and must be captured and securely stored at that time as it is not saved to the Chef server database. A user can reset their private key through the use of the Reset Key feature available when viewing the user profile on a Chef server. A user resetting their private key will have no negative impact on other users or the organization, so it is relatively safe to do.

Finally, you need the `knife.rb` file. This file is the easy one. It can be downloaded from the Chef server any time by logging in and browsing to the organization. From there, you can click on any of the Generate Knife Config links in the UI. This will create the `knife.rb` file and download it to your workstation. Another option is to use the `knife configure` command. This will prompt you through the process of creating your knife.rb file.

Put all three of these files into the `.chef` folder of your new chef-repo. Make sure that you save the two key files using the names in the `knife.rb` file (or conversely, update the contents of the `knife.rb` file to match the file names used to save your key files).

```
                                                      .chef — bash — 160×60
Earls-Mac:.chef earlwaud$ pwd
/Users/earlwaud/chef-repo/.chef
Earls-Mac:.chef earlwaud$ cat knife.rb
# See https://docs.getchef.com/config_rb_knife.html for more information on knife configuration options

current_dir = File.dirname(__FILE__)
log_level                :info
log_location             STDOUT
node_name                "earlwaud"
client_key               "#{current_dir}/earlwaud.pem"
validation_client_name   "sdearl-validator"
validation_key           "#{current_dir}/sdearl-validator.pem"
chef_server_url          "https://chefserver/organizations/sdearl"
cookbook_path            ["#{current_dir}/../cookbooks"]
Earls-Mac:.chef earlwaud$
```

Growing your own tree

OS X doesn't come with a version of the tree command installed so, if you like that tool and use a Mac, I've found a clever way to have your cake and eat it too by creating your own tree script. This script was used to create the "tree" output shown in the preceding screenshot. This idea was shared by users Ahmed Masud and JakeGould on http://superuser.com. It goes like this:

There isn't a formal `tree` command per se however you can do this:

Save the following script to /usr/local/bin/tree

```bash
#!/bin/bash

SEDMAGIC='s;[^/]*/;|____;g;s;____|; |;g'

if [ "$#" -gt 0 ] ; then
   dirlist="$@"
else
   dirlist="."
fi

for x in $dirlist; do
     find "$x" -print | sed -e "$SEDMAGIC"
done
```

Change the permissions so you can run it:

```
chmod 755 /usr/local/bin/tree
```

Of course you may have to create `/usr/local/bin`:

```
sudo mkdir -p /usr/local/bin/tree
```

share improve this answer

edited Jan 21 at 22:17
JakeGould
17.1k ● 5 ● 49 ● 61

answered Nov 21 '11 at 10:53
Ahmed Masud
356 ● 1 ● 6

Self-signed certificates

When you are using an On Premise Chef server, you need to do one more thing to finish setting up your chef-repo. If the Chef server you are connecting to has a self-signed certificate, then you will need to add the server's certificate to your chef-repo to allow your workstation to trust your Chef server. An easy way to check if this applies to you is to run the `ssl check` command. It goes like this:

```
knife ssl check
```

If the Chef Server you are communicating with has a self-signed certificate, you will
see a message like this:

```
Earls-Mac:chef-repo earlwaud$ knife ssl check
Connecting to host chefserver:443
ERROR: The SSL certificate of chefserver could not be verified
Certificate issuer data: /C=US/O=YouCorp/OU=Operations/CN=chefserver

Configuration Info:

OpenSSL Configuration:
* Version: OpenSSL 1.0.1p 9 Jul 2015
* Certificate file: /opt/chefdk/embedded/ssl/cert.pem
* Certificate directory: /opt/chefdk/embedded/ssl/certs
Chef SSL Configuration:
* ssl_ca_path: nil
* ssl_ca_file: nil
* trusted_certs_dir: "/Users/earlwaud/chef-repo/.chef/trusted_certs"

TO FIX THIS ERROR:

If the server you are connecting to uses a self-signed certificate, you must
configure chef to trust that server's certificate.

By default, the certificate is stored in the following location on the host
where your chef-server runs:

  /var/opt/opscode/nginx/ca/SERVER_HOSTNAME.crt

Copy that file to your trusted_certs_dir (currently: /Users/earlwaud/chef-repo/.chef/trusted_certs)
using SSH/SCP or some other secure method, then re-run this command to confirm
that the server's certificate is now trusted.

Earls-Mac:chef-repo earlwaud$
```

As you can see in the error message generated by the `ssl check` command, the Chef
server's certificate needs to be obtained and placed into a `trusted_certs` folder in
your `chef-repo/.chef` folder. Again, you will need to contact your Chef server
administrator to get a copy of the certificate file. Once you have it, just place it in the
trusted `certs` folder; when you run your `ssl check` command again, you should
get a message back that says something like:

`knife ssl check`

`Connecting to host chefserver:443`

`Successfully verified certificates from 'chefserver'`

With that successful knife command completed, you have verified that you have
successfully set up your chef-repo and are ready to start creating your infrastructure
as code.

References

- Learn about setting up your Chef repo at the link `https://docs.chef.io/chef_repo.html`.

- Learn more about setting up a chef-repo at the link `https://learn.chef.io/manage-a-web-app/ubuntu/get-set-up/`.

- OS X doesn't come with a version of tree installed so, if you like that tool and use Mac, there is a clever way to have your cake and eat it too by creating your own a tree script. You can find an example shared by Ahmed Masud and JakeGould at the link `http://superuser.com/questions/359723/mac-os-x-equivalent-of-the-ubuntu-tree-command`.

- Keep up-to-date on the Starter Kit resetting the organization's validator key at the link `https://feedback.chef.io/forums/301644-chef-product-feedback/suggestions/9618459-starter-kit-should-not-reset-validator-and-user-ke`.

What else do you need?

You will need just a few more things to round out your workstation toolbox. First, you will want to make sure that you have your favorite text editor and have it configured to integrate with Chef. Next, since you are creating infrastructure code, you really must use a source code control system. I don't want to give anything away on that topic yet but … Git Git Git! Then, you will want to add a hypervisor to your workstation to deploy test nodes. Finally, you'll want to add Vagrant to manage those test nodes. So, let's take a look at these finishing touches for your workstation.

Using your favorite editor

Everyone has their favorite text editor. For a lot of people that editor is Sublime Text, but there are many other choices available. A lot of old schoolers still prefer to use a flavor of the vi editor. Many OS X users swear by Mac-only TextMate. And now there's a new kid on the block from the makers of GitHub: `Atom 1.0`. Sublime Text and Atom are both available for multiple platforms, so whatever OS is your poison, they have a version for you.

> I would recommend that, if you don't already use an editor that has a "project space" feature, you switch to one that does. This feature allows you to quickly and easily switch to and edit different files within a project without the delay of the "save current then open new" workflow needed in an editor that does not have the project space feature.

The project space feature is one of the many reasons I usually recommend Sublime Text, but this feature is also present in other editors such as the new Atom 1.0.

To keep things current, I will use the Atom 1.0 editor in the remainder of this book's examples.

Once you have decided on the editor you plan to use for your Chef workstation and have that editor installed and working, there is one more step. You will need to set the configuration to allow you to integrate your editor with the Chef command-line tools. The best way to do that is to edit your .chef/knife.rb file and add a line to set the editor you want to use with your knife commands. (You could also add an export EDITOR= command to your shell's .bashrc or .bash_profile file.)

Here are some sample knife.rb entries:

Sublime Text:

```
knife[:editor] = '/Applications/Sublime\ Text.app/Contents/
SharedSupport/bin/subl -w'
```

Atom:

```
knife[:editor] = '/Applications/Atom.app/Contents/MacOS/Atom -w'
```

On Mac, the Atom editor has a built-in feature to create symbolic links in the /usr/local/bin folder. With the Atom editor running, open the Atom menu and select **Install Shell Commands** from the submenu. This will create two new links for you. If you do this before updating your knife.rb file, the knife[:editor] entry simply becomes this:

```
knife[:editor] = 'atom -w'
```

When you're using a Windows OS for your workstation, you will have to take greater care in formatting your `knife[:editor]` line to escape the slash characters in the path. A convenient way to do that is to use single quotes around the full value and use double quotes for the path. For Sublime Text, it might look something like this:

```
knife[:editor] = '"C:\Program Files\Sublime Text 2\sublime_text.exe"
--wait'
```

You can test your editor setting by issuing a knife command that requires using the editor. For example, try the command:

knife client create editor-tester

If your editor integration is configured correctly, you will see your editor open up and show you some code. Save the code and exit the editor, and you should see the private key value print out. (This key is not important at this time because we are just testing the editor, and will immediately delete the client.)

If your editor opens, you are done. If you get an error that says **Please set EDITOR environment variable**, then your knife[:editor] value is incorrect. There is probably a typo in the path or some other error. Double-check the value and try again until you successfully launch the editor with your knife client create command.

Once you have validated the integration with your editor, you can delete the test client with the following command:

knife client delete editor-tester

Now you are ready to edit your infrastructure code! When you are creating amazing infrastructure code, you are going to want to make sure that it gets preserved and to ensure that happens you going to want to use a source control tool. Say hello to my little friend, Git.

Version control systems

Git, initially designed and developed by Linus Torvalds for Linux kernel development back in 2005, is now the most widely used version control system for developers everywhere. It's the number-one choice due to its speed, data integrity, and its distributed workflow model. Git is certainly the primary choice as the version control system to be used when developing infrastructure code with Chef.

I will be emphasizing the use of Git throughout the examples in the rest of the book. Git is included with Mac OS X, but it will need to be installed on Windows and Ubuntu workstations. I recommend you to use the GitHub desktop installer where available (Windows and OS X) and allow it to deploy the command-line tools as part of the installation. This installation of Git is easy and will be left to the reader to execute.

Virtualization hypervisor

There are several virtualization choices you can use for your Chef testing. The overall goal is to have a system that you can use to deploy a temporary Chef node to test your infrastructure code. One of the best ways to accomplish this is to install a local virtualization tool on your workstation. Among the choices for a local hypervisor are:

- VirtualBox
- Docker
- VMware Workstation or Fusion

One of the best choices for this kind of Chef testing is VirtualBox. The reasons include its functionality, its ease of use, and its free price tag. Either of the VMware solutions will cost you not only for the hypervisor layer, but also for the integration plugins we'll use with Vagrant to manage our test nodes.

Visit the VirtualBox downloads page at `https://www.virtualbox.org/wiki/Downloads` to download the installer. Once downloaded, it is an easy matter to install it, so I'll leave that to the reader to take care of.

Vagrant

Last, but certainly not least, is Vagrant. Vagrant is another item I consider to be one of the key pieces of the Chef testing puzzle. It is the "glue" between Chef and the hypervisor that deploys the test nodes during testing. You will want to download and install Vagrant on your workstation. You can find the downloaders at `https://www.vagrantup.com/downloads.html`. Vagrant is also an easy install, so I'll leave that to the reader to handle.

I'll go into using Vagrant with VitualBox (and Docker) in some detail in a later chapter.

References

- You can download Sublime Text 2 from `http://www.sublimetext.com/`

- If you want to try the long-running beta of Sublime Text 3, it can be found at `http://www.sublimetext.com/3`

- If you are looking to try Atom 1.0, you can get it at `https://atom.io/`

- The OS X editor, TextMate, can be had at `https://macromates.com`

- Learn more about GitHub at `https://github.com/`

- Learn about and download VirtualBox from `https://www.virtualbox.org/`

- Learn more about Docker at `https://www.docker.com/`

- To get VMware Workstation go to `https://www.vmware.com/products/workstation`

- Or for Mac OS X, get VMware Fusion at `https://www.vmware.com/products/fusion`

What is chef-apply?

One often overlooked tool that is installed with the ChefDK is `chef-apply`. This tool basically allows you to execute chef to converge a single recipe on your local machine. There is no Chef server involved. Everything is local.

Note that chef-apply is not a tool for the deployment of production nodes. It's just a quick and easy way to use Chef to configure your local system.

Why is that useful?

One use case for chef-apply is to learn what a recipe does. You can use `chef-apply` to run a recipe in a "test only" mode by using the `-W` or --why-run parameter. This will converge the recipe, showing you everything that would happen with the recipe without making actual changes to your system.

You can also execute some one-liner scripts. You can easily use `chef-apply` in a scripting-like manner to install software. For example, if you need to use Git on your system and you find it's not installed. Just issue the command:

```
sudo chef-apply -e "package 'git'"
```

This will check to see if Git is currently installed. If it is, then the command will just inform you that that is the case and exit. If Git is not installed, then it will go about using the correct installer (aka Provider) to obtain and install the package.

Testing this on my Ubuntu workstation, you can see that Git was not installed initially. Then, by using the chef-apply command, the git package is installed. Then to confirm that nothing happens if you try to use chef-apply to install a package that is already installed, I ran the same chef-apply again to show what happens:

```
earlwaud@ubuntu: ~
earlwaud@ubuntu:~$ git
The program 'git' is currently not installed. You can install it by typing:
sudo apt-get install git
earlwaud@ubuntu:~$ sudo chef-apply -e "package 'git'"
Recipe: (chef-apply cookbook)::(chef-apply recipe)
  * apt_package[git] action install
    - install version 1:1.9.1-1ubuntu0.1 of package git
earlwaud@ubuntu:~$ sudo chef-apply -e "package 'git'"
Recipe: (chef-apply cookbook)::(chef-apply recipe)
  * apt_package[git] action install (up to date)
earlwaud@ubuntu:~$
```

How about creating a "workstation" recipe to set up all the "missing" items from a new ChefDK workstations setup? You create the recipe that defines the state of having your editor installed and integrated with Chef, defines the state of having git installed, and defines the state of having your custom OS X "tree" script created in /usr/local/bin. You create this recipe once, and you (and anyone in your organization) can quickly complete their workstation setup by using chef-apply with your workstation recipe.

References

- The link to get the details of an interesting use case for chef-apply posted by Chris Doherty on chef.io is https://www.chef.io/blog/2015/01/16/convert-your-bash-scripts-with-chef-apply/.
- The link to the chef.io documentation on chef-apply is https://docs.chef.io/ctl_chef_apply.html.

Summary

In this chapter, we've taken a quick stroll down memory lane and reviewed some Chef basics so that those concepts are fresh and easy to mentally access during the rest of the journey through this book. Next up, we took a deeper dive into the Chef Development Kit and learned how to download, install, and configure it for our Chef workstation. We've exposed the small gap in the ChefDK installer when used on Mac OS X and Linux systems, which is the setup of the shell environment and learned the simple way (provided by the new Chef tool) to fill that gap. We also explored the setup and configuration of your very own on-premise Chef server, including creating your admin user and the first organization. After this, we took a look at setting up our Chef repo, giving a BIG WARNING about the starter kit. And then we considered what was still missing from a well-rounded Chef workstation. That will be our favorite editor, a version control system, a virtualization layer to simplify our testing flow, and Vagrant to glue things together. Finally, as an added bonus, we talked about the ChefDK tool chef-apply.

Wow! That was a lot of ground for a single chapter, but I hope that you were able to stick with me till the end. This chapter is a great foundation for the Chef knowledge transfer coming your way in the chapters ahead.

So without any further delay, let's charge ahead into *Chapter 2*, *Knife Tooling and Plugins*, and carve things up with some Swiss Army knife skills.

Knife Tooling and Plugins

2

In this chapter, we're going to cover the primary command-line tool in the Chef repertoire. Basic Knife functionality is detailed, as well as the use of community plugins and instructions on how to create your own new plugins.

"Knife skills are the gateway drug to good cooking" – *Chef Todd Mohr,* **Certified Culinary Educator (CCE)**

In this chapter, the reader will learn to wield Knife and extend its capabilities as needed. Here is the list of topics that will be covered in this chapter:

- Knife help
- Knife subcommands
- Knife to editor integration
- Knife Windows plugin
- Knife EC2 plugin
- Creating new Knife plugins

Knife help

Let's begin with the basics. As with all command-line tools in the Chef toolbox, knife has a rich help system built in. Issuing the command `knife --help` will display the basic knife syntax help contents. When you issue the `knife --help` command, you get a list of all the optional parameters, plus a list of all the knife subcommands. In addition, each of the subcommands has its own help content. For example, ask for help with the subcommand `node`, and you will get the syntax for the full set of node-specific subcommands and options.

Here is what it will look like when you issue the `knife node --help` command:

```
● ● ●                                          1. bash
Earls-Mac:chef-repo earlwaud$ knife node --help
FATAL: Cannot find subcommand for: 'node --help'
Available node subcommands: (for details, knife SUB-COMMAND --help)

** NODE COMMANDS **
knife node bulk delete REGEX (options)
knife node create NODE (options)
knife node delete NODE (options)
knife node edit NODE (options)
knife node environment set NODE ENVIRONMENT
knife node from file FILE (options)
knife node list (options)
knife node run_list add [NODE] [ENTRY[,ENTRY]] (options)
knife node run_list remove [NODE] [ENTRY[,ENTRY]] (options)
knife node run_list set NODE ENTRIES (options)
knife node show NODE (options)

Earls-Mac:chef-repo earlwaud$ █
```

You can see from this help text that, using the `knife node` command, you can create nodes, delete nodes, list nodes, show the details of nodes, and much more. Each subcommand available to the knife command has a similar set of rich help details available on demand.

Most of the actions associated with the subcommands have additional syntax help details available, and they can be accessed in the same fashion as earlier. For example, issuing the command `knife node show --help` will give you all of the options available for the action "show" of the subcommand `node`.

The frequency of use of the knife subcommands vary greatly, and having this level of syntax help at your fingertips is very valuable. When you are trying to use a subcommand that you don't regularly execute, remembering to check the syntax and options using this help system will help you avoid frustration and mistakes.

However, if you need more than syntax help on a specific subcommand, you can invoke the full help text for that command by using the full knife help command. For example, entering the command `knife help node` will present you with the full knife-node help man page. This content will detail all of the options available to the subcommand, in this case, the `node` subcommand. It includes a description of the function of the subcommand, the syntax, the options, and example uses of the subcommand—in short, a rich man page for the subcommand.

References

There is an excellent help reference available on GitHub that takes the built-in syntax help information to the next level. You can download and print out your own reference guide from `https://github.com/chef/quick-reference`.

Knife subcommands

Now that we have some help skills under our belt, let's take a look at some of the other knife subcommands in greater detail. Using the various knife subcommands, we will manage nodes, cookbooks, recipes, roles, and environments. We will also use knife to do searching of our Chef server data. All of this and more is available using Knife.

We will have a look at some of the most used commands, but also dig deeper into some of the less frequently used commands to better understand what they can do for us.

Knife Bootstrap

You use the knife bootstrap subcommand to install the chef-client on systems so that it can be used on those systems to communicate with the Chef server. The bootstrap process also registers the system with the Chef server to facilitate communication between the two. In addition to installing the chef-client and registering it with the Chef server, bootstrapping also creates a Node object on the Chef server that is used to manage the configuration of the bootstrapped system.

The primary syntax of the bootstrap command is knife bootstrap <IP | FQDN>. For example, to bootstrap a server by IP address, you would use a command like `knife bootstrap 192.168.10.44`. This instructs knife to install the chef-client on the system with the IP address 192.168.10.44, register that system with the Chef server, and create a node representing the system on the Chef server.

 To obtain the Chef server's SSL certificate, you can use the knife subcommand `ssl_fetch` to download the on-premise Chef server's SSL certificate and install it in your `trusted certs` folder. This certificate is used in the knife bootstrap subcommands.

Here is an example knife bootstrap command that I used to bootstrap an opscode-centos-7.1 vagrant node running on VirtualBox:

```
knife bootstrap 127.0.0.1 --node-name vagrant-node01 --ssh-port 2222
--ssh-user vagrant --identity-file ~/chef-repo/.vagrant/machines/default/
virtualbox/private_key --sudo
```

Here is the result of running that bootstrap command:

```
1. bash
Earls-Mac:chef-repo earlwaud$ knife bootstrap 127.0.0.1 --node-name vagrant-node01 --ssh-port 2222 --ssh-user
  vagrant --identity-file ~/chef-repo/.vagrant/machines/default/virtualbox/private_key --sudo
Doing old-style registration with the validation key at /Users/earlwaud/chef-repo/.chef/hosted/sdearl-validat
or.pem...
Delete your validation key in order to use your user credentials instead

Connecting to 127.0.0.1
127.0.0.1 -----> Installing Chef Omnibus (-v 12)
127.0.0.1 downloading https://omnitruck-direct.chef.io/chef/install.sh
127.0.0.1   to file /tmp/install.sh.12437/install.sh
127.0.0.1 trying wget...
127.0.0.1 el 7 x86_64
127.0.0.1 Getting information for chef stable 12 for el...
127.0.0.1 downloading https://www.chef.io/stable/chef/metadata?v=12&p=el&pv=7&m=x86_64
127.0.0.1   to file /tmp/install.sh.12442/metadata.txt
127.0.0.1 trying wget...
127.0.0.1 sha1    5907edce1a3b0f7bd42359fe64960da8833385e9
127.0.0.1 sha256        1c3e680f106ab6829c3713307e447116f7bb3f2d9c30fd3943638b01d6246fe2
127.0.0.1 url    https://packages.chef.io/stable/el/7/chef-12.9.38-1.el7.x86_64.rpm
127.0.0.1 version       12.9.38
127.0.0.1 downloaded metadata file looks valid...
127.0.0.1 downloading https://packages.chef.io/stable/el/7/chef-12.9.38-1.el7.x86_64.rpm
127.0.0.1   to file /tmp/install.sh.12442/chef-12.9.38-1.el7.x86_64.rpm
127.0.0.1 trying wget...
127.0.0.1 Comparing checksum with sha256sum...
127.0.0.1 Installing chef 12
127.0.0.1 installing with rpm...
127.0.0.1 warning: /tmp/install.sh.12442/chef-12.9.38-1.el7.x86_64.rpm: Header V4 DSA/SHA1 Signature, key ID
83ef826a: NOKEY
127.0.0.1 Preparing...                      ############################### [100%]
127.0.0.1 Updating / installing...
127.0.0.1   1:chef-12.9.38-1.el7            ############################### [100%]
127.0.0.1 Thank you for installing Chef!
127.0.0.1 Starting the first Chef Client run...
127.0.0.1 Starting Chef Client, version 12.9.38
127.0.0.1 Creating a new client identity for vagrant-node01 using the validator key.
127.0.0.1 resolving cookbooks for run list: []
127.0.0.1 Synchronizing Cookbooks:
127.0.0.1 Installing Cookbook Gems:
127.0.0.1 Compiling Cookbooks...
127.0.0.1 [2016-04-17T22:59:55+00:00] WARN: Node vagrant-node01 has an empty run list.
127.0.0.1 Converging 0 resources
127.0.0.1
127.0.0.1 Running handlers:
127.0.0.1 Running handlers complete
127.0.0.1 Chef Client finished, 0/0 resources updated in 24 seconds
Earls-Mac:chef-repo earlwaud$
```

The optional parameters that I used in this command are:

- `--node-name vagrant`: Create a Node object on the Chef server with the name "vagrant".

- `--ssh-port 2222`: Use port "2222" when connecting to the system being bootstrapped.

- `--ssh-user vagrant`: When ssh'ing to the system, log in with username "vagrant".
- `--identity-file ~/chef-repo/`: Use key-based authentication and use the listed key file "~/chef-repo/...".
- `--sudo`: Execute the commands on the bootstrapped system using sudo.

There is one significant option that I did not include in the example shown earlier. Did you notice its absence? That optional parameter is `--run-list <RUN_LIST>`. The run list option allows you to specify a comma-separated list of policies, roles, and recipes, that are used in the initial chef-client run.

Another common optional parameter used is `--environment`. This parameter can be used to associate an environment with the system/node, so that only policies, roles, and recipes that are part of the associated environment are used when configuring the server.

Knife Node

The knife node subcommand is used to query and set the various configuration values for a node. One of the most common uses of this subcommand is to get a list of nodes known to your Chef server. The command to do this is `knife node list`. This will return the complete list of nodes on your Chef server. The node subcommand can also be used to create, delete, or edit node objects on your Chef server.

 Make sure that you have set up your editor to work with Knife, as shown in the *Knife to editor integration* section of this chapter.

Other uses for the node subcommand include adding or removing a node's run list. And of course, there is the `knife node show <node name>` command to let you see the current configuration settings stored in the Node object on the Chef server.

Knife Diff

Another useful knife subcommand is knife diff. Knife diff is used to compare the files in your current Workstation repo with what is stored on the Chef server. You can compare files before you upload them to the Chef server. You can also use knife diff to compare the repo files with versions used for different environments. You will find this subcommand to be very valuable when modifying resources, such as cookbooks and recipes, to compare your changes to the state of the resource on the Chef server. It provides an excellent sanity check on your work.

Remember that you can use knife diff to compare individual files, like a single recipe file, or you can use it to compare folders, like an entire cookbook.

Knife Exec

Exec is a knife subcommand that lets you run Ruby scripts against the Chef server in the context of a fully configured chef-client. What that means is that you can do things to the Chef server via Ruby scripts that would be much more difficult or impossible to accomplish using other subcommands. For example, if you want to move nodes from one environment to another, you can issue a knife exec subcommand. Here is what a knife exec command to move all nodes in the "_default" environment into the "development" environment:

```
knife exec -E 'nodes.transform("chef_environment:_default") { |n| n.chef_
environment("development") }'
```

This is something that you would not need to do very often, but having the ability to do it with a single knife exec command would still save you a lot of time. Another example use case would be adding a role or recipe to a subset of your nodes, such as all the nodes in production. If, for example, you want to add the recipe "base" to all of your nodes in production, you could issue a knife exec command like this:

```
knife exec -E 'nodes.transform("chef_environment:production") {|n| puts
n.run_list << "recipe[base]"; n.save }'
```

Executing this command will update the run_list for all of the nodes in the production environment adding the recipe "base".

 Issuing the command without the n.save as a test run

If you issue the preceding command without including the n.save first, then you can see the effects of the knife exec command without applying the changes to the server. If everything looks right, run it again with the n.save to apply the changes. This lets you try test your commands before they make changes to your environment.

Issue the following command first to test the results:

```
knife exec -E 'nodes.transform("chef_environment:production") {|n| puts
n.run_list << "recipe[base]"}'
```

Then, issue the command again with `n.save` to apply the changes:

```
knife exec -E 'nodes.transform("chef_environment:production") {|n| puts
n.run_list << "recipe[base]"; n.save }'
```

Knife SSH

The knife ssh subcommand lets you run ssh commands on all or a subset of the nodes known to your Chef Server. The nodes that will have the ssh command invoked on them are determined by a search or a query against the Chef Server's nodes. For example, if you want to run the uptime command on all of the nodes in the production environment, you can issue a command like this one:

```
knife ssh "chef_environment:production" "uptime" -p 2222 -x earl -P
MyPW99
```

The search used is `chef_environment:production`. The command being issued on the matching nodes is "uptime". In this case, the port being used for `ssh` is `2222`, and the credentials are self-explanatory.

Another good use of the knife ssh subcommand is to combine it with the knife exec subcommand. This combination lets you do some very powerful things. For example, you can check the status of the ntpd service on all your production nodes with a command something like this:

```
knife ssh -p 2222 -x earl -P MyPW99 -m "`knife exec -E "search(:node,
'chef_environment:production').each {|host| puts host[:hostname] }" |
xargs`" '/etc/init.d/ntpd status'
```

Here, we are searching for all of the nodes in the production environment, and for each node, we are sshing into the system and issuing the command `/etc/init.d/ntpd status`.

Using a combination of the knife ssh subcommand and the knife exec command is an excellent and easy way to create ad hoc reports.

Knife Search

The knife search subcommand is one of the most used commands in the knife set. knife search lets you do queries against all of the data stored in the Chef server. Since the chef-client run sends system data collected via the Ohai command to the Chef server, there is a wealth of search criteria that is available to search against. The knife search subcommand uses two main parts: an index and a query. A knife search is executed against one of the indexes on the Chef server. The possible indexes are "client," "environment," "node," or "role."

Note that if you do not specify an index, knife search uses the default of "node". The other half of the knife search subcommand is the query. The query is the filter applied to the index to limit the results of the search. In addition, there are several optional parameters that modify the data returned from the search. For example, you can use the optional parameter of "-i" to instruct knife search to return only the ID of the objects in the index that match the filter used. Here, a sample command will better explain. If you want to see a list of all the nodes in your Chef server, you can issue the following command:

```
knife search node '*:*' -i
```

Here, the knife search command is using the index of "node" and the query or filter is *:*, and the -i says to just give me the index IDs for the matching objects. The index IDs for the node index are the node names.

Remember that the default index is "node", so the same results will be delivered if you issue the command like this:

```
knife search '*:*' -i
```

Without the optional -i, the knife search command will return the Node object details, and there are varying levels of detail you can have the search command return. Here are the options:

- The -i parameter: just the node name, no object details
- No parameter: short list of the object's details
- The -m parameter: medium list of the object's details
- The -l parameter: full list of all of the object's details

You can also specify specific attributes of the node object, that is, the IP Address, with the -a parameter. The following command will return the IP address of all the nodes in the Chef server:

```
knife search node '*:*' -a server_ip
```

This is only the tip of the knife search iceberg. In these basic examples, we are essentially ignoring the query part of the search command by using a "*:*". Say that you need to see a list of all of the Nodes that are in the 192.168.112.x subnet. You can issue the following knife search command to create the list:

```
knife search node 'server_ip*:192.168.112.*' -i
```

Truly, the only limit to what you can search for is your imagination. The knife search command is one of the most powerful commands in the knife set.

References

- You can read more about the knife command and all of its subcommands on the Chef site at `https://docs.chef.io/knife.html`.
- The link to the Chef documentation on knife search is at `https://docs.chef.io/knife_search.html`.
- The link to the Chef bootstrapping data is at `https://docs.chef.io/knife_bootstrap.html`.

Knife to editor integration

Many of the interactive knife subcommands use an editor to create or modify the infrastructure code. The proper integration of your favorite editor is important to a fluid knife experience.

Using the "wait" option

The key to successfully using your editor with knife is to configure it to use the editor's "wait" option. The wait option tells your editor to launch, open the specified file or content, but not return or exit from the launch command until the editor is exited.

In your standard modern OS, launching most applications from the command line will invoke the application and then immediately return control to the command-line shell. The command, in this case, invokes the editor; actually, it executes completely by launching the editor. This is the behavior that needs to be avoided when using the knife commands. Depending on the editor of choice and OS, we may need to configure the "invoke the editor" command so that it does not return as soon as the editor is invoked, but instead waits until the editor is closed before it returns control to the command-line shell. Each editor has its own way of indicating a desire to wait for exit before returning control. The best way to configure your editor to use its wait option is to add the parameter to the editor line in your `~/.chef/knife.rb` file. When needed, the setting will take the following format:

```
knife[:editor] = '<path to your editor> <wait option>'
```

Does my editor require the wait option?

As you might expect, every editor has its own unique features and behaviors. Two common editors, Sublime Text and Atom, both require a wait parameter to allow them to be used successfully with knife. Both use a "-w" for the wait parameter. If you use VI or TextMate, then no wait option is necessary, as both editors, when invoked, hold control until the editor is exited.

Use Sublime Text for your interactive knife commands

When I issue a knife command, I want my editor to open quickly and to contain just the contents related to the issued knife command. Sublime Text does this way better than any other editor I've tried so far.

On my OS X system, I use Sublime Text as my editor of choice for the interactive knife commands. The `knife.rb` file entry that I use looks as follows:

```
knife[:editor] = '/Applications/Sublime\ Text.app/Contents/
SharedSupport/bin/subl -w'
```

Moreover, even though I am using Atom as my current code editor of choice, I still prefer to use Sublime Text with my interactive knife commands. This is because I have not found a way to have Atom launch the knife command into a new window that does not also open tabs for the files that were open the last time Atom was launched. In addition to this being an undesirable behavior for me, it also slows down the launch of the editor. I have tried all the various combinations of the command-line parameters available for Atom, including --wait, --foreground, and --new-window, without finding a combination that works for me. Your mileage may vary.

References

- You can get the Sublime Text editor from `http://www.sublimetext.com/2`.

- You can get the Atom editor from `https://atom.io/`.

- You can get TextMate (Mac OS only) from `https://macromates.com/download`.

Knife Windows plugin

Now, let's take a look at a couple of community knife plugins. We'll start with the Windows plugin. We use the knife Windows plugin when we are working with nodes running the Windows operating system. First, you will need to install the knife Windows plugin and then we will review how to use it to bootstrap a Windows node. Then, we will use some of the search features to see some of the Windows-specific node data.

Installing the Knife Windows plugin

Like many things related to the new ChefDK, installing Chef-specific gems is pretty straightforward and easy. In this case, we want to install the knife-windows gem. The command to do this is:

```
chef gem install knife-windows
```

That is all it takes. You are now ready to use the knife Windows plugin.

Bootstrapping a Windows node

Now that we have the knife Windows plugin installed, we can bootstrap our Windows nodes. There are two methods to interface with a Windows system when bootstrapping a node using the knife Windows plugin. One uses ssh just as though the node is a Linux system. The other is using the WinRM interface. The benefit of using the WinRM protocol is that it allows the use of standard Windows objects to be used, such as batch scripts and PowerShell scripts. Here is an example of using the WinRM method to bootstrap a node named "node03":

```
knife bootstrap windows winrm node03 -p 55985 -x Administrator -P MyPW99
-r 'recipe[winbase]'
```

In the preceding command, you can see that we are using the Windows plugin, and the WinRM protocol to bootstrap a node named "node03." We are specifying port 55985 and using the Administrator credentials.

Remember to use a local admin account

Although a node can be connected to an Active Directory domain, it is still necessary to bootstrap the node using a local administrator account.

The last part of the bootstrap command was to tell the node to use the recipe "winbase" in the first chef-client run.

Searching for Windows node data

Now that we know how to bootstrap some Windows nodes, let's take a look at some knife searches that use some Windows-specific attributes. Starting off with something easy, say we need to create a list of all the windows nodes in production:

```
knife search node 'chef_environment:production && os:windows' -i
```

But now we've been asked to provide a list of all the production Windows nodes that have not been properly joined to the domain (that is, they still have a domain of WORKGROUP). This one is a bit tricky because the knife search command does not handle nested attributes all that well, and the attribute we need is very nested (kernel.cs_info.domain). We can see the values with a command like this:

```
knife search node 'chef_environment:production && os:windows' -a kernel.
cs_info.domain
```

This will provide a list of all production windows nodes, but we will still have to manually filter that list down to those nodes that aren't joined to the domain.

If we try to use a command that includes a nested attribute, the search will find zero matches. That is, a command like this will not work for us:

```
knife search node 'chef_environment:production && os:windows && kernel.
cs_info.domain:WORKGROUP' -i
```

So, what can we do? It's the knife exec subcommand that comes to the rescue. We can use nested attributes in the find of a knife exec command, something like this:

```
knife exec -E 'nodes.find("chef_environment:production && os:windows &&
kernel.cs_info.domain:WORKGROUP"){|n| puts "#{n.name}"}'
```

Here, we are using all three conditions in nodes.find to provide a list of nodes that are in the production environment, have windows as the OS, and have the (nested) attribute kernel.cs_info.domain equal to WORKGROUP. Using this type of "search" will net us the list of nodes we desire. Hurray!

References

- The knife Windows plugin on the Chef site is discussed in detail at https://docs.chef.io/plugin_knife_windows.html.
- The GitHub repo for the knife Windows plugin is discussed in detail at https://github.com/chef/knife-windows.

Knife EC2 plugin

Let's continue our community plugin exploration with the knife EC2 plugin. This plugin is used to integrate knife with Amazon cloud instances that allow you to create and manage instances from the command line.

Installing the Knife EC2 plugin

Much like installing the knife Windows plugin, the installation process for the knife EC2 plugin is super easy. The Chef command-line tool comes to our aid once again. Simply issue the following command:

```
chef gem install knife-ec2
```

Your installation will be done in a few seconds. You might note that there is a dependent gem installed; it is the fog-aws gem, which the EC2 plugin uses.

Unlike the knife Windows plugin, after the plugin is installed, there is still more to configure to be able to use it. The knife EC2 plugin requires some specific data related to your Amazon account. There are several ways to make the Amazon data available to the EC2 plugin. The data can be used via environment variables, or as `knife.rb` configuration settings, or by creating an AWS credential file and referring to it in your `knife.rb` file. This is the method I would recommend because sometimes, the `knife.rb` file is uploaded to your git repo and that would put your AWS access key ID and secret access key at risk. However, if you still want to add the Amazon data to your `knife.rb` file, it should be added in this format:

```
knife[:aws_access_key_id] = "Your AWS Access Key ID"
knife[:aws_secret_access_key] = "Your AWS Secret Access Key"
```

If, instead, you want to use the safer AWS credential file method, decide on or create a location to store the credential file, and create a new file entering in the credential data in the format shown later. Note that you do not enclose your ID or Key in any kind of quotes like you would if you are adding them directly to the `knife.rb` file:

```
[default]
aws_access_key_id = Your AWS Access Key ID
aws_secret_access_key = Your AWS Secret Access Key
```

Now update your `knife.rb` file to point to the credential file, by adding a line as follows:

```
knife[:aws_credential_file] = "/path/to/credentials/file"
```

Okay, now you are ready to use the knife EC2 plugin. If you already have some EC2 instances running, go ahead and test your new plugin by listing them out. You can issue a command like this:

```
knife ec2 server list -r us-west-2
```

The -r option tells the EC2 plugin what region you are accessing.

Create a "default" region by adding it to your `knife.rb` file.

If you want to save yourself the extra typing needed to add the -r `<region>` to all of your EC2 plugin commands, you can add an entry into your knife.rb file to specify a "default" region. The entry will look as follows:

```
knife[:region] = "us-west-2"
```

With a default region defined in your `knife.rb` file, you can skip the -r parameter and your knife ec2 plugin will use the region specified in the `knife.rb` file.

If you need to temporarily access a different region, you can still override the default region by using the -r `<some other region>` parameter again.

Creating an EC2 instance

Using the Knife EC2 command to create a new EC2 instance is somewhat complicated. A "simple" version of the command might look something like this:

```
knife ec2 server create --node-name ec2-node08 \
    --groups=launch-wizard-1 \
    --region=us-west-2 \
    --availability-zone=us-west-2a \
    --image=ami-5189a661 \
    --server-connect-attribute=public_ip_address \
    --flavor=t2.micro \
    --ssh-user=ubuntu \
    --ssh-key=my_chef_service \
    --identity-file=/Users/earlwaud/.aws/my_chef_service.pem \
    --run-list=recipe['base']
```

There is a lot going on there, so let's go over each part of the command:

- `knife ec2 server create`: This is the syntax of the create command
- `--node-name ec2-node08`: Name to give the new instance and the Chef node
- `--groups=launch-wizard-1`: Use the pre-existing security group named launch-wizard-1
- `--region=us-west-2`: Selects the region to create instance into
- `--availability-zone=us-west-2a`: The AZ to use
- `--image=ami-5189a661`: The specific AMI image to deploy
- `--server-connect-attribute=public_ip_address`: Use the public IP for ssh
- `--flavor=t2.micro`: The size of the image to deploy
- `--ssh-user=ubuntu`: The user to use in ssh commands
- `--ssh-key=my_chef_service`: The user access key name
- `--identity-file=/Users/earlwaud/.aws/my_chef_service.pem`: This is a key file
- `--run-list=recipe['base']`: The initial run list for the new node

When you run the command, you will see that the knife ec2 server create command details the progression of the instance creation plus the node bootstrap process. That's right, the create command also bootstraps the node and converges the specified run list. Pretty handy, right?

In addition to listing the actions done to create the new instance, the server create command also provides the data needed to access the new instance, including DNS name and both the public and private IP addresses.

So what about existing EC2 instances? You can bootstrap an existing instance pretty much the same way you would bootstrap any other server. Let's take a look.

Bootstrapping an existing EC2 instance

To bootstrap an existing EC2 instance, you will issue a command much like the one used to bootstrap any other server. It might look something like this:

```
knife bootstrap 54.213.235.40 \
    --node-name my_old_ec2_node \
    --ssh-user ubuntu \
    --identity-file /Users/earlwaud/.aws/my_chef_service.pem \
    --sudo
```

There is a significant consideration here. If your Chef server is an on-premise server, you may not have access to it from your EC2 instance. This same consideration applies to the knife ec2 server create command.

Deleting EC2 instances

Eventually, you are going to want to delete some instances. You can use the knife EC2 plugin in order to handle this task. The command you use is `knife ec2 server delete --node-name <node-name> --purge`. The `--purge` option tells knife that you also want to remove the corresponding node and client from the Chef server. Here is what deleting the instance we created earlier looks like:

```
Earls-Mac:chef-repo earlwaud$ knife ec2 server delete --node-name ec2-node08 --purge
no instance id is specific, trying to retrieve it from node name
Instance ID: i-2c9781eb
Instance Name: ec2-node08
Flavor: t2.micro
Image: ami-5189a661
Region: us-west-2
Availability Zone: us-west-2a
Security Groups: launch-wizard-1
SSH Key: my_chef_service
Root Device Type: ebs
Public DNS Name: ec2-54-213-66-101.us-west-2.compute.amazonaws.com
Public IP Address: 54.213.66.101
Private DNS Name: ip-172-31-24-37.us-west-2.compute.internal
Private IP Address: 172.31.24.37
\n
Do you really want to delete this server? (Y/N) Y
WARNING: Deleted server i-2c9781eb
WARNING: Deleted node ec2-node08
WARNING: Deleted client ec2-node08
Earls-Mac:chef-repo earlwaud$ 
```

References

- The link to the Chef knife EC2 plugin page is https://docs.chef.io/plugin_knife_ec2.html.

- Another excellent reference can be found on the GitHub page for the knife EC2 plugin at https://github.com/chef/knife-ec2.

- The link to the knife Cloud plugins at https://docs.chef.io/plugin_knife.html.

- The GitHub knife EC2 plugin link is https://github.com/chef/knife-ec2.

- There is an interesting blog post by Mark Birbeck on using the knife EC2 plugin to create and manage EC2 instances without a Chef server at http://markbirbeck.com/2012/03/16/using-knife-to-launch-ec2-instances-without-a-chef-server/.

Creating new Knife plugins

Sometimes, you will be dealing with unique situations and need to create your own knife plugin. In this section, we will review how that is accomplished.

The basic plugin file format

A custom knife plugin begins by creating a new plugin ruby file. The plugin file has to have a specific format. That format, in its simplest form, looks like this:

```ruby
require 'chef/knife'

module ModuleName
  class SubclassName < Chef::Knife

  deps do
    require 'chef/dependency'
  end

  banner 'knife subcommand argument VALUE (options)'

  option :name_of_option,
    :short => "-l VALUE",
    :long => "--long-option-name VALUE",
    :description => "The description for the option.",
    :proc => Proc.new { code_to_run }
    :boolean => true | false
    :default => default_value

  def run
  end
end
```

The essential sections of this file are:

- The required `chef/knife` directive provides the calls all knife plugins inherit from
- `ModuleName` is the name space for our plugin
- `SubClassName` is important because it defines how the knife plugin will be called
- The `deps do` block provides the list of module-specific dependencies
- The `banner` method call provides the header that is shown when the user needs help

- The `option` method call defines the optional parameters for your plugin
- The `run` definition is the method knife calls to execute our plugin

Once you have created the plugin's ruby file, you have the choice of saving the file to one of two places. You can save it within your chef-repo, in a location like `~/chef-repo/.chef/plugins/knife/shinnynewplugin.rb`. Otherwise, you can save the file in a location outside of any chef-repo, which would be like `~/.chef/plugins/knife/shinnynewplugin.rb`. This second option, outside of any chef-repo, is where I would recommend placing the file. Remember that the file name must have the `.rb` extension.

Example – A simpler EC2 Create Server plugin

If you are like me and don't want to type in all those parameter names and values every time you create new EC2 instances, then this example is for you. We're going to create a shortcut plugin that allows us to create EC2 instances using a predefined set of parameters, so that we don't have to do all that typing every time we want to spin up another instance. Of course, this is an exaggerated example, and if you were going to create such a shortcut plugin, you would use the `knife.rb` file to hold the predefined parameters so that it would not require a code change to update a parameter value. Hmmmm…. Anyway, here is the example code:

```
require 'chef/knife'

module EasyCreate
  class EasyCreate < Chef::Knife
    deps do
    end

    banner 'knife easy create NODENAME'

    def run
      puts "node-name #{name_args.first}"

      cmd = "knife ec2 server create \
        --node-name #{name_args.first} \
        --groups=launch-wizard-1 \
        --region=us-west-2 \
        --availability-zone=us-west-2a \
        --image=ami-5189a661 \
        --server-connect-attribute=public_ip_address \
        --flavor=t2.micro \
        --ssh-user=ubuntu \
        --ssh-key=my_chef_service \
```

```
            --identity-file=/Users/earlwaud/.aws/my_chef_service.pem\
            --run-list=recipe['base']"

        system( cmd )
    end
  end
end
```

Now when you want to create a new EC2 instance, you can issue a command such as the following:

```
knife easy create ec2-node10
```

References

For the complete custom knife plugins documentation, go to `https://docs.chef.io/plugin_knife_custom.html`.

Summary

In this chapter, we've seen how to quickly verify the syntax of a knife subcommand or to review at length the full wealth of the help system contents. We have looked at some of the most often used knife subcommands as well as a few that may be generally overlooked. We also took a deep dive into the knife search subcommand. Then, we shifted gears to explore some existing community knife plugins—one for Windows and and one for EC2. Finally, we cut our way through the exciting topic of creating our own knife plugins. Now, with our newly sharpened knife skills, let's begin to explore the management of your infrastructure code with the use of roles, environments, and the new and exciting feature that is policies, in the next chapter.

3
Leveraging Roles, Environments, and Policies

In this chapter, the reader will learn the power of using roles and to follow the best practices to manage large-scale environments by leveraging roles, environments, organizations, and policies.

> *"My doctor told me I had to stop throwing intimate dinners for four unless there are three other people."* – *Orson Welles*

Here is a list of the topics covered in this chapter:

- Using Chef roles
- Using Chef environments
- Using Chef organizations
- Understanding nested roles
- Learning precedence hierarchy
- Exploring policies

Using Chef roles

Roles provide a way of looking at our infrastructure code as a representation of the functions performed by the servers we associate with them. Said another way, a "web server" role is created and assigned to a server that performs the function of a web server.

The benefit here is functional consistency. Whether your goal is to be able to reproduce a server in the event of failure or upgrade, or to deploy multiple identical servers to load balance a function, using a role will allow you to achieve that functional consistency.

A role's definition can be anywhere between very general, such as "Base" role, to very specific, such as "App-A Inventory Backup PostgreSQL DB Server". It is a common practice to use a role to group functionality that goes together, like all the recipes that should be run on every node grouped in a "Base" role.

Sometimes, servers will be assigned a single role, such as "UI Server". Other times, a server will be assigned more than one role. For example, when you want to deploy a server as a 3-tier all in one, that server might have the roles of "UI Server", "DB Server", and "App Server" assigned to it. This distinction can be one of environment. For example, in a development environment, you may deploy a server as an all in one, with all three roles assigned to it, but in production, you deploy each role to a separate server or multiple servers, as load necessitates.

How to create a role

There are two ways to create a new Chef role. The first way to create a role is to use a Knife create command that will allow you to edit a role template and then transfer that edited template to the Chef server directly, creating the role (without creating a saved copy of the role on your workstation). The format of the create command is:

```
knife role create <role_name> [options]
```

For example to create a "base" role using default options, you would issue a command like this:

```
knife role create base
```

That command will launch your editor with a template that contains the various parts of a role, in JSON data format. Here is an example of using the Knife command to create the "base" role:

Of course, you will need to populate the various parts of the role, such as the description and the run_list. Once you have added the content desired for your role, you will save and then exit the editor. This will allow Knife to upload your new role directly to the Chef server. Similarly, you can edit an existing role by using the Knife command in this format:

```
knife role edit <role_name> [options]
```

For example, to edit the "base" role using default options, you can issue the following command:

```
knife role edit base
```

When creating or editing roles this way, you will get a confirmation message that indicates success, such as "Created role[base]" or "Saved role[base]".

The second way, which is the way I would recommend, is to first create a role file on your workstation and then use Knife to upload the role from that file to the Chef server. A role file can be created in one of two formats. One is a JSON data file that is in the same form as the template used in the `knife role create` command. The other is to create the role file as a ruby file that contains domain-specific language. Either way, the file contains the definition of the role it represents. The standard practice is to have the name of the role file equal to the name of the role and to save the role file in the `repo/roles` folder. For example, a ruby-formatted role file for the "Web Server" role would be saved as `~/chef-repo/roles/webserver.rb`.

 This is the best practice way to create roles because you can save the role file in your git repo, like the other aspects of your infrastructure code, and capture the history of the changes made to the role over time.

Once the role file is created, it is then uploaded to the Chef server with an upload command that takes the following form:

```
knife role from file <path to the role file> [options]
```

For example, to update the webserver role, you would have a command like this:

```
knife role from file roles/webserver.rb
```

When all goes well, you will get a message back that says "`Updated Role webserver!`".

Using per-environment run-lists in roles

You may have noted that the section for the env_run_lists in the JSON data role template is shown in the previous section. That section allows you to create different run lists that get used when the role is applied to the various environments in your organization, such as development and production. Per environment run lists can provide a powerful way to deploy server functionality that differs between the stages of the development process.

Per environment run lists in roles can be defined for any number of environments, but there can only be one run list per environment. When a role that has env_run_lists defined is applied to an environment not defined in the role, the default run list, defined in the run_list section of the role, is applied to the server. Similarly, when an environment defined in the env_run_list section has an empty run list, the default run list defined in run_list will be used. Here is a sample role that uses env_run_lists:

```
name 'big_app'
description 'Big App server role'
run_list 'role[base]'
env_run_lists(
  'production' => ['role[base] \
                      recipe[app_insall] \
                      recipe[prod_monitoring]'],
   'development' => ['role[base] \
                      recipe[mysql] \
                      recipe[app_install] \
                      recipe[load_test_data]'],
   'stage' => [],
   '_default' => []
)
override_attributes(
   'base_name' => 'primary',
   'user_name' => 'prod_svc_acct'
)
```

You can see that if the sample role is applied to a server in either the production or the development environments, there are specifically defined run lists that will be used. It is also anticipated that if this role is applied to a server in the stage environment or the _default environment, the default run_list will be used. Also, note that if the role is applied to a server in an environment not listed in the role file, say the "test" environment, then the default run_list will be used. This is exactly what happens when there are no values in the role file for the env_run_lists, that is, all servers that have this role get the default run_list regardless of what environment they are in.

Using nested roles

Having recipes grouped together into a role is very useful, and extending this idea by adding or nesting roles into the run_list of other roles makes for a powerful way to organize and define the functionality of a role or node. For example, if you have created a base role that includes all the recipes that should be applied to every node, it is much easier to add all of that functionality to your web server role by including the base role in its run_list before the other recipes that define a webserver. The resulting run_list is also much easier to understand. For example, a simple web server role might look like this:

```
name 'webserver'
description 'Simple Web Server'
run_list 'role[base] recipe[apache]'
default_attributes(
  'apache' => {
    'sites' => {
      'customers' => {
        'port' => 8080
      },
      'admins' => {
        'port' => 8081
      }
    }
  }
)
```

It is very clear that the web server role will always have the recipes that are part of the base role applied to the server before the apache recipe is applied.

The way this works is that during a chef-client run, the run_list is expanded. In the case of the preceding web server role, the recipes (and possibly roles) found in the "base" role will be evaluated first. You can think of it like this: if the base role has two recipes, say, recipe[motd] and recipe[ntp], then the resulting expanded run_list would look like this:

```
run_list 'recipe[motd] recipe[ntp] recipe[apache]'
```

> It is important to remember that everything is expanded in the order it is listed. If the base role had another role in between the motd and ntp recipes, the resulting expanded run_list would have the recipes from that role in between the motd and ntp recipes.

There are some important considerations here. The first is that during a chef-client run, a recipe will only be applied to a server once, the first time it appears in the expanded run_list. That is why the order in which roles are expanded is an important consideration. Next, this order or sequence is important to the order of the attributes. It contributes to the determination of attribute precedence. We will talk more about the precedence hierarchy later in this chapter. Finally, you will want to review the run_lists containing roles when we discuss policies, because currently, policies don't support roles in the run_list.

There is a downside to roles

Roles provide a lot of benefits to our infrastructure code, and until recently, they were the best way to encapsulate the cookbooks and related data into a single construct to be applied to our servers to define their functional purpose. But they have a major shortcoming. That shortcoming is the absence of any versioning capability.

What this means to you is that any changes to a role used in servers deployed to your environment will always be applied to those servers during the next chef-client run. There is no way to use a single role and define something like "use DB Server role version 1.0 in production and DB Server role version 1.1 in development". When the dev team updates the DB Server role for their ongoing development, that updated role is now the de facto standard for DB servers across all servers that the role is assigned to.

The Chef team knows that this is a shortcoming and has recently provided a solution. That solution is policies, and we will explore policies later in this chapter.

References

- The Chef.io documentation for roles can be found at `https://docs.chef.io/roles.html`.

- There is a nice tutorial on using roles and environments by Justin Ellingwood that can be found at `https://www.digitalocean.com/community/tutorials/how-to-use-roles-and-environments-in-chef-to-control-server-configurations`.

Using Chef environments

If your code development cycle goes through phases, such as development, test, stage, preproduction, and production, then you should also have servers that represent those same phases of development. Environments allow us to reproduce the workflow of the development life cycle by assigning servers to the different phases of that life cycle. Environments offer a way to designate a server as being within a specific part of the development process, such as test or production. Each server can be in one and only one environment. Put another way, a server cannot be in both development and production at the same time. The obvious benefit of using environments is that changes made to one environment will not impact other environments.

The _default environment

Every Chef server will have an environment created automatically when the server is deployed. That environment is named "_default". It is a permanent environment that cannot be renamed, modified, or deleted. Any node that is created on the Chef server will automatically be assigned to the _default environment unless another environment is specifically used.

Creating environments

The creation of an environment is done in much the same way as the creation of a role. There are two methods when using Knife — creating the environment using a `knife environment create` command — or creating an environment file in your chef repo and then uploading that file to create the environment using the `knife environment from file` command. Just like with roles, I recommend that you always create environment files in your chef repo and then upload those files to the Chef server to create the environment. This allows the environment to be checked into your source code control system (that is, Git) and have a history of all the changes made to the environment.

Again, like role files, the environment file can be created in one of two formats: either the JSON data format, or the Ruby DSL format. Here is a sample environment file for a development environment created using the Ruby format:

```
name 'test'
description 'The test environment for the bigapp project'
cookbook_versions(
  'bigapp' => '>= 2.1',
  'testdata' => '= 2.1.1'
)
override_attributes(
```

```
  'bigapp' => {
    'listen' => ['8080', '4443']
  },
  'testdata' => {
    'testset' => 'customer'
  }
)
```

You create environment files in a folder named environments off your `chef-repo` folder. For example, the test environment file would be saved to `~/chef-repo/environments/test.rb`. The best practice is to name the file using the name of the environment. Once you've created the environment file, you would upload that file to the Chef Server with a command in the following format:

`knife environment from file <path to environment file> [options]`

For example, to upload the test environment, you would use the following command:

`knife environment from file environments/test.rb`

A successful upload will result in a response such as `Updated Environment test`. Note that changes that you make to the environment file are uploaded using the same command used to create the environment, and the resulting success message will also be the same.

Use the `-a` or `--all` parameter to upload all environments or roles at once.

Both the Knife environment from a file and the knife role from a file can be used to upload all of the environments or roles at once if you supply a folder instead of a file name and use the `-a` or `--all` parameter. For example, `knife environment from file environments/ -a` would upload all environment files in the `environments` folder.

Specifying cookbook versions in environments

Chef provides a method of specifying cookbook versions to be used within an environment via the "cookbook" or "cookbook_versions" attributes. In the sample shown in the previous section, you saw the use of the "cookbook_versions" attribute. This attribute allows you to specify the version or versions of multiple cookbooks that can be applied to nodes within the environment, in this case, the "bigapp" and "testdata" cookbooks. You can specify the version of a single cookbook by using the "cookbook" attribute instead of "cookbook_versions" (although a single cookbook could also be specified using the "cookbook_versions" attribute).

The limits or constraints that you can specify for the cookbooks used in an environment are the standard operators that you are probably already familiar with, such as "=" (exactly this version), ">=" (this version or any greater version), "~>" (this version or any greater version that does not exceed the specified version number element), and others. If a version constraint is not specified for a cookbook in an environment, it is assumed that any version of that cookbook is acceptable for nodes within that environment.

References

- The Chef.io documentation for roles can be found at `https://docs.chef.io/environments.html`.

- A complete description of the cookbook version constraints can be found at `https://docs.chef.io/cookbook_versions.html`.

When you want to move nodes from one environment to another, you can use the Knife Exec command. Read more about that in the Knife subcommands section found in *Chapter 2*, *Knife Tooling and Plugins*.

Using Chef organizations

A single Chef Server can be configured to manage the infrastructure of multiple organizations. For example, if your company has different business units that each have their own application and infrastructure servers, they can all use the same Chef server or set of Chef servers by defining unique organizations for each business unit on those Chef servers. Organizations allow the siloing of your infrastructure code, including the cookbooks, nodes, roles, environments, and so on. Said another way, cookbooks, nodes, roles, and so on, are not shared across organizations. A cookbook with the same name can exist in multiple organizations and have completely different content in each organization. This is the mechanism that allows for multitenancy on a Chef server. Each organization will have its own set of users. It is possible for a user to have access to multiple organizations, but such a user would have to be invited into each organization.

Creating organizations

An organization can be created on the Chef server via the `chef-server-ctl` command, as shown in the *Setting Up an On-premise Chef Server* section of *Chapter 1, Setting Up a Development Environment on Your Workstation*. For reference, the format of that command goes like this:

```
chef-server-ctl org-create short_name "full_organization_name"
--association_user user_name --filename ORGANIZATION-validator.pem
```

The initial (default) organization will always be created with this command. Additional organizations can be created using this command or through the Chef UI when the Chef Management Console has been installed on the Chef server (also shown in *Chapter 1, Setting Up a Development Environment on Your Workstation*).

Access control

Chef provides access control through a role-based system that uses organizations, groups, and users. The organization is the top-level entity for controlling access. The organization allows for access to the Chef server itself. Users need to be invited into an organization, and they have to accept that invitation to access the Chef server content belonging to that organization.

Each organization will contain a set of groups, some default, for example, "admins" and "users," and optionally some custom groups. Groups control access to object types and objects within an organization. Depending on the need, custom groups can be created within an organization to further fine tune the access control within that organization.

A default user is created during the initial setup of the Chef server, which is automatically added to the admins group. In addition, the Chef server can have any number of other users, all of which will belong to one or more organizations.

References

- The link to the Chef.io reference on organization and groups is `https://docs.chef.io/server_orgs.html`.

- There is a Knife plugin that can be useful when it is necessary to work with multiple organizations or multiple Chef servers. It is named Knife Block, and you can find it at `https://github.com/knife-block/knife-block`.

- The information on the Chef Management Console is at `https://docs.chef.io/ctl_manage.html`.

Learning the attribute precedence hierarchy

With roles, environments, cookbooks, recipes, and so on, there are many places that attributes can be defined. In addition, there are many types of attributes that can be used. If, as a slight exaggeration, the same attribute is defined in all possible resources, each with a different value, how do you know which value would be applied when chef-client converges the node? Consider a more real-world example if you use an application cookbook that has a default attribute defined for the install directory, and you need that app to install into a different directory, what type of attribute can you use, and where should you set it so that your value would be used instead of the default? The answer to these questions is found in the precedence hierarchy. The factors that determine precedence include the type of attribute, the source of the attribute, and of course, the order evaluated. Let's take a closer look at these factors now.

Understanding attribute precedence factors

There are six types of attributes. Each one represents a different level of precedence. The six types, in order of precedence, are: "default", "force_default", "normal", "override", "force_override", and "automatic."

When developing cookbooks, it is the best practice to always provide a default value for the attributes defined in your cookbook. And it is the best practice to use the type "default" when assigning those values. The reason you should use the "default" attribute type is that "default" attributes are at the lowest level of precedence in the hierarchy, and they are always reset at the start of a chef-client run. By using the "default" type of attribute, you allow users of your cookbooks to supply role- and environment-specific values for the attributes using the same "default" type and still supersede your defaults with theirs. And when a developer decides to create a wrapper cookbook, having your cookbook attributes defined with the "default" type makes it easy for the developer to assign new attribute values that will be used instead of yours.

> Remember that the "default" attribute type is the best choice for your cookbook's default attribute values.

Again, the "default" attribute type is the type with the lowest level of precedence. The attribute type that is the next level up in the precedence hierarchy is the "force_default". When you use the attribute type force_default in your cookbooks, you are stating that the attribute values set should take precedence over the "default" attribute values set in any roles or environments.

Next up in the precedence hierarchy is the "normal" type of attribute, sometimes referred to as the "set" type. Normal attribute values have a higher precedence than both default and force_default attributes. In addition, the normal type attribute values are preserved on the node between chef-client runs. This is unlike the "default" type attributes, which are reset on every chef-client run.

The next higher level of attribute is the "override" attribute. While override attributes can be set in roles or environments, typically if necessary, you will use override attributes directly in a recipe. There is also a "force_override" attribute type that has a higher level of precedence than an override attribute. A force_override attribute would be used to make sure that the attribute value set in a cookbook was used instead of any defined in a role or environment.

Finally, at the highest precedence level, we have the "automatic" type attributes. The automatic type of attribute is set by Ohai on the node and always has the highest level of precedence. Examples of automatic attributes would be things specific to the node, like CPU speed or amount of RAM. Automatic attributes cannot be modified during a chef-client run.

> With all of these attribute types available, it can be challenging to know which type to use. I have found that it is usually best to limit your use of attribute types to the default type. There will be situations when you will need to use the other types, but if most of the attribute values you create are type default, you will be successful.

Attribute values can come from a variety of sources. These include nodes, cookbooks (in attribute files), recipes, environments, and roles. These sources, combined with the attribute types listed earlier, generate 15 possible levels of precedence.

Resulting precedence hierarchy

So what does all this mean? When chef-client converges the attributes in a run, the attributes collected from all the various sources are evaluated to determine which value is actually used when applying the recipes. Since there are 15 levels of precedence, there is a mapping of those levels. Chef.io has provided a very nice table to be able to understand the order of precedence. The higher the number in this table, the higher the level of precedence. Said another way, if an attribute is assigned a value in more than one place, the place with the highest number in this table is the value that will be used:

	Attribute Files	**Node/Recipe**	**Environment**	**Role**
default	1	2	3	4
force_default	5	6		
normal	7	8		
override	9	10	12	11
force_override	13	14		
automatic	15			

Let's consider a specific example. You have a `default.rb` file in your apache cookbook/attributes/ folder that contains the following default attribute values:

```
default['apache']['dir']          = '/etc/apache2'
default['apache']['listen_ports'] = [ '80','443' ]
```

Your organization requires that all web servers get installed into /var/www folder and that they use the ports 8080 and 4443 instead of the standard defaults.

Armed with the knowledge provided in the precedence table earlier, you can add "default" type attributes to your web server role, as follows:

```
name 'webserver'
description 'webserver'
run_list 'role[base] recipe[apache]'
default_attributes(
  'apache' => {
    'dir' => '/var/www',
    'listen_ports' => %w(8080 4443)
  }
)
```

And know that your values will be used instead of the cookbook's defaults because a "default" attribute type in a role has a higher level of precedence than the same default type attributes defined in the cookbook's attributes file.

Exploring policies

One of the best things about cookbooks is that they can be versioned. And as you have learned, the best application of cookbooks is to combine them into roles. Unfortunately, there is no concept of version for roles. The proper application of roles to your infrastructure obscures the desirable standard of versions.

Enter policies. Policies allow you to group all of the various resources into a high-level object that defines the specific versions that are used to create the object. Policies combine the best parts of roles, environments, and tools such as Berkshelf, into a single-versioned resource. You can apply a policy in a development environment, test it thoroughly, and promote that policy into the stage and then production environments, progressing your infrastructure code through its lifecycle in a safe, reliable way.

What exactly is a policy?

A policy is built by creating a policyfile. A policyfile is kind of like a Chef role mixed with a Berkshelf berksfile. Policyfiles are used to create artifacts that are used by the chef-client to configure a node. These artifacts are a lock file and a cookbook bundle. They are versioned and cannot be modified without changing the version, and because of this, your chef-client runs become 100 percent reproducible.

A policyfile contains the policy description for a node. They are written using Ruby DSL and contain the `run_list` of recipes, where to get the recipe's cookbooks (including the version of the cookbooks that are valid), and the attributes needed for the recipes. Using ChefDK's `chef generate` command with the policyfile, you create a policy lock file and cache the required cookbooks. The policy and cookbooks can then be uploaded to the Chef server or export the policy and cookbooks into a directory to be used with chef-client or chef solo.

Caching the cookbooks provides several benefits. For example, each cookbook becomes a unique artifact, including each version of the cookbook used. Each of these artifacts can be tracked in a source control. This provides a guarantee that policies will be consistently applied to nodes. The `chef generate` command creates a policy lock file that includes a checksum. Any change in any of the cookbooks used causes a change in the checksum value, which prevents any unexpected cookbook changes being applied to your nodes. This allows a level of certainty that you can deploy a policy to a node across the full development life cycle with 100 percent consistency.

Why would I use a policy?

Although the use of roles can be very effective, there are still significant challenges that are not addressed very well by them, the biggest of the challenges being that roles don't have versions. Another big challenge is that the effort of dependency resolution for cookbooks requires the use of an external tool to work effectively. For most Chef users, that tool is Berkshelf. Chef Environments fills in some of the version deficiency, but the combination of roles, environments, and dependency resolvers like Berkshelf quickly become a source of confusion and potential mistakes. To be clear, I am not saying that there is anything wrong with using Berkshelf. Frankly, until now, it was a must-use tool. But with the introduction of Chef Policy, Berkshelf is no longer needed. The Policyfile includes all the necessary details to resolve all cookbook dependencies.

Another reason that you would want to use Chef Policy is the attribute precedence hierarchy that was covered in a previous section. With the use of Chef Policy, the 15 levels of precedence are effectively reduced by about seven. This removes nearly half of the attribute precedence complexity. This alone can be a compelling reason to switch from roles to policy.

How do I use a policy?

Aha! The part you have been waiting for: how to create and use Chef Policy. First, you will create a Policyfile that describes the desired node state. Let's begin by showing a very simplified example that uses the "example" cookbook that is generated with a `chef generate repo` command (which we explored in *Chapter 1, Setting Up a Development Environment on Your Workstation*). Here is our policyfile:

```
name 'cookbook-dir'
default_source :chef_repo, File.dirname(__FILE__)

run_list 'example'
```

To create the policy lock file from a Policyfile, execute a command in the following format:

```
chef install <path to policy file> [options]
```

For example, here is what it looked like when I created our policy lock file for "cookbook-dir":

```
chef install cookbook-dir.rb

Building policy cookbook-dir

Expanded run list: recipe[example]

Caching Cookbooks...
```

```
Installing example 1.0.0
```

```
Lockfile written to /Users/earlwaud/chef-repo/cookbook-dir.lock.json
```

Let's take a look at the generated policy lock file. Inside the `cookbook-dir.lock.json` file, you will find quite a bit of specific information about our policy. One bit of data to notice is a key "revision_id". Look at the value that was created for it. Here is the one from my lock file:

```
"revision_id":
 "66d367a388f645c251b15db7586830a36be2aadaf9f2aaa96065b1691d0d5995"
```

This is the unique identifier for this lock file and serves as its version number. You can see the name of the policy in the "name" field. You see the run_list that was specified in the policyfile.

 Note that it expanded the recipe to identify the specific cookbook recipe that is used, in this case "default."

Next, you see the specifics about the cookbook captured in this lock file. There is the friendly version number and then a unique identifier. Even if a developer makes changes to this cookbook without updating the friendly version number, the identifier version generated will change, thus providing a new "version number" for the lock file. This makes sure that you get the exact version of the cookbook you intended when you apply the policy to your nodes. There's more data in the lock file, mostly related to attributes. Note that if the values for the attributes change, so will the lock file identifier.

When changes are made to the underlying cookbooks, and a new version of the policy is desired, you issue the command to update the policy in the following format:

chef update <path to policy file> [options]

For example, after changes were made to the "examples" recipe, I updated the policy look file with the chef update command. Here is the command I used:

chef update cookbook-dir.rb

The policy lock file is updated, and it contains a new `revision_id` and a new cookbook identifier (even though I didn't update the cookbook-friendly version number from 1.0.0). Here is the new "revision_id" from the updated lock file for comparison with the higher version:

```
"revision_id":
 "f80ae69ae021e0b577a8c0b9dd23f4bb5ea4b91c66ce921cf868721b9a01cafa"
```

You still need to update the friendly version number

Even though the policy lock file has its own unique version number, it is still going to be the best practice to update the friendly version number in the metadata of your cookbooks. The version number will always play an important role for cookbook versions when collaborating with others or publishing cookbooks to the supermarket.

Another example

So now, let's walk through the workflow of creating and using a new policy. Begin by changing into your home or preferred working directory. Then, execute the following commands:

```
chef generate repo policyfile-book
cd policyfile-book/
git init
git add .
git commit -m 'Initial repo commit'
chef generate policyfile
```

So far, you have created a new repo, initialized git, and then added and committed all the files in the new repo. Finally, you generated a new policyfile template. Since you didn't specify a name for the policy file, you created a template file named `Policyfile.rb`. Here is what that policy file template looks like:

```
cat Policyfile.rb
# Policyfile.rb - Describe how you want Chef to build your system.
#
# For more information on the Policyfile feature, visit
# https://github.com/opscode/chef-dk/blob/master/POLICYFILE_README.md

# A name that describes what the system you're building with Chef does.
name "example-application-service"
```

```
# Where to find external cookbooks:
default_source :supermarket


# run_list: chef-client will run these recipes in the order specified.
run_list "example_cookbook::default"


# Specify a custom source for a single cookbook:
# cookbook "example_cookbook", path: "../cookbooks/example_cookbook"
```

Now you will want to make changes to the policy file template to turn it into the desired policy file. I've edited my `Policyfile.rb` file, making the simple changes resulting in the contents shown here:

```
cat Policyfile.rb
name "policyfile-book"
default_source :supermarket
run_list "motd", 'ntp'
le_cookbook", path: "../cookbooks/example_cookbook"
```

Specifically, I changed the name of the policy to `policyfile-book`. I set the run_list to include two recipes, motd and ntp.

 It is important to note that the `run_list` of a policy can only use recipes. You cannot specify a role, or another policy. These options may be available in future releases, but for now, it is only recipes in the run_list of your policies.

Next we need to generate our policy lock file and cache our desired cookbooks. We do that by issuing the `chef install` command. It will look something like this:

```
chef install
Building policy policyfile-book
Expanded run list: recipe[motd], recipe[ntp]
Caching Cookbooks...
Installing motd          0.6.3
Installing ntp           1.8.6
Installing chef_handler 1.2.0


Lockfile written to /Users/earlwaud/policyfile-book/Policyfile.lock.json
```

Note that in my example, there is a dependency on the chef_handler cookbook, and it was automatically dealt with, and that cookbook was also cached. So, if the cookbooks are cached, where do they go? Well, if you don't specify otherwise, they go into a cache folder off your home directory. For me, that is `~/.chefdk/cache/cookbooks/`. Here is what you will find if you look in that folder, at this point in the example:

```
ls -la ~/.chefdk/cache/cookbooks/

total 0

drwxr-xr-x    7 earlwaud   staff   238 Dec 13 23:07 .

drwxr-xr-x    5 earlwaud   staff   170 Dec 13 22:42 ..

drwxr-xr-x   11 earlwaud   staff   374 Dec 13 23:07 chef_handler-1.2.0-
supermarket.chef.io

drwxr-xr-x   22 earlwaud   staff   748 Dec 13 23:07 motd-0.6.3-supermarket.
chef.io

drwxr-xr-x   10 earlwaud   staff   340 Dec 13 23:07 ntp-1.8.6-supermarket.
chef.io
```

 Note that the specific versions have been identified in the name of the cookbooks.

Next up, we are going to upload our policy and the related files to our Chef server. Remember that we just created a new repo, and it will be necessary to configure that repo to communicate with our Chef server before we can upload the policy. I took care of that by using a shortcut. I copied the contents of the `.chef` folder from another repo into this new one. Here is what that looks like:

```
mkdir .chef

cp -r ../chef-repo/.chef/* ./.chef/
```

Okay, so now we are ready to upload our policy. We upload the policy and its related files with the `chef push` command. You will provide a name for this policy so that it can be identified for use later. In my case, I am using the name "book". Here is what that looks like:

```
chef push book

Uploading policy to policy group book

Uploaded vim 2.0.0 (8f81a5b1)

Uploaded zsh 1.0.3 (cb687099)
```

Alternatively, you can export the policy and related files to a local folder or to a tar file using the `chef export` command. Here is what using those commands looks like, first the export to a folder:

```
chef export chef-repo
Exported policy 'policyfile-book' to chef-repo


ls -la chef-repo/
total 16
drwxr-xr-x    6 earlwaud    staff     204 Dec 13 22:54 .
drwxr-xr-x   15 earlwaud    staff     510 Dec 13 22:54 ..
-rw-r--r--    1 earlwaud    staff    1566 Dec 13 22:54 Policyfile.lock.json
-rw-r--r--    1 earlwaud    staff     396 Dec 13 22:54 client.rb
drwxr-xr-x    4 earlwaud    staff     136 Dec 13 22:54 cookbooks
drwxr-xr-x    3 earlwaud    staff     102 Dec 13 22:54 data_bags
```

Or exporting to create a tar file:

```
chef export -a chef-repo
Exported policy 'policyfile-book' to /Users/earlwaud/policyfile-book/
chef-repo/policyfile-book-c465f6433cc209d0fd8ba9196a9e90beaccb3ab88161556
8f2041aa433cb54c5.tgz
```

Now you have two artifacts you can use to configure your "Book" nodes. Using these exact same artifacts, first in dev, then in test, and finally in production, assures that the configuration of the servers in each stage of your lifecycle is 100 percent consistent.

How to specify the source options for cookbooks

Since you can specify the source you want to obtain cookbooks from in your Policyfile, you need to know the options you have for those sources. Here is a list of sources, with examples:

```
# cookbooks with version constraint
cookbook 'yum', '= 3.6.1'
cookbook 'yum', '~> 3.6.0'

# cookbooks from a local path
cookbook 'yum', '/Users/earlwaud/chef-repo/cookbooks/yum'
```

```
# cookbooks from a git repository
cookbook 'yum', git: 'https://github.com/chef-cookbooks/yum'

# cookbooks from a github repository
cookbook 'yum', github: 'chef-cookbooks/yum'

# cookbooks from a github repo with a release tag
cookbook 'yum', github: 'chef-cookbooks/yum', tag: '3.7.0'
```

Also, there are options for what you want to use as a default source for when you don't specify a cookbook source. The default is defined in the default_source value, and here are the options you have, with examples:

```
# use the chef supermarket
default_source :supermarket
default_source :community

# use a local or private supermarket
default_source :supermarket, 'https://mysupermarket.domain.com'

# use the cookbooks in the current working directory
default_source :chef_repo, FILE.dirname(__FILE__)

# use the cookbooks in another filesystem location
default_source :chef_repo, '/home/src/other-chef-repo'
```

:community = :supermarket

In early versions of the policy generator, the default_source for cookbooks was set to ":community". Later, this was updated to ":supermarket". If you see :community used in policy files, know that it is the same as using :supermarket.

What are the "Gotchas"?

The number one consideration before using Chef Policy is that at the time of this writing, it is just now "nearing" 1.0 status. With the latest Chef release, all of the major features are available, but there is still significant development in flight that will make policies better in the near future.

If you want to know the specific limitations in the current release, here is my list:

- Must be using the latest released versions of Chef, ChefDK, and Chef Server
- There is no support for Chef roles

- You cannot "nest" or "include" other policies like you can with Chef roles
- Using Chef zero, which is a local in-memory Chef Server, requires compatibility mode
- Not yet officially branded as version 1.0 by Chef.io
- And my #1 limitation... Not yet implemented for use with Knife bootstrap

References

- The (limited) documentation about policies on the Chef.io site can be found at `https://docs.chef.io/policy.html`. Hopefully, it will be expanded by the time you visit it.
- You will probably want to check out the policyfile documentation on GitHub found at `https://github.com/chef/chef-dk/blob/master/POLICYFILE_README.md`.
- You will find the chef-zero repo on GitHub at `https://github.com/chef/chef-zero`.
- The link to the Chef.io blog post titled "Policyfiles: A Guided Tour" at `https://www.chef.io/blog/2015/08/18/policyfiles-a-guided-tour`.
- There is an excellent Chef.io webinar recording on the why, what, and how of Chef policies, that can be watched at `https://www.chef.io/webinars/?commid=171697&utm_campaign=add-to-calendar&utm_medium=calendar&utm_source=brighttalk-transact`.

Summary

In this chapter, you learned about Chef roles and how valuable they are to deploying fully functional servers. We saw that even though they are a global resource, they can be leveraged across environments to deliver different content, based on the environment of the node. We also discussed the big shortcoming of roles, that being their lack of a version component. Then, we looked at using Chef Environments to mimic the development life cycle of your infrastructure code. That was followed by talking about how to provide multitenancy with your Chef servers using organizations. Next, we took a deep dive into the attribute precedence hierarchy, and then we finished up with a visit to the exciting new policy feature, which delivers an object that combines the best of roles and environments (and dependency tools such as Berkshelf too).

In out next chapter, we will investigate custom resources, explaining how to create and use them effectively. Are you ready? Then read on...

4
Custom Resources

In this chapter, we're going to discuss the exciting changes released in Chef 12.5 that transform the old LWRPs and HWRPs into the much easier-to-create and use Custom Resources. We'll start with a look at the differences between the old and new, but by the end of the chapter, the reader will know how to build and use Custom Resources.

"To me, my recipes are priceless." – Colonel Sanders

Here is a list of the topics covered in this chapter:

- Out with the old (LWRPs), in with the new (Custom Resources)
- Creating an example use case
- Creating and using a Custom Resource
- Making a Custom Resource more reusable
- Subclassing a Custom Resource

Out with the old (LWRPs), in with the new (Custom Resources)

When Chef was created, the Chef developers delivered a tool that had a lot of capabilities right out of the box. The variety of resources that it supported natively was very useful and quite extensive. But, of course, being a finite tool, it could not handle every possible type of resource that existed or could exist in the future. Knowing this, the Chef developers built in a feature set to allow users to augment the capabilities and support an ever-growing set of resources.

This feature set is known as **Lightweight Resource Providers (LWRP)** and **Heavyweight Resource Providers (HWRP)**. These features allow users to define new resources and create the providers to support those resources, making Chef infinitely customizable.

The two types, LWRP and HWRP, are differentiated by the level of complexity used to define the resources and the providers being created. LWRPs are created using the **Chef DSL (Domain-specific Language)** and are capable of handling most customization needs. HWRP are created using pure Ruby. HWRPs are the go-to feature when the requirements are too complex to be handled by straight Chef DSL.

Unfortunately, creating and using LWRPs and HWRPs is more challenging than most of the other features of Chef. This is because the Chef developers created Custom Resources. Custom Resources provide the same feature set as LWRP and HWRP, but do it in a way that is much easier to create and use. None of the capabilities are lost in translation either. A Custom Resource can easily handle the task of providing new resources using the Chef DSL, but it can also handle the times when you need to support more complex scenarios that require using pure Ruby.

What is the difference between the old way and the new way of defining resources?

As of version 12.5, LWRPs and HWRPs are no longer used. All existing code that creates and uses them will still work because version 12.5 is backward compatible with cookbooks from previous versions, but new resources should now be created only as Custom Resources.

LWRP and HWRP required you to create both the Resource and the Provider. With Custom Resources, it is only necessary to create the Resource. There is no need to create a folder named providers in the cookbook when creating Custom Resources.

Creating and using Custom Resources is much easier than it was to create and use LWRPs and HWRPs.

Custom Resources use "properties". LWRPs and HWRPs used attributes, which was easily confused with Node attributes.

It is much easier to create OS-specific resources by subclassing a base class, and we will take a look at doing that later in the chapter.

 Although Custom Resources are not deprecating "Definitions", it is recommended that going forward, you should create Custom Resources instead.

There are many other differences between the old Resource Provider model and the Custom Resource model introduced in version 12.5, but what is listed earlier should provide reason enough to embrace the change.

What is a Custom Resource?

A Custom Resource is an extension to Chef. It is a way to create and use new resources that were not provided by Chef. A Custom Resource is created as part of a cookbook. A Custom Resource can be created with Chef DSL and can use built-in resources, or you can create a Custom Resource using Ruby if the need is complex enough. A Custom Resource provides the mechanism to create and use resources that are not built in to Chef. For example, Chef has built-in resources for things, such as directories, files, and services. However, there is no built-in resource for websites. So, as a way to demonstrate Custom Resources, we will create a website Custom Resource later in this chapter.

References

- The link to Chef's new Custom Resources information is `https://docs.chef.io/custom_resources.html`.

- The link to the Chef page for Custom Resources prior to version 12.5 is `https://docs.chef.io/release/12-4/custom_resources.html`. It describes LWRP and HWRP.

- The Chef documentation for (almost deprecated) definitions is at `https://docs.chef.io/definitions.html`.

- There is an excellent book that really details the creation and use of LWRPs and HWRPs. The book is titled *Customizing Chef* and is by *Jon Cowie*. You can check out a sample at `https://books.google.com/books/about/Customizing_Chef.html?id=XOBdBAAAQBAJ&printsec=frontcover&source=kp_read_button&hl=en#v=onepage&q&f=false`.

Creating an example use case

In order to understand the creation and use of Custom Resources, let's create a somewhat contrived example use case. In order to avoid getting lost in the details, we'll keep the example simple, using just enough detail so that you can see the power of Custom Resources.

What is the goal?

We have been asked to create a new cookbook to support a brand new web application. The application is going to use several different websites such as a "Users" site, a "Suppliers" site, and a "Customers" site. The developers are saying that there will be several other sites needed in the future, but they want to get started now with these three.

Based on this short user story, we are going to create a new cookbook named "mywebapp", and it is going to create the beginnings of three websites: "Users", "Suppliers", and "Customers". We should keep in mind that these three sites are only the beginning, and our cookbook should be written to make adding more websites easy. We are going to begin with the non-custom resource model, so let's get started.

Creating the cookbook

As described in *Chapter 1, Setting Up a Development Environment on Your Workstation*, we will use the chef command-line tool to create our cookbook template. We do that by issuing the following commands:

```
cd ~/chef-repo/cookbooks
chef generate cookbook mywebapp
```

Let's take a look at what we are starting with. Go into the new cookbook folder and issue the tree command like this:

```
cd mywebapp
tree
```

This is what you should see:

We have a new cookbook template named `mywebapp` ready to customize to our needs.

Creating the default recipe

Now that we have our cookbook template ready to go, let's create our default recipe. Adding the following code to the `default.rb` file will give us the resources needed to create three (very simplistic) websites. The code is as follows:

```
#
# Cookbook Name:: mywebapp
# Recipe:: default
#
# Copyright (c) 2016 The Authors, All Rights Reserved.

directory '/var/www/users' do
  recursive true
  mode 0755
```

```
  user 'earlwaud'
  group 'wheel'
  action :create
end

file '/var/www/users/index.html' do
  content '<html><title>Users</title><body><h1>Hello to our Users</
h1></body></html>'
  mode 0755
  user 'earlwaud'
  group 'wheel'
  notifies :restart, 'service[httpd]'
end

service 'httpd' do
  action :nothing
end

directory '/var/www/suppliers' do
  recursive true
  mode 0755
  user 'earlwaud'
  group 'wheel'
  action :create
end

file '/var/www/suppliers/index.html' do
  content '<html><title>Suppliers</title><body><h1>Hello to our
Suppliers</h1></body></html>'
  mode 0755
  user 'earlwaud'
  group 'wheel'
  notifies :restart, 'service[httpd]'
end

service 'httpd' do
  action :nothing
end

directory '/var/www/customers' do
  recursive true
  mode 0755
  user 'earlwaud'
  group 'wheel'
```

```
  action :create
end

file '/var/www/customers/index.html' do
  content '<html><title>Customers</title><body><h1>Hello to our
Customers</h1></body></html>'
  mode 0755
  user 'earlwaud'
  group 'wheel'
  notifies :restart, 'service[httpd]'
end

service 'httpd' do
  action :nothing
end
```

Looking at the preceding code, we can see that we have repeated a "set" of resources three times, one for each of the three websites we wish to create. First, we have the directory resource that defines the location where we want to put our website files. The description includes instructions to recursively create the segments of the folder path and apply the permissions, owner, and group values to each one. Next, we have a file resource that creates an index.html file in the target folder, again applying the permissions, owner, and group values. Also, we are providing a very basic description of the content for the file. In this case, it is a site-specific title, and a site-specific "Hello" message for the body of the web page.

If we want to validate that what we have created so far is working, we can execute a local override chef-client run with the -z and -o parameters, as follows:

cd ~/chef-repo

sudo chef-client -z -o mywebapp

This chef-client run will generate a lot of output. Here is a subset of what you will see:

```
(truncated) ...
Synchronizing Cookbooks:
[2016-01-18T12:20:02-08:00] INFO: Storing updated cookbooks/mywebapp/
recipes/default.rb in the cache.
  - mywebapp (0.1.0)
Compiling Cookbooks...
Converging 9 resources
Recipe: mywebapp::default
  * directory[/var/www/users] action create[2016-01-18T12:20:02-08:00]
INFO: Processing directory[/var/www/users] action create
(mywebapp::default line 7)
```

```
[2016-01-18T12:20:02-08:00] INFO: directory[/var/www/users] created
directory /var/www/users

    - create new directory /var/www/users[2016-01-18T12:20:02-08:00]
INFO: directory[/var/www/users] owner changed to 501
[2016-01-18T12:20:02-08:00] INFO: directory[/var/www/users] group
changed to 0
[2016-01-18T12:20:02-08:00] INFO: directory[/var/www/users] mode
changed to 755

    - change mode from '' to '0755'
    - change owner from '' to 'earlwaud'
    - change group from '' to 'wheel'
  * file[/var/www/users/index.html] action create[2016-01-
18T12:20:02-08:00] INFO: Processing file[/var/www/users/index.html]
action create (mywebapp::default line 15)
[2016-01-18T12:20:02-08:00] INFO: file[/var/www/users/index.html]
created file /var/www/users/index.html

    - create new file /var/www/users/index.html[2016-01-
18T12:20:02-08:00] INFO: file[/var/www/users/index.html] updated file
contents /var/www/users/index.html

    - update content in file /var/www/users/index.html from none to
23195b
    --- /var/www/users/index.html    2016-01-18 12:20:02.000000000
-0800
    +++ /var/www/users/.index.html20160118-4946-1nzzlcz  2016-01-18
12:20:02.000000000 -0800
    @@ -1 +1,2 @@
    +<html><title>Users</title><body><h1>Hello to our Users</h1></
body></html>[2016-01-18T12:20:02-08:00] INFO: file[/var/www/users/
index.html] owner changed to 501
[2016-01-18T12:20:02-08:00] INFO: file[/var/www/users/index.html]
group changed to 0
[2016-01-18T12:20:02-08:00] INFO: file[/var/www/users/index.html] mode
changed to 755
…(truncated)
```

The preceding subset of the chef-client run output is related to the set of resources creating the first website, "**Users**". You will note that it creates the new /var/www/users directory and then applies the owner, group, and permissions to it. Next, it creates the new /var/www/users/index.html file. Then, it sets the index.html file contents to the desired site content described in the file resource. Finally, it sets the owner, group, and permissions for the newly created file. All of this is as expected.

Our simple, but repetitive, recipe did the job. It created three "**websites**" as requested. Although that recipe worked, it does not meet all of the requirements of the developers. So what is missing?

The recipe worked, but what is missing?

Although the recipe worked and created our three websites, there is a significant request made by the developers that was not addressed. They wanted the recipe to be written so that it could be easily expanded to create many more additional websites.

Of course, we could copy the resources of one of the websites and paste them in at the bottom, editing the definitions to reflect a new website. This would work, but it is not very efficient, and it will make an already repetitive recipe even more repetitive. Also, this plan is a potential source of errors. For example, after pasting the copied resources, the person editing the recipe might forget to update one or more of the "custom" values, forgetting to change the file location, for example. What's more is that if there needs to be a change made, say changing the permissions from 755 to 644, it would be necessary to update the recipe in six places, even with just our three websites. Again, this method would be inefficient and error-prone.

So what can we do about meeting the developers' request, and at the same time, address all this inefficient repetition and potential for errors? Say hello to my little friend, "Custom Resources".

References

The link to chef-client documentation that includes the details for using local mode is `https://docs.chef.io/ctl_chef_client.html#run-in-local-mode`.

Creating and using a Custom Resource

Now that we have our use case defined and a working solution created, we want to introduce updates to the cookbook to turn what we have into a better solution that uses Custom Resources. Specifically, we are going to create a "website" Custom Resource.

What makes up a Custom Resource?

Custom Resources are created by making a Ruby file in the cookbook's resources folder. The resource name will be the name of the file created. For example, if we want to create a "website" Custom Resource, we would create a new Ruby file named website.rb, as follows:

```
mkdir -p ~/chef-repo/cookbooks/mywebapp/resources
touch ~/chef-repo/cookbooks/mywebapp/resources/website.rb
```

This will create a new folder named resources and create an empty file named website.rb in that folder.

 Creating a default.rb resource file: If you create a resource file named default.rb, the resource will have the same name as the cookbook.

A cookbook can have multiple resources. Each one would be defined in a separate Ruby file in the resources folder.

The contents of the resource file will have three basic parts:

- Declarations of the properties used in the Custom Resource
- Loading of the current value of the properties, if they already exist
- Definitions of the actions that the Custom Resource can take

A Custom Resource is much simpler to create when compared with the LWRP and HWRP.

Creating the "website" Custom Resource

We are going to "re-use" some of the code in the default.rb recipe to create our new "website" Custom Resource. First, let's create a new file to hold our Custom Resource:

```
mkdir ~/chef-repo/cookbooks/mywebapp/resources
touch ~/chef-repo/cookbooks/mywebapp/resources/website.rb
```

Next, let's copy one set of the website resources from our recipe/default.rb file, the Users site resources, and paste them into our new website.rb file. Here is the section we are copying and/or pasting:

```
directory '/var/www/users' do
  recursive true
  mode 0755
  user 'earlwaud'
```

```
    group 'wheel'
    action :create
end


file '/var/www/users/index.html' do
    content '<html><title>Users</title><body><h1>Hello to our Users</
h1></body></html>'
    mode 0755
    user 'earlwaud'
    group 'wheel'
    notifies :restart, 'service[httpd]'
end


service 'httpd' do
    action :nothing
end
```

Next, we need to "wrap" our copied code in an action block with the format
action :start do ... end. Now our website Custom Resource looks as follows:

```
action :start do
    directory '/var/www/users' do
        recursive true
        mode 0755
        user 'earlwaud'
        group 'wheel'
        action :create
    end


    file '/var/www/users/index.html' do
        content '<html><title>Users</title><body><h1>Hello to our Users</
h1></body></html>'
        mode 0755
        user 'earlwaud'
        group 'wheel'
        notifies :restart, 'service[httpd]'
    end


    service 'httpd' do
        action :nothing
    end
end
```

This code block is our action definition for our "website" Custom Resource.

 When you have more than one action defined in a Custom Resource file, the first action listed will be the default action.

In our example, you can plainly see that we have some "constants" defined in our action block, and because we want this to be a highly reusable Custom Resource, this simply will not do. So, let's create some properties for our Custom Resource, which we'll use to replace these constants.

At the top of our `website.rb` file, let's add two new properties. One will be the "site name" and the other will be the "title". Add the following two lines to the `website.rb` file:

```
property :site_name, String, name_property: true
property :title, String
```

The first line is for the site name. This property is defined to be a string and includes the `name_property` setting, which says to use the value of the resource name for the value of this property.

All resources defined in Chef have a `name_property`. For example, our directory resource for the Users site has the `name_property` of `/var/www/users`.

When a recipe uses our new website resource, the name it provides will be the value that gets set for our `site_name` property. This will make more sense when you see how we use our Custom Resource in the section ahead.

Second, we are adding a title property, also of type string.

Once we have our properties declared, we need to do some modifications to our Custom Resource's action to use the new properties instead of using the constant values currently defined.

Let's update our `website.rb` file to use the new properties now. Once updated, our file should contain the following:

```
property :site_name, String, name_property: true
property :title, String

action :start do
  directory "/var/www/#{site_name}" do
    recursive true
    mode 0755
    user 'earlwaud'
```

```
      group 'wheel'
      action :create
   end

   file "/var/www/#{site_name}/index.html" do
      content "<html><title>#{title}</title><body><h1>Hello to our
#{title}</h1></body></html>"
      mode 0755
      user 'earlwaud'
      group 'wheel'
      notifies :restart, 'service[httpd]'
   end

   service 'httpd' do
      action :nothing
   end
end
```

That is all we need for this very simplified example of a Custom Resource. Let's move on to how to use our new website Custom Resource.

Using our Custom Resource

Now that we have created our "website" Custom Resource, let's put it to use. We are going to update our cookbook's recipe file. Edit the `default.rb` file we created earlier, and cut out all of the code. Then, add the following three blocks of code to the now empty file:

```
mywebapp_website 'users' do
   title 'Users'
end

mywebapp_website 'suppliers' do
   title 'Suppliers'
end

mywebapp_website 'customers' do
   title 'Customers'
end
```

These three blocks of code are using our new Custom Resource. You will note from this example that the way you use a Custom Resource is to use the name of the cookbook, an underscore, and the name of the resource. In this case, our cookbook is named "mywebapp", and our Custom Resource is named (from the file that defines it) "website". Based on this, we can use our newly defined resource as "mywebapp_website".

Our two properties are given values for each instance of our Custom Resource. First, site_name is given the values from the resource names, such as "users", "suppliers", and "customers". Second, the title is given its values from the title properties.

Using our new Custom Resource has delivered on the request made by the developers. We have a new recipe that will be easy to expand to create future websites. In addition, we have removed a lot of repetition from the first version of our cookbook, and the result is a more user-friendly cookbook that is much less error-prone and easier to understand and use. Not bad, right?

So, let's take it for a spin. Use the local override chef-client run again to see how this has changed the way our resources are converged. Issue the same commands used earlier:

```
cd ~/chef-repo
sudo chef-client -z -o mywebapp
```

Here is what you should see in the chef-client output this time:

```
(truncated)...

Synchronizing Cookbooks:

[2016-01-18T14:03:42-08:00] INFO: Storing updated cookbooks/mywebapp/
recipes/default.rb in the cache.

[2016-01-18T14:03:42-08:00] INFO: Storing updated cookbooks/mywebapp/
resources/website.rb in the cache.

  - mywebapp (0.1.0)

Compiling Cookbooks...

Converging 3 resources

Recipe: mywebapp::default

  * mywebapp_website[users] action start[2016-01-18T14:03:42-08:00] INFO:
Processing mywebapp_website[users] action start (mywebapp::default line
7)


    * directory[/var/www/users] action create[2016-01-18T14:03:42-08:00]
INFO: Processing directory[/var/www/users] action create (/Users/
earlwaud/chef-repo/.chef/local-mode-cache/cache/cookbooks/mywebapp/
resources/website.rb line 5)

  (up to date)

    * file[/var/www/users/index.html] action create[2016-01-
18T14:03:42-08:00] INFO: Processing file[/var/www/users/index.html]
action create (/Users/earlwaud/chef-repo/.chef/local-mode-cache/cache/
cookbooks/mywebapp/resources/website.rb line 13)

  (up to date)
```

```
  * macosx_service[httpd] action nothing[2016-01-18T14:03:42-08:00]
INFO: Processing macosx_service[httpd] action nothing (/Users/earlwaud/
chef-repo/.chef/local-mode-cache/cache/cookbooks/mywebapp/resources/
website.rb line 21)

  (skipped due to action :nothing)

    (up to date)
...(truncated)
```

As in the output sample shown earlier, I have included only the subset of the output that relates to the creation of the Users website.

A couple of differences you should notice here are:

Only three resources are converged this time, compared to nine before. These three are our new Custom Resources. Also note that pretty much everything resulted in no action taken (up to date). This is because the new Custom Resource we created does the same work that was done (using nine resources) in our model that didn't use Custom Resources.

Both versions converge to the same state, but by using Custom Resources, we have achieved that desired state much more efficiently and in a way that is much more extensible.

References

The link to a Chef.io slide deck on creating Custom Resources is https://docs.chef.io/decks/custom_resources.html.

Making a Custom Resource more reusable

The Custom Resource we just created, "mywebapp_website", is easily reusable within our mywebapp cookbook and could be used with other cookbooks, but what if we want to expand on its reusability? What if we want to make a cookbook that only has a Custom Resource that we want to use in several cookbooks? The answer is pretty simple. Let's walk through the steps to convert our "website" Custom Resource into a more reusable Custom Resource-only cookbook.

Making a Custom Resource-only cookbook

The Custom Resource website.rb file in the cookbook mywebapp, which we created in the previous section, is almost all we need to create our more reusable Custom Resource-only cookbook. Let's create a new cookbook named appsite, which will be our new reusable cookbook:

```
cd ~/chef-repo/cookbooks

chef generate cookbook appsite
```

Now delete the entire recipe folder. The best practice for reusable Custom Resource cookbooks is that they do not have a recipe folder at all. They should only include the resources folder (and maybe a libraries folder if it uses helper functions, which we will talk about in the next section). Our reusable Custom Resource cookbook will not have its own recipes, but it will only contain the website Custom Resource found in the resources folder from our previous example.

Reuse the code from the "mywebapp" example

Now that we have a new cookbook (with no recipe folder), let's move the resources folder from our previous example into the "appsite" cookbook. This will completely remove the resources folder and the website.rb file within from the "mywebapp" cookbook and place them in our new "appsite" cookbook.

You're done. This completes the work on our reusable Custom Resource-only cookbook. Wow, that was really easy, right? So how do we use it?

Using the reusable Custom Resource-only cookbook

We now have a brand new shiny cookbook that supplies a Custom Resource to create websites. Using the cookbook is pretty easy. We need to do two things to our "mywebapp" cookbook example to leverage our "appsite" cookbook.

First, we need to add a "depends" directive to our cookbook metadata.rb file. Making this one line change will result in a metadata.rb file that looks like this:

```
name 'mywebapp'
maintainer 'The Authors'
maintainer_email 'you@example.com'
license 'all_rights'
description 'Installs/Configures mywebapp'
```

```
long_description 'Installs/Configures mywebapp'
version '0.1.0'
depends 'appsite'
```

Adding the `depends` directive to our cookbook ensures that the specified cookbook will be loaded and available when our cookbook converges. If the specified cookbook, in this case "appsite", is not available for some reason, the chef-client r un would fail to converge.

Secondly, we need to change the name we use when calling our Custom Resource. In the `default.rb` file of our "mywebapp" cookbook, change the three resource calls so that they use the new name for our Custom Resource. The resulting `default.rb` file will look like this:

```
appsite_website 'customers' do
  title 'Customers'
end

appsite_website 'suppliers' do
  title 'Suppliers'
end

appsite_website 'users' do
  title 'Users'
end
```

That was pretty easy too, right? When `Chef.io` created the Custom Resource feature, a driving goal was to make it much easier to create and use compared with LWRP and HWRP, and I think they have succeeded very well in that goal.

However, with that said, what if you need to do something a little more complex? For example, if you want to handle websites installed to different operating systems? We can do that too, and we'll take a look at doing it later in the chapter, with an example that uses subclassing in a Custom Resource. But now, let's have a quick look at handling idempotence.

Handling idempotence

In our simple example, the resources handle the check for idempotence, making sure that actions are only executed when the resulting state would be different than the existing state. But if we were doing something more complex, such as using Ruby code in our actions or making calls to APIs to affect change, then we need our code to handle the idempotence tasks. Fortunately, Chef has the helper functions "load_current_value" and "converge_if_changed" to help us with this need.

Without actually changing our action so that it truly needs to handle the idempotence, let's look at what the Custom Resource code might look like using the previously-mentioned helper functions.

 I'm simplifying the contents of `index.html` to keep the example simple.

If we needed to check the state of the contents of the `index.html` file and only change it if the resulting state (or contents) would be different than it currently is, then we can update the code to look like this:

```
property :site_name, String, name_property: true
property :title, String

load_current_value do
  title IO.read("/var/www/#{site_name}/index.html")
end

action :start do
  converge_if_changed do
    directory "/var/www/#{site_name}" do
      recursive true
      mode 0755
      user 'earlwaud'
      group 'wheel'
      action :create
    end

    file "/var/www/#{site_name}/index.html" do
      content title
      mode 0755
      user 'earlwaud'
      group 'wheel'
      notifies :restart, 'service[httpd]'
    end

    service 'httpd' do
      action :nothing
    end
  end
end
```

You can see in the preceding example that we are checking whether there is a change to "title" by using the call to `load_current_value`. Then, with converge_if_ changed, we are executing the action only if there was a change to the value of title. This is a somewhat forced example, but it should serve as a template to handling idempotence in your Custom Resources.

> Remember that this type of custom test and set code is not necessary when leveraging the built-in resources provided by Chef within your Custom Resource. You will only need to add this type of functionality if your Custom Resources are using Ruby for your actions, or coding for some other, more complex scenario.

References

The link to the Chef Documentation for Custom Resource DSL with details about converge_if_changed and load_current_value is `https://docs.chef.io/dsl_custom_resource.html`.

Subclassing a Custom Resource

Sometimes, you need to handle more complex situations, such as supporting distinctly different operating systems, such as Linux and Windows. This can easily be handled by subclassing your Custom Resource. Let's consider a new requirement for our use case, that is, we need to extend our new appsite Custom Resource cookbook so that it will allow us to create websites on OS X and Linux using Apache, and on Windows using IIS.

In order to provide for subclassing of our Custom Resource, we will need to convert them into a library module, so let's start there.

Convert our resource into a library module

We begin by creating a new folder named "libraries" in our cookbook. Next, we create a new file in our libraries folder named `website.rb` and add the following contents to the file:

```
module AppsiteCookbook
  class Website < Chef::Resource
    resource_name :appsite_website

  end
end
```

This is the template used to define our library module. We are creating a new library module that will be used by calling the name "appsite_website". It is a new class that is of type Chef::Resource.

Next, we can copy all of the code from our resource/website.rb file and paste it into our new library module definition. The resulting file will then look like this:

```
module AppsiteCookbook
  class Website < Chef::Resource
    resource_name :appsite_website

    property :site_name, String, name_property: true
    property :title, String

    action :start do
      directory "/var/www/#{site_name}" do
        recursive true
        mode 0755
        user 'earlwaud'
        group 'wheel'
        action :create
      end

      file "/var/www/#{site_name}/index.html" do
        content "<html><title>#{title}</title><body><h1>Hello to our
#{title}</h1></body></html>"
        mode 0755
        user 'earlwaud'
        group 'wheel'
        notifies :restart, 'service[httpd]'
      end

      service 'httpd' do
        action :nothing
      end

    end
  end
end
```

So far, we have only converted our Custom Resource into a library module Custom Resource. At this point, you can delete the folder named resources and then run the override local chef-client command again. The results will be the same state as before with no actions taken because everything is "(up to date)".

So, let's move on to the subclassing of the Custom Resource now.

Subclassing the library module Custom Resource

Now we are going to convert our library module Custom Resource into a subclassed Custom Resource. In this example, we are going to handle the scenario of deploying our websites for either Apache on Linux and OS X systems, or for IIS on Windows systems. Let's change the base class first. We are going to simplify our libraries/website.rb file changing the contents to the following:

```
module AppsiteCookbook
  class Website < Chef::Resource
    resource_name :appsite_website

    property :site_name, String, name_property: true
    property :title, String

    action :start do
      puts "Executing Base Class"
    end

  end
end
```

This simple base class is just going to provide the class name, provide for the properties, and execute any required base class actions — in this case, just writing out a message.

Next, let's create our first base class for the Linux-based operating systems. Create a new file in the libraries folder named website_linux.rb. Put the following code into the file:

```
module AppsiteCookbook
  class WebsiteLinux < Website
    resource_name :appsite_website_linux
    provides :appsite_website, os: [ 'linux', 'darwin' ]

    action :start do
      puts 'Installing on Linux OS'
      super()
      puts 'Executing Linux Sub-Class'
```

```
        directory "/var/www/#{site_name}" do
          recursive true
          mode 0755
          user 'earlwaud'
          group 'wheel'
          action :create
        end

        file "/var/www/#{site_name}/index.html" do
          content "<html><title>#{title}</title><body><h1>Hello to our
#{title}</h1></body></html>"
          mode 0755
          user 'earlwaud'
          group 'wheel'
          notifies :restart, 'service[httpd]'
        end

        service 'httpd' do
          supports :restart => true
          action :nothing
        end

      end
    end
end
```

This is the code that will get executed for the OS types "Linux" or "Darwin" (OS X).

The key things to notice are that the class is named
WebsiteLinux and is derived from our base class
Website. Next, note the "provides" directive. This is what
instructs chef-client to use this subclass when the OS type
matches either "linux" or "darwin". The rest of the code is
pretty much identical to our earlier example.

Finally, let's create the Windows subclass file for completeness. Again in the libraries folder, create a new file named website_windows.rb. Put the following code into the new file:

```
module AppsiteCookbook
  class WebsiteWindows < Website
    resource_name :appsite_website_windows
    provides :appsite_website, os: 'windows'
```

```
action :start do
  puts 'Installing on Windows OS'
  super()
  puts 'Executing Windows Sub-Class'

  directory "#{ENV['SYSTEMDRIVE']}\\inetpub\\wwwroot\\#{site_
name}" do
    recursive true
    mode 0755
    user 'earlwaud'
    group 'wheel'
    action :create
  end

  file "#{ENV['SYSTEMDRIVE']}\\inetpub\\wwwroot\\#{site_name}\\
index.html" do
    content "<html><title>#{title}</title><body><h1>Hello to our
#{title}</h1></body></html>"
    mode 0755
    user 'earlwaud'
    group 'wheel'
    notifies :restart, 'service[w3svc]'
  end

  service 'w3svc' do
    action :nothing
  end
end
  end
end
```

Again, notice the class line—it defines the class name as `WebsiteWindows` and says that the class is derived from our `Website` base class. And like in the Linux subclass, we have a "providers" directive that instructs the chef-client to use this base class only when running on a "windows" OS.

Because all of this code is functionally equivalent to our earlier examples, executing our override local chef-client run will result in no state modifying actions taken, as everything is (up to date).

References

The link to the Chef documentation on Libraries is `https://docs.chef.io/libraries.html`.

Summary

In this chapter, we saw how the new 12.5 version of Chef has brought us the Custom Resource, and we explored how the Custom Resource has improved upon the old concept of LWRPs and HWRPs. We realized that Chef has built-in resources for a lot of things, but not for creating websites. Therefore, you learned how to create a new "website" Custom Resource. We expanded on the website resource to make it easy to use in different cookbooks, and expanded it even further so that we can use it for cookbooks that will be converged in multiple operating systems. By now, you should really appreciate the humble Custom Resource. It is a great improvement over the old Resource Provider model and can greatly simplify your recipes.

Next, let's dive into the use of Chef to provision into the traditional datacenter. There is a lot to cover, so let's get started.

5
Provisioning in the Traditional Data Center

In this chapter, we're going to pull together the concepts of the earlier chapters to deliver the software-defined data center in the traditional on-premise model. The reader will take control of their traditional data center, integrating Chef into industry-wide compute deployment and configuration environments.

> *"The secret of success in life is to eat what you like and let the food fight it out inside."* –
> *Mark Twain*

The following topics will be covered in this chapter:

- VMware provisioning
- Open Stack provisioning
- Network automation

VMware provisioning

VMware is the blue 600-pound gorilla in the data center. If you have any exposure to virtualization in a corporate setting, then the odds are that you have worked extensively with VMware's product line.

Since early 2000s, VMware has had an ever-increasing presence in the data center, which started initially as a way to deliver more computing power in the same space through server consolidation. Then, VMware continued to grow as a way to provide faster server provisioning to meet the ever-increasing demands for rapid deployment.

And now, VMware is the fast, fault-tolerant, and highly available on-site data center cloud provider. Regardless of the reasons, VMware virtualization environments are here to stay in our data centers (at least in the short term).

Because of this, you will need to be able to leverage Chef to manage the configuration of all VMware virtual machines.

Since VMware deployments are such a common part of the traditional data center, I am not going to take you through vSphere environment deployment. If for some reason, you do not already have access to a vSphere environment, you can deploy a "lab in a box" using VMware workstation or fusion. There are many guides available on the Internet that can detail the requirements and steps needed to set up your lab. For example, there is a fairly complete guide on the EnterpriseDaddy website, and the link is `http://www.enterprisedaddy.com/building-a-home-lab-for-vmware-vsphere-6-0/`. You can download a PDF of their guide or review the steps in the pages of their blog.

Let's proceed now with the expectation that you have access to a vSphere environment or that you've created your own vSphere lab to work with. There are many ways to leverage Chef in the VMware-centric data center environment. Starting with just post-provisioning customization, the knife command will very effectively integrate with a VM previously provisioned in any number of ways, allowing the DevOps person to manage the configuration and application deployment on their VMs with relative ease. You can bootstrap a VM with knife, installing the chef-client and applying any desired run lists or perhaps, with the new feature, a policy.

But if you want to provision your VMs with Chef, there are many ways to do that. You can use Chef to work directly with ESX hosts using the knife-esx plugin. With this plugin, you can clone, bootstrap, and manage virtual machines on your ESX or ESXi hosts. Although this is very useful, most large VMware deployments don't stop with the utilization of this free version of VMware's hypervisor. Instead, they will opt for the more complete solution, paying for the feature-rich vSphere product line.

So, another Chef to VMware provisioning option is to use the knife-vsphere plugin and interact directly with the vSphere server. This plugin provides a lot of functionality beyond just creating virtual machines. You are also able to handle some management tasks, such as powering on or off your VMs and adding additional drives by adding VMDKs. We will talk more about some of these features shortly.

Then, there is a knife plugin for VMware's **vCloud Director** (**vCD**) product. It is appropriately named knife-vcloud. If you have an active deployment of vCloud Director, like my company does, then you might be very interested in the knife plugin that lets you work with vCD. However, as the vCloud Director product line is nearing the end of its life, I'll not be talking about using the knife-vcloud plugin here. However, I will provide a link in the references section if you want to investigate it on your own.

There's also integration between Chef and **VMware vCloud Automation Center** (**vCAC**). This is a great area to familiarize yourself with because it is the direction that VMware is moving its product line. There's a plugin named knife-vrealize. This is in the same vein because VMware vRealize is the new product branding for vCAC. There's also another, relatively new, VMware knife plugin named knife-vcair. This plugin allows you to create, bootstrap, and manage instances in VMware's Hybrid Service known as vCloud Air (vcair). I will provide references to these plugins later, but due to space limitations, I will leave the discovery of these to the reader's discretion.

Because this chapter focuses on the traditional data center where vSphere is certain to be found, we will continue to look at the knife-vsphere plugin, starting with the installation of the plugin itself.

Installing the knife-vsphere plugin

Like many other plugins we have installed so far, we will use Chef to install our new knife gem. Here is the command:

```
chef gem install knife-vsphere
```

Once you've executed the gem install, you need to configure your `knife.rb` file. So, edit your file with the following command:

```
vi ~/chef-repo/.chef/knife.rb
```

Add the following lines to your knife file, replacing the values with values appropriate to your vSphere environment:

```
knife[:vsphere_host] = 'vcenter-hostname'
knife[:vsphere_user] = 'privileged username'
knife[:vsphere_pass] = 'your password'
knife[:vsphere_dc]   = 'your-datacenter'
```

Here are the values I've used in my `knife.rb` file:

```
knife[:vsphere_host] = 'vcenter6.nat.local.net'
knife[:vsphere_user] = 'earlwaud'
knife[:vsphere_pass] = '1Password'
knife[:vsphere_dc]   = 'SanDiego'
```

One big concern here is the public nature of your password. This is very undesirable in a real production environment. So, the knife-vsphere plugin provides the ability to use a base64 encoded version. To do this, you would need to prepend the tag `base64:` to your password value string. That would look something like this:

```
knife[:vsphere_pass] = 'base64:Yk2nZuJwHp=='
```

An alternative to saving the password in the `knife.rb` file is to pass the credentials on the command line when you execute your knife commands.

Also, depending on your environment, you may experience SSL connection issues when you run your knife commands. This is usually due to certificate errors, and you can configure your `knife.rb` file to just ignore these errors with the additional setting as follows:

```
knife[:vsphere_insecure] = true
```

With these commands saved in our `knife.rb` file, we are ready to start provisioning to our vSphere environment. Of course, you are going to need a template in your vSphere environment, so let's check our `knife.rb` configuration with a quick query to see the templates that are available to provision (or clone) from. The command you will use for this check is as follows:

`knife vsphere template list`

Another query you will want to try is to list out the available datastores. Use the following command:

`knife vsphere datastore list`

Similarly, you can get a list of several object types, such as `hosts`, `vm`, `cluster`, `folder`, `pool`, and `vlan` by issuing a command in the same format:

`knife vsphere hosts list`

`knife vsphere vm list`

`knife vsphere cluster list`

`knife vsphere vlan list`

Here is what running these commands looks like in my shiny new vSphere 6 lab:

```
● ● ●                          1. bash
Earls-Mac:chef-repo earlwaud$ knife vsphere template list
Template Name: dsl-template
Earls-Mac:chef-repo earlwaud$ knife vsphere datastore list
Datastore: esxi6-01-datastore1 (31.31 GB / 32.50 GB)
Datastore: esxi6-02-datastore1 (31.55 GB / 32.50 GB)
Earls-Mac:chef-repo earlwaud$ knife vsphere hosts list
Pool: Prod
   Host: esxi6-01.nat.local.net
   Host: esxi6-02.nat.local.net
Earls-Mac:chef-repo earlwaud$ knife vsphere vm list
Folder:
        VM Name: DSL-4.4.10
                 IP:
                 RAM: 64
                 State: off
Earls-Mac:chef-repo earlwaud$ knife vsphere cluster list
Cluster: Prod
Earls-Mac:chef-repo earlwaud$ knife vsphere vlan list
VLAN: VM Network
Earls-Mac:chef-repo earlwaud$ █
```

Next, let's take a look at how we provision using the knife-vsphere plugin.

Provisioning VMs using the knife-vsphere plugin

Using the knife-vsphere plugin to provision VMs into VMware Vsphere can range from a fairly simple command to a very complex command.

Starting out with baby steps, here is an example of a simple knife command to clone a VM template to create a new VM:

```
knife vsphere vm clone api_vm01 \
    --template centos6-template \
    --cspec centos6 \
    -V
```

Examining the preceding command, we start off, with the typical format for a knife plugin command, using knife vsphere for the vsphere plugin. Then, we provide the name of the VM we wish to create. In this case, name is api_vm01.

Next, we provide the parameter `--template` with a value of the name of the VM template that we want to clone. This is typically one of your company's baseline templates. In my case, it is a simple centos6 template I created for my lab.

Next, using the `--cspec` parameter, you tell knife the name of the customization spec to use to customize the VM to your environment once it has been provisioned. In my case, I have a Linux customization spec named "centos6".

Finally, we are using the `-v` parameter to tell knife to provide verbose output.

Remember that we can use a second V, as in `-vv`, to get very verbose, debug-level output from the command. You might consider using the double V when you are trying these commands out for the first few times.

Now, let's take our provisioning command up a notch. Let's do some additional VM customization with our knife command. Here is another example of using the knife-vsphere plugin to provision a VM:

```
knife vsphere vm clone api_vm02 \
    --template centos6-template \
    --cspec centos6 \
    --ccpu 1 \
    --cram 2 \
    --dest-folder Public \
    --datastore esxi6-01-datastore1 \
    --resource-pool Production \
    --annotation "This VM was provisioned using the knife-vsphere plugin.
The VM is owned by Earl Waud" \
    --start \
    -V
```

So, what is new here. We have added the parameter `--ccpu`. The value used for this parameter tells knife to provision the VM with that number of vCPUs. Similarly, the `--cram` parameter and value tells knife to provision the VM with that many GB of RAM. The next new parameter is the `--dest-folder`. The value of this parameter tells knife the name of the folder you want your VM placed in (visible in the **Inventory | VMs and Templates vCenter view**). Remember that the folder has to exist in vCenter for the knife command to execute successfully. If the folder does not exist, your knife command will fail with a "no such folder" error. The next parameter in our knife command is the `--datastore`. The value provided to this parameter is the exact name of the datastore that you want to house the VMs files when it is provisioned. If the datastore does not exist, the knife command will fail with a "no such datastore" error.

Next, we added the `--resource-pool` parameter and value. This parameter is somewhat overloaded. At its most basic use, the value is the name of the vSphere cluster that you want to provision into. But as the name would imply, you are actually targeting the automatic default resource pool that exists in every cluster. You can, as desired, specify the name of a resource pool that exists, and the VM will be added to that resource pool.

> Note that to target a resource pool, you need to provide the value in the form of "Cluster/ResourcePool". For example, if you have a cluster named Production and you have resource pools within that cluster named Gold, Silver, and Bronze, and you want your new VM to go into the Silver resource pool, the parameter value should be provided as "Production/Silver".

Finally, we added the `--annotation` parameter and value. The value provided for this parameter will be inserted into the **Annotations** section shown on the VM's **Summary** view. Oh yeah, we also added the parameter `--start`, which as you might expect, tells knife to have the VM started after the successful provision completes.

So, you may have noted that while we did provision a VM, and we did some pretty awesome customizations, we didn't do anything Chef to our VM. So, let's Chef this thing up. We are going to do another provision, and this time, we're going to add two Chef-specific parameters, one parameter to tell Knife to bootstrap our VM and the other parameter to provide the node name to our Chef Server to register the VM under. We also need to add some authentication parameters. For this example, I am using ssh user credentials, so the new knife command looks like this:

```
knife vsphere vm clone api_vm03 \
    --template "centos6-template" \
    --cspec centos6 \
    --ccpu 1 \
    --cram 2 \
    --dest-folder Public \
    --datastore esxi6-01-datastore1 \
    --resource-pool "Development" \
    --annotation "This VM is owned by Earl Waud." \
    --start \
    --node-name api_vm03 \
    --bootstrap \
    --bootstrap-protocol ssh \
```

```
--ssh-user centos \
--ssh-password password \
--ssh-port 22 \
--run-list "recipe[base]" \
-V
```

This is not the best way to authenticate when cloning a VM with knife for several reasons, not the least of which is that your password is right there for all to see. But in addition, when Knife gets to the step where it uses sudo to gain root-level privileges on your new VM, it may ask you for the sudo password (unless the user is configured for NOPASSWD access in the sudoers file). This does not lend itself to automation very well. This of course implies that the ssh user you provide on the command line must be added to the sudoers file in the template for the chef-client install to work.

Now we have a Knife command that will provision VM, customize that VM, bootstrap the VM, and set the desired state to converge with the run list specified. The VM will be registered with the Chef Server and can be managed from there. Not too shabby.

Cleaning up our vSphere and Chef environments

Perhaps we have been doing a lot of test provisions, or we have system that have been around for a while that we need to retire to reclaim our compute resources. For whatever the reason maybe, we need to get rid of some of our VMs. The knife-vsphere plugin has been covered. We can control the power state of our VMs using the `state` subcommand. For example, if we want to power off our VM, we can issue a command in this format:

```
knife vsphere vm state <VM NAME> --state off
```

For example, if we want to power off the VM we provisioned previously, we can use the command:

```
knife vsphere vm state api_vm03 -state off
```

This command will do a hard power off of the VM. If we want to be more respectful of the guest OS running within VM, we can add the `--shutdown` parameter to the command, and the knife plugin will execute a guest shutdown on the VM instead of a hard power off. Once we are completely finished with our VM, we can remove them from vCenter by issuing a `delete` command. The command takes the following form:

```
knife vsphere vm delete <VM NAME>
```

Big note! This command is destructive in that it not only removes the VM from vCenter, but it does it with the "Delete from Disk" command, resulting in the VM being removed from vCenter and all of the VM's files get deleted from the datastore that contained them. They are gone, and unless you have some external backup (such as NAS snapshots and many more), they are gone for good. So, be careful with using this feature.

As an example of using this command, if we want to delete the VM we recently provisioned, we can issue the following command:

```
knife vsphere vm delete api_vm03
```

There is a very useful parameter that we can apply with the delete subcommand. It is --purge. When we add this parameter to the delete subcommand, the node representing the VM in the Chef Server will also be deleted.

Using Chef with VMware and Vagrant

Even though this chapter focuses on using Chef in the traditional data center, I want to take a few minutes to cover using Chef with either VMware Workstation or VMware Fusion and a tool named Vagrant to provision development environments. This is an important technology because it creates development environments that are running the same Chef code that is used in production vSphere environments. "Sounds good," you say; "How do I do it," you say, well let's take a look now.

Disclaimer

The Vagrant plugins for either VMware Workstation or VMware Fusion are commercial (not open source) products and must be purchased from HashiCorp. At the time of this writing, they are $79 per license. The licenses are unique between Workstation and Fusion, so if you work using both desktop hypervisors, you would need to purchase a separate license for each. If you are in a corporate setting and developing Chef cookbooks and your company is providing Workstation or Fusion software, then they should willingly spring for the Vagrant plugin license. If you are not able or not willing to purchase the license for the VMware desktop hypervisor, then there is a popular alternative that does not require the purchase of a commercial product. That alternative is using VirtualBox from Oracle as the desktop hypervisor. The general functionality is the same, although the templates used for provisioning will differ.

Once you have purchased your Vagrant license, you will get an e-mail from HashiCorp that details instructions on downloading your plugin and license file. Once you have them downloaded and have Vagrant installed (of course), you can install and license your new plugin. The command will be slightly different depending on if you are using Workstation or Fusion.

Here are the commands to install and license the Fusion plugin:

```
vagrant plugin install vagrant-vmware-fusion
vagrant plugin license vagrant-vmware-fusion license.lic
```

And here are the commands to install and license the Workstation plugin (it should be run from a command prompt with Administrator privileges):

```
vagrant plugin install vagrant-vmware-workstation
vagrant plugin license vagrant-vmware-workstation license.lic
```

The license.lic parameter in these commands is the filename (and path) to the downloaded plugin license key file.

You can confirm that the plugin and license were successfully deployed by issuing the following command:

```
vagrant plugin list
```

We want to download some VM boxes to use in our development environment. You can find many options in the Vagrant box share found at http://www.vagrantbox. es. For my testing, I have downloaded a CentOS5.10 box. Here is the command:

```
vagrant box add centos-5.10 https://dl.dropboxusercontent.com/s/
r5okkx8330h3tzh/vagrant-centos-5.10-x86_64.box
```

This will download the VM box and deploy it in your VMware Workstation environment. The box is placed into a common Vagrant cache area so that you won't need to download the box file each time you deploy a new environment. You can see a list of the boxes that have been downloaded and are stored in the cache with the following command:

```
vagrant box list
```

Now we're ready to provision some VMs with our desktop hypervisor. For brevity, in the remaining examples in this section, I will be using Workstation. The Fusion commands are nearly identical.

Now you need to initialize your new project. Issue the following command:

```
cd ~/chef-repo
vagrant init centos-5.10
```

Now we want to bring up our new Vagrant box with the following command:

```
vagrant up --provider vmware_workstation
```

You can see a list of the templates that have been downloaded and are stored in the cache with the following command:

```
vagrant box list
```

We now have a new VM running in our VMware Workstation system. However, here is another case where we haven't done anything with Chef yet. So, let's go ahead and get rid of this environment with the following command:

```
vagrant destroy
```

This will power down the VM and then delete it from the workstation (and from the hard drive).

OK, with our first test system deployed and cleaned up, we are ready to add some Chef to this party. We need to edit the Vagrantfile that was created for us when we ran the `vagrant init` command earlier. Initially, this default Vagrantfile will comprise mostly comments. For the sake of space in this chapter, we will remove the comments and only share the active content of the Vagrantfile. Here is what a simple Vagrant file looks like:

```ruby
# -*- mode: ruby -*-
# vi: set ft=ruby :

VAGRANTFILE_API_VERSION = '2'

Vagrant.configure(VAGRANTFILE_API_VERSION) do |config|
  config.vm.box = 'centos-5.10'

  config.vm.network 'public_network'

  config.vm.hostname = 'vagrant-vm01'

  config.vm.provision :chef_client do |chef|
    chef.chef_server_url = \
        'https://chefserver/organizations/sdearl'
    chef.validation_client_name = 'sdearl-validator'
    chef.validation_key_path = \
```

```
        '/Users/earlwaud/chef-repo/.chef/sdearl-validator.pem'
    chef.run_list = 'recipe[base] '
    chef.validation_client_name = 'sdearl-validator'
    chef.environment = 'production'
  end
end
```

Now, when we issue the command `vagrant up`, the VM being provisioned will also have the chef-client installed and will be registered with the Chef server, and will converge with the run list of `"recipe[base] "`.

Now that we are deploying VMs using Vagrant and registering them with our Chef server, when we clean up those VMs, we also want to clean up the Chef-client and node in our Chef Server. Of course, you can do this manually every time, but that is not what we are all about. We want automation. Well, there's a Vagrant plugin for that. It is called **Butcher**. What the plugin does for us is when we issue our vagrant destroy commands, it will not only destroy the VM but will also reach out to the Chef Server and do the necessary cleanup of the Node there as well. Installing the plugin is easy. Just enter the following command:

```
vagrant plugin install vagrant-butcher
```

Once it is installed, there are a few additional configuration lines you will want to add to your Vagrantfile. Here are the lines to add:

```
config.butcher.client_key = \
    '/Users/earlwaud/chef-repo/.vagrant/butcher/default-client.pem'
config.butcher.enabled = true
config.butcher.verify_ssl = false
```

Now when you execute your vagrant destroy commands, everything will be cleaned up automatically. Great.

References

- You can read about the knife-vsphere plugin at `https://github.com/chef-partners/knife-vsphere`.

- How to guide on setting up a vSphere 6 lab in VMware Workstation is at `http://www.enterprisedaddy.com/building-a-home-lab-for-vmware-vsphere-6-0/`.

- Learn more about the many Chef + VMware integrations at `https://www.chef.io/solutions/vmware/`.

- You can read about the knife-vcair plugin at `https://github.com/chef-partners/knife-vcair`.

- If you are working directly with ESX instead of vSphere, you might like the info for the knife-esx plugin, which can be found at `https://github.com/maintux/knife-esx`.

- Finally, if you want to work with VMware Fusion or VMware Workstation, you can integrate with Vagrant and the corresponding plugin. Learn more at `https://www.vagrantup.com` and `https://www.vagrantup.com/docs/vmware/installation.html`.

- You can find a variety of Vagrant base boxes at `http://www.vagrantbox.es`.

- If you are interested in making your own templates or boxes for Vagrant, there is an excellent tutorial found at `https://blog.engineyard.com/2014/building-a-vagrant-box`.

- You can read about the Vagrant Plugin Butcher at `https://github.com/cassianoleal/vagrant-butcher`.

OpenStack provisioning

Using Chef to provision to OpenStack instances requires an OpenStack environment to work with. This seems obvious and simple, but with OpenStack, nothing is really obvious and simple. To emphasize this point, let me tell you a story.

My first exposure to OpenStack was in early 2014, when the company I was working for hired a well-respected training company to come onsite and train our team in the setup and use of OpenStack. It was a very expensive engagement, but we were considering the possibility of reducing our reliance on VMware and were looking at OpenStack as a path toward that end. The training was scheduled for full 5 days for about a dozen people. The instructor arrived on Monday morning, and after introductions, we got down to it. After 3 full days of "work," only two people in the class had a working OpenStack environment. Even the instructor's example environment was not functional. On that day, the instructor apologized and bowed out, ending our training early. The costs were refunded by the training company, and our team decided that, at least for the short term, OpenStack was not our path to VMware independence.

OpenStack has come a long way since then, and it is much less troublesome to get an environment up and running today. Still, it is a complex deployment and can present a lot of challenges. So, before we dive into our use of Chef to provision to OpenStack instances, let's take a look at the way we can set up a development OpenStack environment.

Know that the information in the section ahead was not easily obtained. Bits and pieces had to be learned from all over the place, refined, and reworked to be able to detail a way to deploy a fully functional DevStack OpenStack environment using Neutron networking in a VMware Workstation VM. Even though this is a book on Chef Provisioning, the following section alone is worth the price of the book!

> To paraphrase a quote by Matt Damon's character in the move The Martian -- "I had to science the crap out of this".

So, let's get to work…

Setting up a DevStack OpenStack all-in-one environment

There is a community production of OpenStack named DevStack. This "tool" is not something meant for production use and does not support all configuration and platforms. However, it is a perfect tool for education and dev and test scenarios. You can quickly set up a working OpenStack environment on a workstation or a beefy laptop. So, if you want to use OpenStack for development, the DevStack production is a good option for you. Let's walk through the setup so that if you don't already have access to OpenStack, you can test out the Chef provisioning examples coming up later in the chapter. Let's begin with the setup of the "host" of our DevStack.

Deploying the DevStack Host VM

You can set up DevStack directly on physical hardware, but I would highly recommend that you use a desktop virtualization tool such as VMware Workstation or Fusion. You probably already have it installed in your system. We are going to set up a new VM for our DevStack and set up specific networking for that VM to assure that everything works as desired.

I suggest you to download the Ubuntu 14.04 desktop 64-bit installer ISO for your host VM. At the time of this writing, the current master repo for DevStack works well with this version of Ubuntu. Plus, it is painless to install in the latest version of VMware's desktop hypervisors, using the "Easy Install" feature, which answers nearly all of the deployment questions automatically.

Because we are in fact going to install all of our OpenStack environment into this host VM, you will want to set the configuration a little larger than you might be used to for normal desktop OS VMs. I would recommend that you give the VM at least 6 GB of memory. With only 4 GB, you will experience a small amount of memory swapping just to stand up the OpenStack environment. It will work, but if you have a system that has the RAM, go ahead and set the VM to 6 GB of memory or more. Since my workstation has 32 GB of RAM, I am using 8 GB for my VM. Next, you will want to give the VM at least 2 CPUs. This is the bare minimum. Since I have a system that can handle it, I am setting my VMs CPU count to 4. Be sure to enable the Virtualization options on the CPUs in **Virtual Machine Settings**, as shown in the following image. Next, you should allow the VM to have some disk breathing room by setting a large hard disk size. I went with a 180 GB drive.

 Remember that the disk will not use the full allocated capacity set here, but it will only use what is actually used by the VM.

I set my disk files to use a single file instead of breaking them into small chunks.

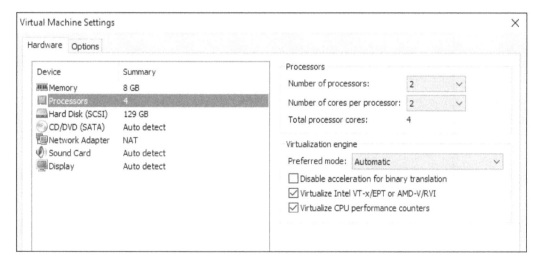

For now, in the networking option, select **NAT** for **Network Adapter**. We will talk more about the networking shortly.

Next, I removed the USB controller and the printer as they are not necessary for the DevStack host. I also turned off the **accelerate 3D Graphics** option on the Display.

Once you've set your Virtual Machine Settings, save them and power on the VM to let it run the OS installer. Enter your name, username, and password and remember them so you can log in once the VM is running. When the installation is complete, log in and make the VM your own by setting your normal desktop things, such as wallpaper, terminal settings, and running software updates (restart as necessary).

In addition, I would recommend installing the ntp, landscape-common (for the landscape-sysinfo command), and htop (it's just a better top). Here is the command:

```
sudo apt-get install ntp landscape-common htop
```

You might want to consider taking a VM Snapshot at this point and labeling something like `Clean Ubuntu 14.04 Install`.

Change host interface from DHCP to static.

We want to control the IP address assigned to our OpenStack host, so we need to change the interface configuration from a DHCP autoassigned IP configuration to one that is static. In my setup, the NAT networking interfaces are on the 192.168.157.0/24 subnet. So, here is what my updated networking will look like:

Save your new settings and then, to make sure the settings take effect, open a terminal window and restart the network manager with the following command:

```
sudo service network-manager restart
```

Now check your settings by with the ifconfig command and pinging some well-known servers such as www.google.com.

Downloading and installing DevStack

Now that we have our host VM up and running, it is time to download and install OpenStack DevStack. First things first, we need to install git. Open up a Terminal session on your host VM and issue the following command:

```
sudo apt-get install git -y
```

This will install git so that we can use it to download the DevStack repo. I would recommend doing an update next with the following command:

```
sudo apt-get update
```

Then, issue the following git command to clone the DevStack repo:

```
cd ~/
git clone https://git.openstack.org/openstack-dev/devstack -b stable/kilo
```

Although you can deploy the master branch for DevStack, or even the Liberty branch, at the time of writing, the knife-openstack plugin has not been blessed for anything later than the OpenStack stable kilo release. Therefore, I am working with stable/kilo branch so that you will have a working example. The earlier stable branches are probably ok, but I would recommend going with kilo since I know that it works with the config file I am about to share.

Now that we have the DevStack installer bits, we can do the installation as soon as we are ready.

Next, we want to create a configuration file to help DevStack configure OpenStack correctly for our Host VM.

Create and edit a file named local.conf:

```
cd ~/
touch devstack/local.conf
vi devstack/local.conf
```

Enter the following data into the new file:

```
[[local|localrc]]

# Passwords (modify to match your VM)
ADMIN_PASSWORD=password

DATABASE_PASSWORD=$ADMIN_PASSWORD
RABBIT_PASSWORD=$ADMIN_PASSWORD
SERVICE_PASSWORD=$ADMIN_PASSWORD
SERVICE_TOKEN=$ADMIN_PASSWORD

# Branches
KEYSTONE_BRANCH=stable/kilo
NOVA_BRANCH=stable/kilo
NEUTRON_BRANCH=stable/kilo
SWIFT_BRANCH=stable/kilo
GLANCE_BRANCH=stable/kilo
CINDER_BRANCH=stable/kilo
HEAT_BRANCH=stable/kilo
TROVE_BRANCH=stable/kilo
HORIZON_BRANCH=stable/kilo
SAHARA_BRANCH=stable/kilo

# Host VM IP address (replace with the IP of your VM)
HOST_IP=192.168.157.134
SERVICE_HOST=192.168.157.134
MYSQL_HOST=192.168.157.134
RABBIT_HOST=192.168.157.134
GLANCE_HOSTPORT=192.168.157.134:9292

# domain (should be the same as chef server domain)
# dhcp_domain=nat.local.net

# Enable the console auth service
enable_service n-cauth

# Disable tempest service to save stack time
disable_service tempest

# Do not use Nova-Network
disable_service n-net

# Enable Neutron
```

```
ENABLED_SERVICES+=,q-svc,q-dhcp,q-meta,q-agt,q-l3

# Neutron options
Q_USE_SECGROUP=True
Q_L3_ENABLED=True
Q_USE_PROVIDERNET_FOR_PUBLIC=True
Q_AGENT=linuxbridge

# IP range for fixed and floating IP assignments
FIXED_RANGE="10.0.0.0/24"
PUBLIC_INTERFACE=eth0
FLOATING_RANGE="192.168.157.0/24"
Q_FLOATING_ALLOCATION_POOL=start=192.168.157.250,end=192.168.157.254
PUBLIC_NETWORK_GATEWAY="192.168.157.1"

# Linuxbridge Settings
LB_PHYSICAL_INTERFACE=eth0
LB_INTERFACE_MAPPINGS=default:eth0
PUBLIC_PHYSICAL_NETWORK=default

# Enable Logging
LOGFILE=/opt/stack/logs/stack.sh.log
VERBOSE=True
LOG_COLOR=True
SCREEN_LOGDIR=/opt/stack/logs
```

You will need to make a few changes to reflect your installation.

First, change the ADMIN_PASSWORD value to the password you use for your login account on the Host VM.

Then, replace all of the 192.168.157.134 values with the IP address you are using for the Host VM.

Then, set the dhcp_domain value to the same domain that your Chef Server belongs to. This value will be to domain that provisioned instances belong to. If they do not match the domain of your Chef Server, they will not be able to register with the Chef Server.

Then, replace the FLOATING_RANGE and Q_FLOATING_ALLOCATION_POOL values with values in the same subnet as your Host VM.

Finally, replace the PUBLIC_NETWORK_GATEWAY value with the gateway address of your NAT network.

Now save the file with all the changes, and you are ready to stack your DevStack.

Don't use root to run DevStack

An important note here is that you do not want to run DevStack as root. The web page documentation suggests you to use a script provided in the repo to create a "stack" user. I have found that there are permission issues that can get introduced if you do that. So, I recommend that you use your own user account to run DevStack, and don't bother with the creation of a specialized "stack" user.

Keep your network active during the stacking of DevStack. When you are "stacking," there is a lot of dependency on the eth0 interface of the Host VM to stay active. I've found that depending on your system's connection, the eth0 interface can temporarily lose connectivity with the NAT network. I've found that if you open another terminal window and start up a continuous ping of the host computer's IP address that the stack is much more likely to run to completion. This might just be a quirk of my systems, but I've found that it really is does the trick for me. Once the stack is up and running, you can stop the ping.

Ok, we have our second terminal window open and pinging our VMs host IP address, so we are ready to install and start our OpenStack environment. Change into the devstack folder and launch DevStack with the following commands:

```
cd devstack
```

```
./stack.sh
```

This will take a while, depending on your system's horsepower and your network bandwidth. It may be a good time to go get a coffee, grab some lunch, or take a nap. Naps are nice. Expect about 30 minutes, give or take, for the stack command to complete.

You will see a lot of messages across the screen, but if everything goes according to plan, you will get a "DevStack Components Timed" message that will look something like this:

```
This is your host ip: 192.168.157.134
Horizon is now available at http://192.168.157.134/
Keystone is serving at http://192.168.157.134:5000/
The default users are: admin and demo
The password: password
```

You can now open up your browser and enter the Horizon URL shown in your stack. sh output and log into your OpenStack environment. However, before you get too far, I would suggest you to take another snapshot of your VM as a safety net.

Downloading the demo project rc file and applying it

We now have a working OpenStack environment, but there is one more thing we want to do. Since this is a test tool and we are going to want to make testing easy, let's configure the system to permit all ping and ssh traffic; so when we use commands to access the instances we are going to provision, we will have no surprises.

The first step will be to log in to our environment, so open up a browser on your DevStack VM and log in as admin. For me, the URL is `http://192.168.157.134/`. Use the user name `admin` and the password that you used in the `local.conf` file described in the preceding section. For me, that was `password`.

Now make sure that you are in the demo project space by selecting **demo** in the projects drop-down menu near the top-left part of the web page. Next, using the menu accordion on the left, select the option **Project**, then **Compute**, and **Access & Security**. Now in the **Access & Security** view, select the tab for **API Access**. Press the **Download OpenStack RC File** button to download the rc file. Save the file to your DevStack Host VM.

Adding the security rules to allow ping and ssh traffic

Now we have the rc file to configure the environment in order to add our security rules. Open up a terminal window and, assuming that you saved the rc file in your `Downloads` folder, issue the following command:

```
source ~/Downloads/demo-openrc.sh
```

You will be prompted for your password. Again, enter the password you used in the `local.conf` file (the same one shown at the end of your successful run of `./stack.sh`).

Shortly, you will be entering two commands, one for the ICMP protocol for ping, and the other for tcp protocol on port 22 for the ssh commands.

The two commands will be in this format:

```
neutron security-group-rule-create \
  <SECURITY GROUP ID> \
  --direction ingress --ethertype IPv4 --protocol icmp \
  --remote-ip-prefix 0.0.0.0/0


neutron security-group-rule-create \
  <SECURITY GROUP ID> \
  --direction ingress --ethertype IPv4 --protocol tcp \
  --port-range-min 22 --port-range-max 22 \
  --remote-ip-prefix 0.0.0.0/0
```

However, you'll first need to get the <SECURITY GROUP ID> value for your DevStack's default security group to use in the commands. To get the security group ID, you will issue the nova secgroup-list command as follows:

```
nova secgroup-list
```

Here is the results from my execution of these commands as an example:

```
earlwaud@ubuntu:~$ source ~/Downloads/demo-openrc.sh
Please enter your OpenStack Password:
earlwaud@ubuntu:~$
earlwaud@ubuntu:~$ nova secgroup-list
+-------------------------------------+---------+----------------------
--+
| Id                                  | Name    | Description
|
+-------------------------------------+---------+----------------------
--+
| a209661a-cb15-4cc7-b42f-45a5c507aba0 | default | Default security group
|
+-------------------------------------+---------+----------------------
--+
earlwaud@ubuntu:~$
earlwaud@ubuntu:~$ neutron security-group-rule-create \
>   a209661a-cb15-4cc7-b42f-45a5c507aba0 \
>   --direction ingress --ethertype IPv4 --protocol icmp \
>   --remote-ip-prefix 0.0.0.0/0
Created a new security_group_rule:
```

```
+-------------------+-----------------------------------------+
| Field             | Value                                   |
+-------------------+-----------------------------------------+
| direction         | ingress                                 |
| ethertype         | IPv4                                    |
| id                | fabb4c57-b2c6-4661-a1a7-f7083b1d1743    |
| port_range_max    |                                         |
| port_range_min    |                                         |
| protocol          | icmp                                    |
| remote_group_id   |                                         |
| remote_ip_prefix  | 0.0.0.0/0                               |
| security_group_id | a209661a-cb15-4cc7-b42f-45a5c507aba0    |
| tenant_id         | e2af8dbd4ae44ecf84b1f9b30ff1aad8        |
+-------------------+-----------------------------------------+
earlwaud@ubuntu:~$
earlwaud@ubuntu:~$ neutron security-group-rule-create \
>   a209661a-cb15-4cc7-b42f-45a5c507aba0 \
>   --direction ingress --ethertype IPv4 --protocol tcp \
>   --port-range-min 22 --port-range-max 22 \
>   --remote-ip-prefix 0.0.0.0/0
Created a new security_group_rule:
+-------------------+-----------------------------------------+
| Field             | Value                                   |
+-------------------+-----------------------------------------+
| direction         | ingress                                 |
| ethertype         | IPv4                                    |
| id                | 5dba1c6e-e57d-4739-82b2-5153270f033f    |
| port_range_max    | 22                                      |
| port_range_min    | 22                                      |
| protocol          | tcp                                     |
| remote_group_id   |                                         |
| remote_ip_prefix  | 0.0.0.0/0                               |
| security_group_id | a209661a-cb15-4cc7-b42f-45a5c507aba0    |
| tenant_id         | e2af8dbd4ae44ecf84b1f9b30ff1aad8        |
+-------------------+-----------------------------------------+
earlwaud@ubuntu:~$
```

With these rules in place, all of the ICMP and TCP traffic on port 22 will past into your provisioned instances. Your new DevStack OpenStack all-in-one system is now ready to use for development and testing.

You will also want to provide a *public* DNS address for your *private* network so that your provisioning VMs are able to resolve external host names. I am using a local DNS address of 192.168.157.101 and a public DNS address of 8.8.8.8. So, the command to do that is as follows:

```
neutron subnet-update private-subnet --dns-nameservers list=true
192.168.157.101 8.8.8.8
```

Since I was rebuilding my DevStack a lot during testing (and writing this book), I created a small script to add rules. The script still needs to source your demo_openrc.sh file, so it will ask for your password, but once that's done, the script to create the security group rules and inject the public DNS server:

```
#!/bin/bash
#new_rules.sh

# load the demo project access settings
source ~/Downloads/demo-openrc.sh

# capture the ID for the "default" security group
ID="$(nova secgroup-list | grep default | awk -F"|" '{ print $2 }')"

# add a rule for ping
neutron security-group-rule-create $ID \
  --direction ingress --ethertype IPv4 \
  --protocol icmp --remote-ip-prefix 0.0.0.0/0

# add a rule for ssh
neutron security-group-rule-create $ID \
  --direction ingress --ethertype IPv4 \
  --protocol tcp --port-range-min 22 --port-range-max 22 \
  --remote-ip-prefix 0.0.0.0/0

# add a rule for dns
neutron security-group-rule-create $ID \
  --direction ingress --ethertype IPv4 \
  --protocol tcp --port-range-min 53 --port-range-max 53 \
  --remote-ip-prefix 0.0.0.0/0

# add a public DNS to the private instances
neutron subnet-update private-subnet --dns-nameservers list=true
192.167.157.101 8.8.8.8
```

With that large task behind us, let's now return to our Chef workstation and do some OpenStack provisioning.

Installing the knife OpenStack plugin

Now that we have a working OpenStack environment, there are some steps we need to take on our Chef workstation to set up for provisioning into that environment. The first of those steps is to install the knife-openstack gem. To accomplish this, back on your Chef development workstation, change directories to your chef-repo folder and issue the chef gem install command, like this:

```
cd ~/chef-repo
sudo chef gem install knife-openstack
```

This command will download and install the gem and make it ready and available for our knife commands to use. There is still more setup work that we need to do; therefore, we will set up some knife OpenStack-specific configuration so that knife can communicate with our OpenStack environment.

We need some data from the OpenStack environment, and the best way to get it is to log in and download it. So, on your Chef workstation, browse to the OpenStack Horizon dashboard and log in. If you are using the DevStack environment that we set up earlier, you will use the URL that you got from running stack.sh. In my case, it is http://192.168.157.134/. You will log in with the admin credentials also provided from running the stack.sh command.

Setting up the DevStack public key

We are going to create and download a security key pair to allow our knife bootstrap commands to ssh into our instances without using username/password credentials.

So, once you log in to OpenStack, set your project to be "admin" by selecting admin from the projects drop-down at the top of the web page. You should see the green "switch to project "admin" successful" message, and your project label should now display as admin.

Next, using the accordion menu on the left, select the **Project** top menu, and from its submenu options, select **Access & Security**. Now in the **Access & Security** area, select the tab for **Key Pairs**.

If you just deployed your DevStack, you probably don't have any existing key pairs to use, so press the **+ Create Key Pair** button to create you first one. Give it a significant **Key Pair Name**, then press the **Create Key Pair** button. I named my key pair admin since I will be working with the admin project and login credentials. Creating the key pair will initiate a download of the public key file. If it does not, be sure to download the key before moving away from the new key pair page. It is important to remember the name you use to create the key pair as it will be vital to the successful use of our provisioning with Chef, (and it is the name given to the public key file).

Now copy the public key file to a location you can access easily from your chef repo. For simplicity of my examples, I am copying the public key file to my chef-repo folder.

```
cp ~/Downloads/admin.pem ~/chef-repo/
```

 One important tip to remember is that public key files need to be secure, and most applications won't use them unless the permissions are tight.

So, the next step will be to make sure to tighten the permissions on the public key file. Issuing the following command will take care of this step:

```
chmod 400 ~/chef-repo/admin.pem
```

The public key is now ready to use in our chef OpenStack provisioning. But before we can start using it, we need to poke some holes in our OpenStack firewall.

Allocating some floating IP addresses to the project

We worked very hard to create an OpenStack environment that allows us to use the knife-openstack plugin to allocate floating IP addresses, so we might as well add some to our project so that we can allocate them when the time comes.

Browse to your horizon dashboard and log in. Make sure that your project is set to demo again (it should default to that because it was used previously, but check to be sure). Select the **Project** menu from the menu accordion on the left and then select **Access & Security** from the **Project** submenu options. Now, select the **Floating IP** tab.

Click on the **Allocate Floating IP Address** button and add an IP to the public group. Repeat this process a few times to give us a few floating IPs to work with.

These public IP addresses will be assigned to the OpenStack instances to allow a route to access the private subnet addresses that are assigned to the instances during provisioning. The floating IP will be used by knife to install the chef-client and to execute the chef-client run that will register the node with the Chef Server. Apply the configuration settings based on the run list used.

Configuring the knife-openstack plugin knife settings

Do you remember the `knife.rb` file we configured in *Chapter 2, Knife Tooling and Plugins*? Well, we are going to update it now to include the settings for the knife-openstack plugin. Once again, we need information from OpenStack, and the best way to get it is to log in and collect it.

Once more, browse to your horizon dashboard and log in. Again, make sure that your project is set to admin. Again, select the **Project** menu from the menu accordion on the left, and select **Access & Security** from the **Project** submenu options. This time, in the **Access & Security** view, select the **API Access** tab.

Once there, you are going to want to view the credentials needed for the API access. As you probably have already figured out, you can view them by clicking on the button marked **+ View Credentials**. Here is what my API access credentials look like:

You will want to capture the values shown in the **User Credentials** dialog as we are going to need them for our knife.rb file. Once you have copied the values, you will want to edit your knife.rb file:

```
cd ~/chef-repo
vi .chef/knife.rb
```

Go to the end of the file and add the following values, replacing the **Project ID** and **Authentication URL** values with the data from your **User Credentials** dialog. Here are my entries:

```
knife[:openstack_auth_url] = 'http://192.168.157.134:5000/v2.0/tokens'
knife[:openstack_username] = 'admin'
knife[:openstack_password] = 'password'
knife[:openstack_tenant] = 'demo'
knife[:openstack_tenant_id] = 'ae3bbe1e367f44189424511bd8c123a0'
knife[:openstack_region] = 'RegionOne'
```

Notice that the openstack_auth_url value has an extra /tokens string at the end that is not shown in the **User Credentials** dialog. Make sure that you add it to your knife.rb file.

Note that each OpenStack entry should be on its own, single line in the knife.rb file. The code shown above may appear to have some lines split into two. The only other comment on these lines is the one for the OpenStack region. This is the default value used for my DevStack environment. It will be the same default value for your environment too. Now, save your changes, so we can test our knife-openstack plugin integration.

Here, for reference, is the full knife.rb file that contains settings for knife, the editor integration, the ec2 plugin, and the OpenStack plugin:

```
# See https://docs.getchef.com/config_rb_knife.html for more
information on knife configuration options

current_dir = File.dirname(__FILE__)
log_level                   :info
log_location                STDOUT
node_name                   'earlwaud'
client_key                  "#{current_dir}/earlwaud.pem"
validation_client_name      'sdearl-validator'
validation_key              "#{current_dir}/sdearl-validator.pem"
chef_server_url             'https://chefserver/organizations/sdearl'
cookbook_path               ["#{current_dir}/../cookbooks"]
```

```
#ssl_verify_mode      :verify_none
knife[:editor] = '/Applications/Sublime\ Text.app/Contents/
SharedSupport/bin/subl -w'
knife[:aws_credential_file] = '/Users/earlwaud/.aws/credential_file'

#knife-vsphere
knife[:vsphere_host] = 'vcenter6.nat.local.net'
knife[:vsphere_user] = 'earlwaud'
knife[:vsphere_pass] = '1Password'
knife[:vsphere_dc] = 'SanDiego'
knife[:vsphere_insecure] = true

#knife-openstack
knife[:openstack_auth_url] = 'http://192.168.157.134:5000/v2.0/tokens'
knife[:openstack_username] = 'admin'
knife[:openstack_password] = 'password'
knife[:openstack_tenant] = 'demo'
knife[:opnestack_tenant_id] = '181735be7b8a4a0c80c68200dffabe77'
knife[:openstack_region] = 'RegionOne'
knife[:openstack_ssh_key_id] = 'admin'
```

Add knife openstack server create parameters to your `knife.rb` file.

You may note the `openstack_ssh_key_id` value shown in this listing. I've added it to my `knife.rb` file so that I can avoid adding it to every `server create` command. I'll include it in the upcoming example, but know that you can add other OpenStack parameters to your `knife.rb` file to shorten your knife commands.

With our updated `knife.rb` file, we should be able to successfully communicate with our OpenStack environment using knife. We can test this integration easily with the following commands:

```
cd ~/chef-repo
```

```
knife openstack server list
```

If your configuration is correct, issuing the server list command shown earlier will return a single header line of information. It is only showing a header line because we haven't deployed any instances yet. Another command you might want to try at this point is the `image list` command. We are going to need the image information when we try to provision an instance. Give this a try now:

```
knife openstack image list
```

You should get back a list of the default images in your OpenStack environment. In my case, issuing that command looks like this:

```
Earls-Mac:chef-repo earlwaud$ sudo knife openstack image list
Name                          ID
Snapshot
cirros-0.3.4-x86_64-uec          84dff654-7f0d-45c8-a20b-b08c0ef39fd1   no
cirros-0.3.4-x86_64-uec-ramdisk  d03ec228-a5c9-4200-8058-3bde074c67a1   no
```

Let's get a better option for our knife-openstack plugin testing.

Adding a CentOS instance image to provision

The default deployment of DevStack detailed earlier comes with some sample cirros images to test and validate the OpenStack deployment. Those images are listed in the output example from the previous section. For our use, we want to deploy a more production-like image. For the examples in the rest of this chapter, I am going to use a CentOS image for provisioning OpenStack instances.

You can obtain the same image by visiting the official Get Images OpenStack page at this URL: `http://docs.openstack.org/image-guide/obtain-images.html`. Near the top of the page, you will find the Official CentOS 6 Images link. Clicking that link will take you to a list of CentOS 6 images you can download. I'll use the CentOS image for the rest of the testing in this chapter. Click on the link for that image and download it to your Chef workstation. The exact name of the image I downloaded for the examples is as follows:

```
CentOS-6-x86_64-GenericCloud-1508.qcow2
```

Once it has been downloaded, you can log in to your OpenStack environment and add the image to the list of available images. Make sure that you are in the demo project, then using the menu accordion on the left, select **Project** | **Compute** | **Images**. Now press the **+ Create Image** button to create our new `centos6` image. A dialog window will open up, and you can populate the inputs as follows:

Leave all of the other inputs blank. Also, since this is an image in the demo project, and we will provision into the demo project, you don't need to check the **Public** check-box, but if you want this image to be available to any other projects, check the public check-box. Now click on the **Create Image** button, and we are ready to provision an OpenStack instance with Chef. Let's give it a try.

Provisioning a new instance

Now that we finally have everything configured for OpenStack provisioning, let's see what our first knife OpenStack provisioning command will look like. Here is a command that I used to provision a new OpenStack instance (and deploy chef-client onto to it and so on):

```
knife openstack server create \
--availability-zone "nova" \
--image "centos6" \
--flavor "m1.small" \
--sudo \
```

```
--bootstrap-protocol ssh \
--ssh-user "centos" \
--identity-file "/Users/earlwaud/chef-repo/admin.pem" \
--openstack-ssh-key-id admin \
--openstack-floating-ip \
--run-list "recipe[base]" \
--node-name api_vm01 \
-V
```

There are a lot of parameters in that command, so let's talk about each one. By the way, if you want to see the full list of parameters for this create command, ask for help with this command:

```
knife openstack server create --help
```

Ok, so here is what's going on:

- `knife openstack server create`: This is telling knife to use the newly installed openstack plugin and to issue a create server command. The `server create` command will talk to OpenStack, and using the API information we added to the `.chef` file, will execute a "Launch Instance" command. Several of the parameters in our knife command are used to provide the inputs for the launch instance command.

- `availability-zone "nova"`: This parameter tells OpenStack that we want our instance to go into the "nova" zone. In our dev environment, we only have the single zone, but if this were a production deployment, we would have multiple zones, which would provide our physical fault isolation. The objective would be to deploy redundant instances in different zones to provide protection against physical failure of the hosting resources.

- `image "centos6"`: This is the name of the image from which we want to build our instance. This is the image we installed in the earlier section.

- `flavor "m1.small"`: This tells OpenStack what resources we want our instance to have. This sets the number of vCPUs, the amount of memory, the disk size, and so on. The configured "Flavors" can be found in your OpenStack dashboard in the **Admin** accordion menu on the left-hand side.

- `sudo`: This tells knife to execute the node bootstrap using sudo.

- `bootstrap-protocol ssh`: This instructs the knife command to use ssh to connect to the new instance when it bootstraps the node.

- `ssh-user "centos"`: This is the username to use when executing the ssh command for bootstrapping the node. All of the images provided on the OpenStack image pages use an OS distro-related user name. For CentOS images, the user name is `centos`, for Ubuntu images, it is `ubuntu`, and for the cirros images, the username is `cirros`.

- `identity-file "/Users/earlwaud/chef-repo/admin.pem"`: This parameter is providing the location on your Chef workstation to the key file that will be used for authentication during the connection of the ssh session.

- `openstack-ssh-key-id admin`: This parameter tells OpenStack the name of the key pair to use when deploying the instance thus providing the access via key authentication in the ssh command. (There is no password access provided for the OpenStack instances deployed.)

- `openstack-floating-ip`: This parameter is telling OpenStack to associate one of the allocated floating IP addresses to the provisioned instance. This IP address will provide the public access to the node. It is an address on the public network interface. In our environment, the instance is provisioned with an IP address in the 10.0.0.x subnet on a private network interface. The floating IP is created in the public subnet (for our example, that is in 192.168.157.250 - 192.168.157.254). OpenStack is configured to with a virtual router to pass traffic between the private and public networks.

- `run-list "recipe[base]"`: This parameter is telling knife to use the run list "base" when it does the initial bootstrap chef-client run.

- `node-name api_vm01`: This parameter is telling OpenStack to name the new instance `api_vm01`. This will also be the name of the node on the Chef Server.

- `v`: Finally, this parameter is telling the knife command to provide verbose debugging output during the execution of the command.

> Note that it is the only parameter we used that has a single dash. You can increase the level of output to debug by adding a second V, making the parameter `-VV`.

Here is a look at the command with its output:

```
knife openstack server create \
> --availability-zone "nova" \
> --image "centos6" \
> --flavor "m1.small" \
> --sudo \
```

```
> --bootstrap-protocol ssh \
> --ssh-user "centos" \
> --identity-file "/Users/earlwaud/chef-repo/admin.pem" \
> --openstack-ssh-key-id admin \
> --openstack-floating-ip \
> --run-list "recipe[base]" \
> --node-name api_vm01 \
> -V


INFO: Using configuration from /Users/earlwaud/chef-repo/.chef/knife.rb


Waiting for server [wait time = 600]....
Instance ID        af367e7f-689a-4c1e-b086-da07da75e03b
Name               api_vm01
Private IP         10.0.0.12
Flavor             2
Image              2135dc5e-9c5a-473d-ace4-f1477a076836
Keypair            admin
State              ACTIVE
Availability Zone  nova
Private IP Address: 10.0.0.12
[fog] [WARNING] Unrecognized arguments: openstack_identity_endpoint
Floating IP Address: 192.168.157.252
Private IP Address: 10.0.0.12
Bootstrapping the server by using bootstrap_protocol: ssh and image_os_
type: linux


Waiting for sshd to host (192.168.157.252).........done
Doing old-style registration with the validation key at /Users/earlwaud/
chef-repo/.chef/sdearl-validator.pem...
Delete your validation key in order to use your user credentials instead


Connecting to 192.168.157.252
192.168.157.252 -----> Installing Chef Omnibus (-v 12)
192.168.157.252 downloading https://www.opscode.com/chef/install.sh
. . .(truncated). . .
```

There you have it. You can now provision new OpenStack instances using the knife-openstack plugin. Go forth and provision!

References

- Learn more about DevStack at this link `http://docs.openstack.org/developer/devstack/`.

- Download the Ubuntu Desktop install bits at `http://www.ubuntu.com/download/desktop`.

- Follow the knife-openstack plugin repo at `https://github.com/chef/knife-openstack`.

- Follow the status of the "Forbidden error" at `https://bugs.launchpad.net/devstack/+bug/1243075`.

- Download your OpenStack instance images from `http://docs.openstack.org/image-guide/obtain-images.html`.

- Read about the OpenStack configuration input settings at `http://docs.openstack.org/developer/devstack/configuration.html`.

- There is a nice OpenStack command cheat sheet `http://docs.openstack.org/user-guide/cli_cheat_sheet.html`.

Network automation

The **Software-defined Networking (SDN)** technology is still in its infancy. Since it is still evolving, it means different things to different people. It is like what the idea of Cloud Computing used to be; in the past, if you asked several different people what Cloud Computing means, you would have received several very different answers. Now, we have refined the definition of Cloud Computing and developed the specific technologies of **Platform as a Service (Paas)**, **Infrastructure as a Service (IaaS)**, and **Software as a Service (SaaS)**.

Like Cloud Computing, SDN comprises many different technologies such as OpenFlow, Virtual Switching, and Data Center Network Fabrics. Because of this, there is no single answer to the question "What is Network Automation?". Every company has a unique network configuration (although with common elements), so every company will have a different need for their network automation. In fact, with the proper attention, this topic could be made into its own, thick, book.

So what can we cover in a few pages that will be valuable to the DevOps, or in this case the NetOps engineer? Let's work from Chef.io's point of view. They consider network devices as any other node that can be managed. Here is how Chef.io describes it:

network device

A network node is any networking device—a switch, a router—that is being managed by a chef-client, such as networking devices by Juniper Networks, Arista, Cisco, and F5. Use Chef to automate common network configurations, such physical and logical Ethernet link properties and VLANs, on these devices.

OK, so let's take a look at how we turn the configuration of some of the more common data center elements into code with Chef. We will start with Juniper devices. Then, we'll explore Cisco devices, and finally, we'll learn about using Chef with F5 LTMs. Let's begin.

Automating juniper devices

As an example, let's look at how to manage a common data center switch from Juniper, the QFX5100 switch. This switch supports virtualized network environments so it will stand as a good representation for our purposes. If you are using the Junos Enhanced Automation software, the image comes with a Chef agent preinstalled. It is a ruby program that uses the NETCONF libraries.

The QFX5100 switch can be treated as a node for the Chef Server to manage. And with the built-in chef-client, we can converge the switch to our desired state. The first step is to register the node with the Chef Server. There is a specific bootstrap process to do this registration for us. You will need a specific bootstrap file for this process. You can use wget to download the bootstrap file with the following command:

```
wget https://github.com/opscode/junos-chef/blob/master/bootstrap/junos-minimal.erb
```

Once you have the bootstrap file, you will execute the knife bootstrap command. It will take the following format:

```
knife bootstrap <SWITCH IP ADDRESS> --template_file junos-minimal.erb -x root
```

For example, if the IP address of your switch is 172.0.0.10, you would use the command:

```
knife bootstrap 172.0.0.1 --template_file junos-minimal.erb -x root
```

You will be prompted for the root password, and when entered, the node will be bootstrapped and registered with the Chef Server. OK, now we have a new node, and we want to configure it for our environment. We are going to employ the cookbook netdev to handle the configuration of our switch. We need to add the cookbook to our repo. You can do this with the following commands:

```
knife cookbook site download netdev
tar zxvf ./netdev-2.0.0.tar.gz -C cookbooks
mkdir ~/chef-repo/cookbooks/netdev/recipes
```

Now you need to create the recipes you will use to configure the switch. Here are some example recipes. Create a create_vlan recipe, as follows:

vi ~/chef-repo/cookbooks/netdev/recipes/create_vlan.rb

```
netdev_vlan 'public' do
    vlan_id 100
    description 'public'
    action :create
end
netdev_vlan 'nonpublic' do
    vlan_id 200
    description 'nonpublic'
    action :create
end
```

Create a create_access recipe , as follows:

vi ~/chef-repo/cookbooks/netdev/recipes/create_access.rb

```
netdev_interface 'xe-0/0/14' do
    description 'access interface 14'
    action :create
end
netdev_interface 'xe-0/0/15' do
    description 'access interface 15'
    action :create
end

netdev_l2_interface 'xe-0/0/14' do
    description 'belongs to public VLAN'
    untagged_vlan 'public'
    vlan_tagging false
    action :create
end
```

```
netdev_l2_interface 'xe-0/0/15' do
    description 'belongs to nonpublic VLAN'
    untagged_vlan 'nonpublic'
    vlan_tagging false
    action :create
end
```

Create a `create_uplink` recipe, as follows:

vi ~/chef-repo/cookbooks/netdev/recipes/create_uplink.rb

```
netdev_l2_interface 'xe-0/0/10' do
    action :delete
end
netdev_l2_interface 'xe-0/0/11' do
    action :delete
end

netdev_lag 'ae0' do
    links ['xe-0/0/10', 'xe-0/0/11']
    minimum_links 1
    lacp 'active'
    action :create
end

netdev_l2_interface 'ae0' do
    description 'Uplink interface'
    tagged_vlans ['public', 'nonpublic']
    vlan_tagging true
    action :create
end
```

Now that you have the new recipes, you need to upload them to the Chef server with the following commands:

cd ~/chef-repo

knife cookbook upload netdev

Now you need to update the Chef server run list for the node that represents the switch. You can do this via the Chef server UI or using the `knife node edit` command. Edit the run list to include the new recipes you created earlier. If you are using the knife command, you would enter the following:

knife node edit qfx5100

"run_list": ["recipe[netdev::create_vlan]","recipe[netdev::create_access]","recipe[netdev::create_uplink]"

Next, we need to update the switch, running the chef-client to have the device's configuration converged to our desired state. To do this, you need to log in to the switch and run the `ruby` command to execute the chef-client. Here is the command:

```
/opt/sdk/chef/bin/ruby /opt/sdk/chef/bin/chef-client -c /var/db/chef/
client.rb
```

This will make the switch download the netdev cookbook and apply the recipes you added to the node's run list. This is the similar process that you are used to doing with your compute nodes, so it should seem very familiar now.

Be mindful of time drift

Although compute nodes are sensitive to small time differences between their clock and that of the Chef server, this sensitivity is greater for switches. It is vital that all elements are using NTP and are syncing to the same source for their clocks. The slightest drift between the clocks on the switches and the Chef server will result in failure to converge issues.

Now, let's take a look at some examples of automating Cisco systems.

Automating Cisco systems

In a way very similar to the automation of Juniper devices, Cisco has added Chef support to their Cisco NX-OS. The installation of the chef-client can be done manually or through automation. In the interest of space, I am going to review a high-level automated method of installing the client. Cisco NX-OS supports three environment types: bash-shell, guest-shell, and Open Agent Container (OAC). The chef client can be run in any of the three but on in one at a time. I will focus on guest-shell as it is a CentOS environment that is enabled by default on most platforms.

Note that the automated Chef client installation is not currently available when using the OAC environment, and if you wanted to use chef-client in that environment, you would need to do a manual installation.

There are two gems needed for the chef-client installation: the chef-provisioning and the chef-provisioning-ssh gems. The first one is installed when you install ChefDK, and the second you will need to install yourself. Use the following commands:

```
cd ~/chef-repo
chef gem install chef-provisioning-ssh
```

Now on the Cisco device, you need to do some setup. Here are the steps:

```
# Enter the guestshell environment using the 'guestshell' command
guestshell

# If using the management interface you must enter the management
namespace
sudo su -
chvrf management

# Set up hostname and DNS configuration
hostname n3k

echo 'n3k' > /etc/hostname

cat >> /etc/resolv.conf << EOF
nameserver 10.0.0.202
domain mycompany.com
search mycompany.com
EOF

configure terminal
  feature ssh
  username devops password password role network-admin
  username devops shelltype guestshell
end
```

Of course, you will need to adjust the values for nameserver, domain, search, and so on to match your systems.

Now you need to create a Chef provisioning input file. We will go into detail on the use of the Chef Provisioning feature in *Chapter 8, Using Chef Provisioning*. For now, just create an input file named chef_provisioning.rb and add the following as the contents of the file:

```
require 'chef/provisioning/ssh_driver'

with_driver 'ssh'

with_chef_server 'https://chefserver.example.com/organizations/chef',
  client_name: 'chefuser',
  signing_key_filename: '/etc/chef/chefuser.pem'
```

```
with_machine_options transport_options: {
  ip_address: '10.100.100.1',
  username: 'devops',
  options: {
    # BASH-SHELL options - uncomment if installing to bash-shell
    # prefix: 'sudo ip netns exec management ',

    # GUESTSHELL options - uncomment if installing to guestshell
    prefix: '/isan/bin/guestshell sudo ip netns exec management ',
    scp_temp_dir: '/bootflash',
  },
  ssh_options: {
    password: 'password',
  },
}

machine "n3k_100_1.example.com" do
  action [:ready, :setup, :converge]
  # Copy the trusted certificate to the newly provisioned node
  file '/Users/earlwaud/chef-repo/.chef/trusted_certs/chefserver.crt'
  converge true
end
```

Again, you need to update the values to match your systems. Once you have done this, save the file. Now run the `chef-client` command:

chef-client -z chef_provisioning.rb

This will install the chef-client into the guestshell environment of the Cisco device. However, you may encounter one of the following errors:

Unable to Connect … or … 401 "Unauthorized"

In the first case, you may have a stale SSH key in your `~/.ssh/known_hosts` file. You can remove it with the `ssh-keygen -R <hostname or IP>` command and then try again.

In the second case, you probably have a time sync issue between your system and the Cisco system.

 Make sure that clocks are in sync and try again.

Once the chef-client has been successfully installed into the guestshell environment of the Cisco device, you can begin to build recipes with the Cisco cookbook. Download and install the cookbook with these commands:

```
cd ~/chef-repo
knife cookbook site download cisco-cookbook
tar zxvf ./cisco-cookbook-1.1.2.tar.gz -C cookbooks
```

You are ready to create and edit recipes, upload them to the Chef server, and modify the run list for the Cisco devices in the same way you did for the Juniper devices described in the earlier section.

Now, let's take a look at automating F5 LTMs.

Automating F5 LTMs

There is an interesting article that discusses using Chef to automatically add web servers to an F5 LTM. It was written several years ago, and while the description of the process is accurate, the execution is no longer valid. We are going to re-engineer the process so that we can add this ability to our own Web Server role.

First, we need to download the cookbook from the article. Visit the link `https://devcentral.f5.com/articles/automating-web-app-deployments-with-opscode-chef-and-icontrol` and find the download link titled `f5-node-initiator.tgz` in the "installing the cookbook" section of the article. Click on the link and download the `tgz` file, saving it into your `~/chef-repo` folder. Now you can review the article for the description of what and why, but ignore the how, it is not relevant to today's versions of Chef. Here are the steps you need to set up and use this cookbook:

Start by extracting the cookbook. Use these commands:

```
cd ~/chef-repo
tar zxvf ./f5-node-initiator.tgz -C cookbooks
```

Unfortunately, the cookbook has a `metadata.rb` file that is missing an attribute for the cookbook name, which is required in current versions of chef. So, we need to edit the `metadata.rb` file to add that attribute:

```
cd ~/chef-repo
vi ./cookbooks/f5-node-initiator/metadata.rb
```

And a line at the top like this:

```
name            'f5-node-initiator'
```

Save the file. Now we need to upload the cookbook to our chef server. Use the following commands:

```
cd ~/chef-repo
knife cookbook upload f5-node-initiator
```

You can confirm the cookbook is available on the chef server with the `knife cookbook list` command. Now we need to create our web server role. Create or edit your `web_server.rb` file accordingly:

```
cd ~/chef-repo
vi ./roles/web_server.rb
```

Update the file contents as follows:

```
name 'webserver'
description 'The Web Server Role'
run_list([
    'recipe[base] ',
    'recipe[apache2] ',
    'recipe[f5-node-initiator] '
])
default_attributes({
  'bigip' => {
      'address' => '10.0.0.245',
      'user' => 'admin',
      'pass' => 'password',
      'pool_name' => 'chef_test_http_pool'
  }
})
override_attributes({
  'base_name' => 'Earl Waud',
  'user_name' => 'Earl Waud',
})
```

Replace the `address`, `user`, `pass`, and `pool_name` values with values appropriate for your environment. Save the file. Now we need to upload the role to our Chef server. Issue the following commands to upload the role:

```
cd ~/chef-repo
knife role from file roles/web_server.rb
```

Next, we need to add the new role to our web server nodes. For example, if we have a web server node named `web01`, we would issue the following commands:

```
cd ~/chef-repo
knife node run_list add web01 "role[webserver]"
```

The node web01 is now ready to re-run the chef-client and converge its configuration to that of our new webserver role that includes the f5-node-initiator.

References

- Check out the junos-chef repo for Juniper switch configuration with Chef at `https://github.com/Juniper/junos-chef`.

- Learn about the Chef Junos integration at the Chef.io site at `https://docs.chef.io/junos.html`.

- Read about the QFX5100 switches from Juniper at `http://www.juniper.net/us/en/products-services/switching/qfx-series/qfx5100/`.

- There is the netdev repo on GitHub at `https://github.com/chef-partners/netdev`.

- There is the Cisco cookbook repo on GitHub at `https://github.com/cisco/cisco-network-chef-cookbook?files=1`.

- There is the manual chef-client installation instructions at `https://github.com/cisco/cisco-network-chef-cookbook/blob/develop/docs/README-agent-install.md`.

- There are the automated chef-client installation instructions at `https://github.com/cisco/cisco-network-chef-cookbook/blob/develop/docs/README-chef-provisioning.md`.

- Learn about the Chef to NX-OS integration at `http://www.cisco.com/c/en/us/td/docs/switches/datacenter/nexus9000/sw/7-x/programmability/guide/b_Cisco_Nexus_9000_Series_NX-OS_Programmability_Guide_7x/b_Cisco_Nexus_9000_Series_NX-OS_Programmability_Guide_7x_chapter_01110.html`.

- Read an excellent article on automating WebApp deployments with Chef at `https://devcentral.f5.com/articles/automating-web-app-deployments-with-opscode-chef-and-icontrol`.

- Take a deep look at the F5 Big IP cookbook that was released into open source by Target: `https://github.com/target/f5-bigip-cookbook`.

- Download the F5 cookbook from the Chef supermarket at `https://supermarket.chef.io/cookbooks/f5/versions/0.2.4`.

Summary

In this chapter, we focused on provisioning in the traditional data center. With the widespread use of VMware vSphere, it is appropriate that we started with using the knife-vsphere plugin to deploy VMs into our vSphere environment. You learned how to provision and manage vSphere VM's configuration with Chef using this plugin. We also covered setting up a personal development environment using VMware's desktop hypervisors and Vagrant. We also provided references for you to do your own homework on several other VMware-related knife plugins, and with the information you have learned so far, you should be able to figure out how to make them work in your environment. Next, we took a look at provisioning into OpenStack environments. With the strong growth of OpenStack deployments and the ever-growing list of developers backing this technology, having a good foundation for provisioning into OpenStack is vital. You definitely have that knowledge now. And following the track of having a place for your development work, you learned how to stand up your own OpenStack development environment. Next, we took a dip into the waters of a NetOps engineer, exploring some areas for network automation. What a journey! This chapter is so full of information that you might have to read it twice!

However, if you are ready for more, then next up, we turn our attention to the clouds with a look at provisioning in Amazon AWS and other cloud based hosting providers.

6
Provisioning in the Cloud

This chapter will expand the previous chapter and explore the use of Chef for deployment and configuration in the cloud. Much like VMware is the 600 pound gorilla in the data center, Amazon is the 600 pound gorilla in the cloud. Amazon is the first provider that comes to mind when people ask about the cloud, and it has the biggest market share, at least so far. They currently host about 30 percent of cloud-based systems, which is a larger percentage than the next three providers combined. With that kind of dominance in the cloud market, you might ask why learn how to provision to any other cloud provider? Well, because Microsoft and Google are currently the fastest growing providers. Microsoft has already grabbed about 12 percent of the market share and is growing at a much faster rate than Amazon. And not one to be out done, Google is not too far behind Microsoft. Let the cloud provider wars begin! So, in this chapter, the reader will learn about provisioning to all three of the top cloud providers. This will help them to manage hybrid solutions for scale and high availability with whichever provider best meets their business needs. We'll begin by expanding the work we did in *Chapter 2, Knife Tooling and Plugins*, with provisioning EC2 instances. Then, you will learn how to leverage Chef to provision into Windows Azure and into Google Cloud Platform. The chapter will end with a look at using Chef to provision containers using Docker.

> *"I like rice. Rice is great if you're hungry and want two thousand of something."*
>
> *– Mitch Hedberg*

The following topics will be covered in this chapter:

- Provisioning AWS EC2 instances
- Provisioning Microsoft Azure instances
- Provisioning in the Google Cloud Platform
- Looking at an honorable mention – Linode
- Provisioning containers in Docker

Provisioning AWS EC2 instances

In *Chapter 2*, *Knife Tooling and Plugins*, you explored installing the knife-ec2 plugin and learned the knife configuration settings required to provision AWS EC2 instances. Now you are going to expand on this base of knowledge and learn more about AWS authentication. Then, we are going to see how easy it is to set up a Chef Server in an EC2 instance.

 Remember that you can set up an AWS account on Amazon and use the service for free, as long as you stay within the "Free Tier Eligible" guidelines. I will note where any of the examples go outside of the free services.

Understanding EC2 authentication

As we saw in *Chapter 2*, *Knife Tooling and Plugins*, you need to configure knife to allow it to use the EC2 plugin to create AWS EC2 instances. You can either add the credentials directly to your `knife.rb` file, or better, create an AWS configuration file with the account credentials in it and point your `knife.rb` file to that credentials file. The contents of the credentials file will look something like this:

```
cat /Users/earlwaud/.aws/credential_file
[default]
aws_access_key_id = TR42UIIKKN73BSROPZGA
aws_secret_access_key = eZMk1OXH2Ish056IkH50fLg7TQ9U2pDHrOh9OUF9
```

Then, you will add the pointer to the credentials in your knife file with a line like this:

```
knife[:aws_credential_file] = '/Users/earlwaud/.aws/credential_file'
```

Okay, we can create our EC2 instances with the knife-ec2 plugin. What else do we need? There are two more authentication areas we need to explore: the first is creating security key pairs, and the second is creating networking security groups. Let's take a deeper look into these two topics.

Creating key pairs

Access to the EC2 instances is handled using public key cryptography that encrypts and decrypts the login information. This method uses a public key to encrypt data like passwords. Then, the private key can be used to decrypt that data. These public and private key combinations are known as key pairs.

To log in to an Amazon EC2 instance, you need to provide the private key. The Linux-based instances are created without passwords, and the only access is via the use of the key pairs. Windows-based instances also use key pairs. But for Windows, you use the private key to obtain the administrator password, which can then be used to access the instance via RDP.

You can create your key pairs through the Amazon user interface, or generate your own key pairs, and upload the public key to Amazon where it can be injected into your created instances. Here are the steps to creating your key pair using Amazon:

1. Browse the Amazon compute EC2 console and login.

2. Select the region that will use the key pair. For me, this is US West (Oregon).

> It is important to remember that key pairs are only valid in the region where they are created or uploaded.

3. Expand the **NETWORK & SECURITY** accordion in the navigation pane on the left and select **Key Pairs**.

4. Click on the **Create Key Pair** button.

5. In the window that pops up, enter the name you want to use for your new key pair and then click on the **Create** button.

6. The private key file will be downloaded automatically via your browser. The filename will match the name you give the key pair and will have the extension of .pem.

> This is the only time you will be given the private key file. Save it in a location that is persistent. I saved mine at the same location as my AWS credentials file, which is at /Users/earlwaud/.aws/credential_file. It is a real big pain if you lose a private key and need to access an instance that was created with the matching public key. You can find documentation for dealing with this on the Amazon site, but trust me, it's not fun. Keep your private keys safe and accessible.

7. In most use cases, as the last step, you need to change the permission on the private key file to be more restrictive. For example, to use the key with ssh, you must lock down the access to it. Use the command chmod 400 ~/.aws/us-west-oregon-earl01.pem.

If you are accessing EC2 instances using PuTTY on your Windows system, you need to generate a private key file in a format that can be used by PuTTY. When you install PuTTY, there is an additional tool named PuTTYgen that is installed as well. PuTTYgen can be used to create an SSH-2 RSA version of your private key file, which PuTTY can use to access your instances. If you've never done this before, you can find the full instructions in the Amazon documentation. I will provide the direct link to that document in the references section later. You're now ready to use key pairs to create and access your new EC2 instances.

Creating security groups

Now, let's take a look at creating security groups. The EC2 security group is essentially a firewall for your instances. Each instance you create needs to have one or more security groups applied to provide the access rules for the instance. You can create a security group that has many rules for inbound or outbound traffic, or you can create multiple security groups where each has a specific rule for traffic, such as a rule to allow ICMP traffic. This multiple security group method is a better choice, allowing you to create protocol-specific security groups that can be applied on an as needed basis. If your application needs SSL access, you can create a security group for HTTPS and apply that group to your instance. Now it's very clear what traffic is permitted in or out of your systems.

For the examples in this book, I am going to describe the steps to create and configure a single security group with very open access. In a real production application, you will want to configure your security groups with very specific and limited access, allowing only the network traffic necessary to use your applications. With that detail noted, here are the steps to create the new security group, which we will use in the next section to deploy an EC2 instance for our new Chef Server.

1. Browse the Amazon compute EC2 console and login.
2. Select the region that will use the security group. For me, this is US West (Oregon). As with key pairs, security groups are only valid in the region where they are created.
3. Expand the **NETWORK & SECURITY** accordion in the navigation pane on the left and select Security Groups.
4. Click on the **Create Security Group** button.
5. In the popup window, enter a name and description.
6. Click on the **Add Rule** button one or more times and create the rules for the new group. In this security group, I added a rule for ICMP, SSH, HTTP, and HTTPS.
7. Once all the rules have been added, click on the **Create** button to create the new security group.

Take a look at the security group I created for the example in this chapter:

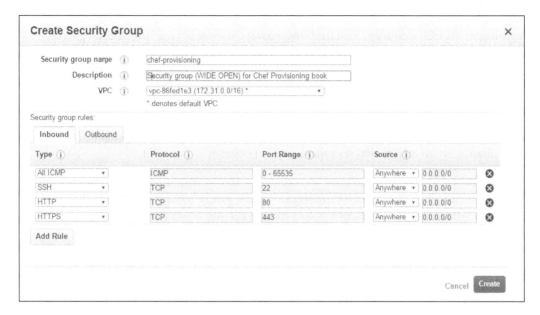

You can see in the preceding image that I added four rules to my security group—one to allow ping traffic, one to allow SSH traffic, and one each for HTTP and HTTPS. Remember that it would be a better idea to create individual security groups for each protocol and then add those groups to your instances only if that protocol is needed for your application. Also note that I left the source of all these inbound rules to be wide open, allowing access from any IP address. You really don't want to do this for a production environment if you can avoid it. Of course, if the system is hosting a public web server, you may need to have an open access rule for HTTP or HTTPS, but you certainly wouldn't want to have SSH wide open like this.

Also, each security group has a default outbound rule that allows all network traffic to flow out of the instance. This too can be narrowed to limit what can exit your systems and should be modified to achieve a hardened environment.

Now that you have your AWS credentials setup to use knife to create EC2 instances and you've created a key pair to use for accessing those instances, and you have created your security group to control the network traffic to and from your instances, let's create a new instance. This time, we are going to use knife, along with our existing public Chef Server, to deploy and configure a new Chef Server in an EC2 instance.

Installing Chef Server into an EC2 instance

There are two ways you can arrive at the destination of having your Chef Server running in an EC2 instance. The first and easiest way is to just "purchase" a Chef Server AMI from the AWS Marketplace. There are different levels of the Chef Server AMIs based on the number of nodes that you plan to manage, starting at 25 nodes, all of which currently offer a 14-day free trial (which, by the way, is not exactly free, you still pay for the AWS infrastructure charges, just not for the hourly software charges). These Chef Server instances all come with an easy way to add additional Chef.io offerings, such as Chef Analytics, Management Console, and Chef Compliance, at an additional software cost, of course.

The second way, which is the way we are going to examine further, is to stand up the Chef Server in an EC2 instance ourselves. We are going to download the chef-server cookbook and its dependent cookbooks form the Chef marketplace. Then, we are going to upload the cookbooks to our current publicly accessible Chef Server. Then, we are going to use the knife-ec2 plugin to create our new instance and converge its configuration to that of a Chef Server. Finally, we are going to use some of the commands you learned in *Chapter 1, Setting Up a Development Environment on Your Workstation*, to round out the setup of our Chef Server. This sounds like a lot to do, but you'll see that it's not too bad. Let's start.

The first step is to download the chef-server cookbook and its dependencies. To do this, we are going to issue the following commands:

```
cd ~/chef-repo
knife cookbook site install chef-server
```

This knife cookbook command will go out to the Chef supermarket and will download the chef-server cookbook archive file. It will extract the contents of that archive into our cookbooks folder and then delete the downloaded archive file. It will then look at the dependencies for the chef-server cookbook, and in turn, download, extract, and delete the archive for each of the dependent cookbooks. This process will be repeated for each of the dependent cookbooks until all the cookbooks necessary to use the chef-server cookbook have been added to our local repo.

Depending on the state of your repo, you may receive an error message telling you that you need to commit your exiting changes before installing new cookbooks. If you get this message, use the git add and git commit commands to "tidy up" your local repo as needed and then run the knife cookbook command again.

Now that we have the chef-server cookbook and all of its dependencies in our local repo, we need to upload them into our publically accessible chef server. In my case, I am using the free version of Chef Server available at http://manage.chef.io. Yes, this is a kind of recursion—we are using a Chef Server to deploy a Chef server. (I have a T-shirt that has a circle of text on the front that says "In order to understand recursion, one must first understand recursion." It is my favorite T-shirt.). To upload our cookbooks to the Chef Server, we will issue the following command:

```
cd ~/chef-repo
knife cookbook upload chef-server --include-dependencies
```

Now we are ready to create out new EC2 instance and converge it into a Chef Server. If you haven't done so yet, install the knife-ec2 plugin now with the following command:

```
chef gem install knife-ec2
```

Before we create our instance, let me point out that you cannot use the t2.micro flavor for your Chef Server instance. Chef Server's minimum memory requirements as stated in the Chef documentation are 4 GB. I have found that you can stand up a Chef Server (for testing and dev) using only 2 GB, which is configured when you use a t2.small flavor. The Chef Server cookbook will not converge successfully if you try to use it in a 1 GB server, which is what you get when you use the t2.micro flavor. So, t2.small is the smallest working environment flavor you have for testing this out. This is of importance because the t2.small flavor is not "Free Tier Eligible", and you will be incurring infrastructure charges when you deploy a t2.small instance. With that advisory said, here is the knife-ec2 command I used for deploying the EC2 instance I'll use for the Chef Server:

```
cd ~/chef-repo
knife ec2 server create \
  --node-name ec2-chef-server \
  --groups=chef-provisioning \
  --region=us-west-2 \
  --availability-zone=us-west-2a \
  --image=ami-9abea4fb \
  --server-connect-attribute=public_ip_address \
  --flavor=t2.small \
  --ssh-user=ubuntu \
  --ssh-key=us-west-oregon-earl01 \
  --identity-file=/Users/earlwaud/.aws/us-west-oregon-earl01.pem \
  --run-list="recipe['chef-server']" \
  -V
```

This will take a little while to complete, but when it is done, the new EC2 instance will be a registered node on your public-facing Chef Server, the chef-server cookbook will have been installed, and the instance will be ready for you to ssh into, to finish up the configuration. Of course, you could have added additional recipes to the run-list and completed some or all of the next steps, but for the sake of space in this chapter, I am going to just list out the steps manually a little later. Right now, let's review the server create command we used to provision our Chef Server;

- `knife ec2 server create`: This is the ec2 server create subcommand.

- `--node-name ec2-chef-server`: This parameter provides the name to use to register the node on the Chef Server. In this example, our node will be registered as "ec2-chef-server". This value will also be used for the instance name in AWS.

- `--groups=chef-provisioning`: The value used in this parameter is the name of the security group you have created in AWS. Remember that the security group provides the firewall settings for your instances. This time, we are referencing the security group "chef-provisioning" that we created earlier.

- `--region=us-west-2`: This parameter identifies the target region for our provisioning. This is one of the parameters that we can set in our knife.rb file so that we wouldn't need to add it to our commands like we did here. This VM will be deployed in the "us-west-2" region.

- `--availability-zone=us-west-2a`: Each region has multiple zones to provide for fault tolerance. This parameter specifies which of the zones to deploy into. In our example here, we are using the "us-west-2a" zone.

- `--image=ami-9abea4fb`: Here, we provide the name of the template image that we want to deploy. You can find the details of all of the available AMI images in the AWS Marketplace. The link for the Marketplace will be in the references section later. An easy way to find AMIs that are available in your target region is to log in to the AWS console. Select the region you are interested in. Then, select "AMIs" from the images navigation pane.

Remember to select "Public Images" in the search bar to see the images that are in the AWS Marketplace. In this example, we are using the AMI named "ami-9abea4fb". This is an Ubuntu 14.04 server image that uses the EBS root device type.

- `--server-connect-attribute=public_ip_address`: This parameter tells Knife that we want to have a public IP address assigned to our instance.

- `--flavor=t2.small`: The flavor parameter provides the resource size to use when provisioning this instance. The "t2" flavors are of general purpose, and "small" indicates that the VM will have 1 vCPU and 2 GB memory. Other sizing options include nano, micro, medium, and large. Note that most of the flavors are outside of the free tier subset, so be aware of this when selecting your flavors.

- `--ssh-user=ubuntu`: With many public AMIs available in the Marketplace, especially the OS-specific AMIs, access is granted with a specific username. In this case, we are using an Ubuntu server AMI, so the username is "ubuntu".

- `--ssh-key=us-west-oregon-earl01`: This parameter provides the name of the key pair we set up in AWS.

- `--identity-file=/Users/earlwaud/.aws/us-west-oregon-earl01.pem`: This parameter's value is the local path and filename for the key file associated with the key referenced in the ssh-key parameter.

- `--run-list="recipe['chef-server']"`: With this parameter, we provide the run-list to be used in the initial chef-client run. It is the state to which we wish to converge this node.

- `-V`: This is the standard verbose output option parameter. We can increase the level of output with a second V, like -VV.

Now that we understand the parameters used, here is a snippet of the output from the server create command used earlier. Make note of the Public DNS Name when you run your command, since we will use that to access the instance when it is deployed.

```
Waiting for EC2 to create the instance.......
Public DNS Name: ec2-54-201-38-94.us-west-2.compute.amazonaws.com
Public IP Address: 54.201.38.94
Private DNS Name: ip-172-31-18-207.us-west-2.compute.internal
Private IP Address: 172.31.18.207

Waiting for sshd access to become available.
```

Let's take care of the final steps needed to turn our EC2 instance into a full-fledged Chef Server. The first of these final steps is to ssh into our new Chef Server. Remember that we need to use the private key that we created earlier along with the Public DNS name of the newly deployed instance.

Since we deployed an Ubuntu instance, the user name we need for our ssh connection is "ubuntu". This is the same user name that we used in the knife command earlier. If we had used a different OS provider for our EC2 instance, say CentOS, then we would be using a different username, that is, "centos" for these commands. And as you can see from the preceding image, the public DNS name is `ec2-54-201-38-94.us-west-2.compute.amazonaws.com`. To ssh into our new system, issue the following commands:

```
cd ~/chef-repo
ssh -i ../.aws/us-west-oregon-earl01.pem ubuntu@ec2-54-201-38-94.us-
west-2.compute.amazonaws.com
```

You will receive a message about not being able to establish the authenticity of the host (a very normal ssh message). Enter `yes` to continue, and you will be logged into your new instance. Now we will issue the last few commands (these are much the same as we saw in *Chapter 1, Setting Up a Development Environment on Your Workstation*) to finish our Chef Server setup. Here are the commands:

```
sudo chef-server-ctl user-create earlwaud Earl Waud earl@sandiegoearl.com
MyPassword99 --filename ~/earlwaud-ec2.pem
sudo chef-server-ctl org-create sdearl "San Diego Earl" --association_
user earlwaud --filename ~/sdearl-validator-ec2.pem
sudo chef-server-ctl install chef-manage
sudo chef-server-ctl reconfigure
sudo opscode-manage-ctl reconfigure
```

You will want to download the two Chef Server .pem files that are created with the preceding commands, so they can be used later to work with this new Chef Server, but other than this, we are done. You can open up a web browser now and visit the URL for your new server. In my case, it is `http://ec2-54-201-38-94.us-west-2.compute.amazonaws.com`. You will be presented with the login for your Chef Server. Enter the username and password you provided in the user create command shown earlier and you are good to go.

Now, let's turn our attention to what Microsoft has been cooking up in the clouds with their hosting solution, Microsoft Azure.

References

- Read about the partnership between Chef.io and Amazon AWS at `https://www.chef.io/solutions/aws/`.

- Visit the Amazon EC2 console at `https://console.aws.amazon.com/ec2/`.

- You can find the knife-ec2 plugin on github at `https://github.com/chef/knife-ec2`.

- Explore the many AMI images available to provision from in the AWS Marketplace at `https://aws.amazon.com/marketplace/ref=csl_ec2_ami`.

- Find the details for the Chef Server-specific AMIs offered on the AWS Marketplace at `https://aws.amazon.com/marketplace/pp/B010OMO0UE/?ref=_ptnr_chef_website#product-details`.

- Learn how to connect to your EC2 instances using PuTTY at `https://docs.aws.amazon.com/AWSEC2/latest/UserGuide/putty.html?icmpid=docs_ec2_console`.

- Amazon's documentation on key pairs is at `https://docs.aws.amazon.com/AWSEC2/latest/UserGuide/ec2-key-pairs.html?icmpid=docs_ec2_console`.

- Amazon's documentation on security groups is at `https://docs.aws.amazon.com/AWSEC2/latest/UserGuide/using-network-security.html?icmpid=docs_ec2_console`.

- The chef-server cookbook repo on Github is at `https://github.com/chef-cookbooks/chef-server`.

- Find all the available flavors that can be used to configure your instance's resource sizing at `https://aws.amazon.com/ec2/instance-types/`.

Provisioning Microsoft Azure instances

Now that we have a solid understanding of using Chef to turn our EC2 cloud infrastructure into code, it is easy to deploy and manage. Let's see how we can do that using Microsoft's cloud hosting provider service, Azure. As I mentioned earlier in the chapter, Azure is the fastest growing cloud provider, currently with about 12 percent of the cloud hosting market. As with Amazon, Microsoft offers a free trial of the service, so you can test out how things work for you with a real-life proof of concept.

At the time of writing this chapter, Microsoft Azure has multiple personalities. By this, I mean that Microsoft has created a newer fresh version of their Azure user interface, that is, Portal. Portal has a new domain name and a new cleaner, customizable UI. Along with this new UI, there is a new deployment model named Resource Manager. You may see this referred to as Azure Resource Manager. The older UI and deployment model, Azure Service Management, is now branded as Classic. Here are the URLs to access both versions of the UI:

- **Classic**: `http://manage.windowsazure.com/`
- **Portal**: `http://portal.azure.com/`

The newer Portal UI allows you to provision "Classic" VMs and will manage those VMs as well as any that are provisioned using the actual Classic UI. However, only Classic VMs (those created with the "Classic" setting using the Portal UI or those created using the Classic UI itself) are currently manageable using Chef. You cannot see or act on the Azure Resource Manager VMs created using the Portal UI.

 So far, you can access both versions of the user interface when you create an account using either. So if you've already created an account via the Portal UI, you can still use all of the following information.

With that framing, if you haven't done so yet, using either of the UIs, create your free trial account now, and let's explore Azure together.

Installing the knife-azure plugin

We begin, like we have several times before, by installing the plugin that will let us use Knife to work with a hosting provider, in this case, Microsoft Azure.

The current release of the knife-azure plugin is version 1.5.0. There is a release candidate of the plugin, version 1.6.0.rc.0, that was released in November 2015. This release candidate version is documented as the first version to support the newer resource model available via the Portal UI. The release candidate version provides access to the new Azure Resource Manager resource model with an additional unique keyword (azurerm), so your commands would start with:

```
knife azurerm …
```

The keyword for working with the Classic model (azure) has not changed in the release candidate version, so those commands would still start with:

```
knife azure …
```

Because the plugin will use separate keywords for each API, you can only execute in one model or the other in a single knife command.

Unfortunately, all of my attempts to get the `knife azurerm` commands to work have failed. Even the documentation says that the release candidate version of the plugin is not ready for production use. Because of this, the examples in this chapter will focus on Classic Azure and not Portal Azure. I am certain that in the near future, maybe by the time you read this book, the knife-azure plugin will get a new release version that also allows Chef Integration with the Portal Azure Resource Manager API to work.

Alright, let's install the plugin. You can easily install the plugin with the following commands:

```
cd ~/chef-repo
chef gem install knife-azure
```

Otherwise, if you want to give the release candidate version a try, use these commands:

```
cd ~/chef-repo
chef gem install knife-azure -v 1.6.0.rc.0
```

You can also use the more generic parameter:

```
cd ~/chef-repo
chef gem install knife-azure -prerelease
```

Either version works perfectly with the Classic model, so all of the commands will work as expected (except for the azurerm commands that I just pointed out earlier). If you are working in a production environment, I would strongly suggest that you stick with the latest release version and not use any release candidate versions).

By now, installing this plugin should seem very familiar and if you've been following along throughout the book, you probably could have installed it without looking at any of the commands shown earlier. Great!

Configuring the plugin

Now we are going to configure the knife-azure plugin. Configuring the plugin is also much like we have done previously. We are going to update the contents of our knife.rb file, adding a line for knife-azure. This time, however, the format is slightly different. This time, we need to have Azure generate a subscription file for us. We'll download the subscription file and save it in a safe location (I created a folder ~/.azure to store the credentials file in so that name and location will be consistent with the name and location we used for AWS).

To have Azure create your credentials file, you need to visit `https://manage.windowsazure.com/publishsettings/index?client=xplat`. When you browse this link and you are already logged in to Azure, Microsoft will generate your subscription file and initiate the download automatically. If you are not logged in, you will be asked for your login credentials, and then you'll be redirected to the download page and your subscription file will download automatically. If the download does not start, you can click the link to restart the download. Note that you need to have your Azure account created for this to work. The webpage has a link to take you to the Sign Up page if you haven't done so yet.

Once you've saved and copied your downloaded subscription file into your safe place folder, you are ready to update your `knife.rb` file. I copied my subscription file to `~/.azure/credentials.publishsettings`. (You want to maintain the file type of `.publishsettings`, especially if you plan to use other tools like PowerShell to integrate with Azure.) Now, edit the `knife.rb` file and add the lines for the Azure plugin configuration:

```
cd ~/chef-repo
vi .chef/knife.rb
```

Add the following lines:

```
#knife-azure
knife[:azure_publish_settings_file] = '/Users/earlwaud/.azure/
credentials.publishsettings'
```

Notice that I used the full path for the location/name of the subscription file. I found that if I use `~/.azure...`, the plugin does not correctly find the credentials.

OK, we have our plugin and credentials installed, and we have our knife configuration file updated accordingly. Let's start working with Azure.

Verifying the configuration

We have our new knife-azure plugin ready to use. So, let's kick the tires on this thing. Start off with a simple command to list our exiting Azure hosted servers. Enter the following:

```
knife azure server list
```

Well, that was probably underwhelming, as you probably haven't created any Azure virtual machines yet. You should still have seen a column header line show up as a response to your command. It would look something like:

```
...

DNS Name   VM Name   Status   IP Address   SSH Port   WinRM Port
```

This at least tells us that our plugin integration is working as desired. Now, let's try another command. This time, we want to list out all of the available images that we can use as a template to provision from. Try this command:

```
knife azure image list
```

Wow, that one gave us some output. You should have seen a very long list of images scroll across the screen. The information returned lists the name of each image, the base OS of each image, and the regions that each image can be deployed into. Much like AWS, many of the resources are associated to specific regions. Here are some of the possible regions you should see in your command results: Southeast Asia, Australia Southeast, West Europe, Central India, Japan East, Central US, East US, and South Central US. Currently, Microsoft provides Azure hosting services in 22 regional data centers.

Generating public/private key pairs

We now know that our knife-azure plugin is working, so it's almost time to use it to provision a new VM. We have one more step before we give provisioning a try though. We need to create a key pair to use for authentication with our Knife commands. I've found it, let's say "challenging" to get the authentication to work with username and password credentials, so I recommend you to focus on using key pairs for authentication and save yourself that headache. So, let's create a key pair for our Azure provisioning purposes. You can use the ssh-keygen command to create the key pair you need. Here is what it looked like when I created my key pair:

```
$ ssh-keygen
Generating public/private rsa key pair.
Enter file in which to save the key (/Users/earlwaud/.ssh/id_rsa): /
Users/earlwaud/.ssh/azure_rsa
Enter passphrase (empty for no passphrase):
Enter same passphrase again:
Your identification has been saved in /Users/earlwaud/.ssh/azure_rsa.
Your public key has been saved in /Users/earlwaud/.ssh/azure_rsa.pub.
The key fingerprint is:
7c:ed:c9:84:ee:7a:ea:48:65:00:d1:2a:ca:d3:89:c1 earlwaud@Earls-Mac.local
The key's randomart image is:
+--[ RSA 2048]----+
|    oo           |
|     ..          |
|.    ..          |
| E. .  o   o     |
|..+..  S o o     |
|.+ o   o o + .   |
| .   .   . +     |
|      . . ..     |
|       ..++.     |
+-----------------+
```

Provisioning virtual machines

OK, now that we have our key pair ready, let's create a new Azure compute resource. Here is the knife-azure plugin command to create a new server named earl-vm01:

```
knife azure server create \
  --azure-dns-name earl-dns01 \
  --azure-vm-name earl-vm01 \
  --azure-source-image
112500ae3b842c8b9c604889f8753c3__OpenLogic-CentOS-71-20160308 \
  --azure-service-location 'Central US' \
  --ssh-user earlwaud \
  --identity-file ~/.ssh/azure_rsa \
  --bootstrap-protocol ssh \
  --node-name earl-node01 \
  --run-list 'recipe['base']' \
  -V
```

The parameters used here should look quite familiar to you because they are very much like the parameters used for our other knife plugin server creates. Let's review the parameters for certainty.

The first part is the command itself:

- `knife azure server create`: This is the normal knife plugin format for a create server command. The keyword is azure, and the subcommand is server create.

- `--azure-dns-name 'earl-dns01'`: This parameter provides the name that will be assigned as the public DNS name. The domain used by Azure is `.cloudapp.net`. This implies that you must create a unique name to use as the value for this parameter, as it will create a public DNS name that must not conflict with any other public names in the same domain. You can actually create more than one server that uses the same DNS name. This supports Azure availability groups. In our example, we will have a public name of `earl-dns01.cloudapp.net`.

- `--azure-vm-name earl-vm01`: This parameter supplies the friendly name of the server. It is what you will see when you use the `knife azure server list` command and must be of 15 characters or less.

- `--azure-source-image 112500ae3b842c8b9c604889f8753c3__ OpenLogic-CentOS-71-20160308`: This parameter tells the plugin the name of the image file to provision our new system from. Again, you can get a full list of the available images with the command `knife azure image list`. I found it helpful to pipe the output into a grep command to "filter" the list. I use `knife azure image list | grep -i "centos-71"` to find the CentOS 7.1 images available.

- `--azure-service-location 'Central US'`: This parameter provides the name of the region to create the new system in.

 I believe that "West US" is not currently accessible with the knife-azure plugin. I would normally have selected that region, but due to the lack of availability for West US, I selected "Central US".

- `--ssh-user earlwaud`: This parameter tells knife what we want our username to be. In my case, I opted with the ever narcissistic "earlwaud" option.

- `--identity-file ~/.ssh/azure_rsa`: Do you remember the key pair we created earlier? This parameter is the path and name of that key file. This file will be injected into the new server so that the public key can be used to provide password-less access.

- `--bootstrap-protocol ssh`: This parameter tells knife to use the ssh protocol to bootstrap the new system. If we had selected a Windows OS-based image file to provision from, then we would have told knife to use the protocol of "winrm". You will usually use a value of "ssh" for deploying Linux systems.

- `--node-name earl-node01`: This parameter tells knife the name you want to register this new server as within your Chef Server. In this example, we will have a node named "earl-node01".

- `--run-list 'recipe['base']'`: This parameter provides the run-list value. As you already know, it supplies the list of recipes to converge the new system to. The value is a comma-separated list of roles or recipes to apply to the new system.

- `-V`: Finally, this is the verbose option, which can be made even more so with a second V as in `-VV`.

When the command completes, we will have a new compute resource hosted in Microsoft Azure named `earl-vm01`. This new system will be registered with our Chef server with the node name `earl-node01` and be bootstrapped to the provided run list, in this case, "base". The system will be configured to allow key pair access using the username "earlwaud" and the public dns name of `earl-dns01.cloudapp.net`, and the access key in this case will be `azure_rsa`. So, we can ssh into our new system with the following command:

```
ssh -i ~/.ssh/azure_rsa earlwaud@earl-dns01.cloudapp.net
```

Provisioning a new Chef server into Azure

Well that was pretty easy, right? So let's try one more and see if we can deploy an Ubuntu image to step up a new Chef server in Microsoft Azure, as we did with our Amazon EC2 instance. We are going to need to change a few of the parameters in our server create command. First, we need an Ubuntu image name for the source image parameter. Then, we need to update the run-list to tell the command to converge on a Chef server configuration, and finally, we need to increase the resources allocated to the system because the default size of "Small" is too small for a Chef Server. With those changes identified, here is the new `server create` command:

```
knife azure server create \
  --azure-dns-name earl-chef \
  --azure-vm-name earl-chefvm01 \
  --azure-vm-size Medium \
  --azure-source-image b39f27a8b8c64d52b05eac6a62ebad85__Ubuntu-14_04_1-
LTS-amd64-server-20150123-en-us-30GB \
  --azure-service-location 'Central US' \
  --ssh-user earlwaud \
  --identity-file ~/.ssh/azure_rsa \
  --bootstrap-protocol ssh \
  --node-name earl-chefvm01 \
  --run-list 'recipe['chef-server']' \
  --tcp-endpoints 80,443,9683 \
  -V
```

Let's take a quick look at the additional parameters we used this time:

- `--azure-vm-size Medium`: With this parameter, we are asking Azure to create our new system with the resources associated with a "Medium" environment (2 cores, 3.5 GB memory). The other options available as values for this parameter include ExtraSmall (shared core, 768 MB memory), Small (1 core, 1.75 GB memory), Large (4 cores, 7 GB memory), and ExtraLarge (8 cores, 14 GB memory).

- `--tcp-endpoints 80,443,9683`: If you recall from the AWS examples, you create Security Groups with permissions for different network protocols. The tcp-endpoints parameter is an Azure shortcut for this same type of feature. In this example, I am creating a new Chef server, and a Chef server needs the TCP ports 80, 443, and 9683 open and accessible to external connections. This parameter is configuring our new server to have that accessibility.

Executing the server create command given previously creates our Chef server successfully. This command does take a long time to complete, and at one point, it may seem to have frozen. Be patient. Allow it time to run to completion, and it will be successful. Note that if you use a larger azure-vm-size value, the execution will complete more quickly.

Okay, now we can go about our business of sshing into our new Chef server using the same format as the ssh command shown earlier:

```
ssh -i ~/.ssh/azure_rsa earlwaud@earl-chef.cloudapp.net
```

Then, we can complete the setup of our Chef server with these commands (which are nearly identical to the ones we used for our Chef server in the EC2 instance:

```
sudo chef-server-ctl user-create earlwaud Earl Waud earl@sandiegoearl.com
MyPassword99 --filename ~/earlwaud-azure.pem

sudo chef-server-ctl org-create sdearl "San Diego Earl" --association_
user earlwaud --filename ~/sdearl-validator-azure.pem

sudo chef-server-ctl install chef-manage

sudo chef-server-ctl reconfigure

sudo opscode-manage-ctl reconfigure
```

Our new Chef server is online and ready for us to log in at `https:\\earl-chef.cloudapp.net`. This is getting easy, right? Now, with this work done, we can begin to manage our infrastructure using our new Chef server hosted in our Azure cloud.

Several of the parameters used in the earlier server create command can be added as `knife.rb` configuration parameters. Setting them in the knife configuration file will allow you to issue your server create commands without need to supply the parameter. Here is a subset of the common parameters available for your `knife.rb` file. Remember to use fully qualified paths for filename configuration parameters:

```
knife[:azure_publish_settings_file] = '/Users/earlwaud/.azure/
credentials.publishsettings'
knife[:azure_dns_name] = 'earl-dns01'
knife[:azure_service_location] = 'Central US'
knife[:azure_source_image] = '112500ae3b842c8b9c604889f8753c3__
OpenLogic-CentOS-71-20160308'
knife[:azure_vm_name] ='earl-vm01'
knife[:ssh_user] = 'earlwaud'
knife[:identity_file] = '/Users/earlwaud/.ssh/azure_rsa'
knife[:tcp-endpoints] = '80,443,9683'
knife[:udp-endpoints] = '123:124'
```

Once we've finished using our new Azure compute resources and they are no longer desired, we can use the knife-azure plugin to delete the virtual machines and remove the nodes from our Chef server. Here is an example of a command to do this:

```
knife azure server delete earl-vm01 -N earl-node01 --purge -y
```

Now that we have the Chef chops to provision into the top two major cloud hosting providers, let's swing for a triple and learn how to provision into the Google Cloud Platform. Are you ready?

References

- Create a Microsoft Azure account using the Classic UI at `https://account.windowsazure.com/SignUp`.

- Or create your account using the Portal UI at `https://azure.microsoft.com/en-us/`.

- Learn about the Chef and Microsoft partnership at `https://www.chef.io/solutions/azure/`.

- Find the knife-azure plugin repo on Github at `https://github.com/chef/knife-azure`.

- Find the azure-cookbook repo on Github at `https://github.com/chef-partners/azure-cookbook`.

- Link to download (Classic UI) Azure PublishSettings file from Microsoft `https://manage.windowsazure.com/publishsettings/index?client=xplat`.

- If you want to do some DevOps work using Microsoft PowerShell and Azure, you can find the instructions at `https://azure.microsoft.com/en-us/documentation/articles/powershell-install-configure/`.

Provisioning in the Google Cloud platform

By now, you should be seeing the similarities between using Chef with Amazon and Microsoft, and as you might expect, the similarities don't end there. As you are about to see, we are going to do much the same as we explore provisioning and managing systems hosted on the Google Cloud Platform in the **Google Compute Engine** (**GCE**). One of the biggest advantages that Google's Engine offers is speed of deployment, so if you need to stand up images quickly, this might be the hosting platform for you. The Google Cloud Platform is feature-rich and offers automation for many of the services under the platform umbrella. Unfortunately, not all of the automation features are available using the associated Knife plugin. Still, there is plenty we can do, so let's explore what Chef provisioning options are available with the GCE and the knife-google plugin.

Installing and configuring the knife-google plugin

We are going to install the knife-google plugin to allow us to provision and manage our GCE hosts. The installation is via a gem, like the previous plugins we have explored. Use the following command for the installation:

```
chef gem install knife-google
```

This gem has many dependencies, and you will see them installed along the knife-google plugin gem. In my case, the command installed 15 gems in total, but other than the additional dependencies, there is nothing unusual here.

Now we need to set up authentication. This is where we get into something different. All of the previous Knife plugin integrations had a parameter that you add to the `knife.rb` file to supply a credential or point to a file to supply the credential for authentication to the specific hosting platform. Google handles this differently. The Google Knife plugin expects a credential file with a specific name to be in a specific location on your workstation and will look there when you run the knife-google plugin commands.

What's more, the credentials file has to be created with the Google Cloud SDK. It is not something that you log in to the Google Cloud Platform UI and download. And, there is no place in the UI where you can gather all of the values you need to build the file yourself. You are literally forced to install the Google Cloud SDK on your Chef workstation, and once it is installed, issue an SDK command that generates a `.json` file in this location:

```
~/.config/gcloud/application_default_credentials.json
```

You can store this credential file in a different location and create an environment variable to point to it, but there does not seem to be the typical `knife.rb` parameter that you can use to point to a different location or name for the file.

This requirement, having to install the Google Cloud SDK on your Chef workstation to be able to use the knife-google plugin, seems to be the least Chef-friendly installation of any of the Cloud integrations explored in this book. This both surprised and disappointed me a little. So with that said, how do you create the credential file you need for the knife-google plugin? Here are the steps for an OSX workstation.

Open a Terminal window and enter the following command:

```
curl https://sdk.cloud.google.com | bash
```

This will download the SDK and execute its installation. Now, restart your shell with the following command:

```
exec -l $SHELL
```

Next, initialize the gcloud environment with the following command:

```
gcloud init
```

This command will launch a browser window, so you can log in to the Google Cloud Platform and it will ask you to provide various selections to set up an environment for using the SDK. When the command finishes, it will have created the credentials file you need to use the knife-google plugin to integrate Chef with the Google Cloud Engine. The resulting `.json` file will have four parameters — `client_id`, `client_secret`, `refresh_token`, and `type`. Okay. That was a long process, but it seems to be the only way to get our needed credential file. And now, with this done, we can get back to the more "normal" Knife integration type stuff.

It is time again to open up our `knife.rb` file and add more configuration data to it. This time, we need to add a value for Google's gce_project parameter. Adding a value for the `gce_zone` parameter makes it so that we don't have to type it repeatedly with each of the knife-google commands. We can also add a parameter for the compute zone. The values of these settings can be determined from the Google Cloud Platform UI, and they were shown when we ran the `gcloud init` command to create our credential file. Here are the values I used in my `knife.rb` file:

```
#knife-google
knife[:gce_project] = 'api-project-167666703318'
knife[:gce_zone] = 'us-central1-a'
```

Now we are almost ready to start issuing knife-google plugin commands that we expect to work. We've got one more step to complete first, that being creating and registering our key pairs.

Creating and registering your key pairs

First, we need to create a key pair that we will then post to our user settings in the Google Cloud Platform. To create a new key pair, follow the instructions shown in the earlier Azure section. Here is the command for reference:

ssh-keygen

Save the keys in your `.ssh` folder. Give them a name that you can remember, letting you identify the key later so you can upload it to Google. I used the following:

/Users/earlwaud/.ssh/gce_rsa

With the keys generated, we now need to upload the public key to Google. Here are the steps required to successfully upload your key:

1. Visit the Google Cloud Platform UI at `https://cloud.google.com/`.
2. Log in to your account.
3. Go to console view by clicking on **My console** to the top-right of the page.
4. Select your project from the project list dropdown in the menu bar (you may only have one project at this point, so it may be preselected for you).
5. Using the **Products and Services** menu button, go to **Compute Engine**.
6. Select the **Metadata** functions from the **Compute Engine** menu options.
7. Change to the **SSH Keys** tab.

8. Click on the **Add item** button.

9. Now copy and paste in the entire contents of your public key into the "username" input field. To change the username automatically detected for the key, prefix your key with the username you plan to use as the `--ssh-user` value when creating a server with Knife. For example, if you plan to connect as "chef-user01", your key should look like: `chef-user01:ssh-rsa AAAAB3NzaC1yc2EAAAA...`

10. Finally, click on **Save** to complete the key entry. If you need to add more than one key, maybe for different users, then you need to hit the **Edit** button and then you get the **Add item** button again.

Here is what the uploaded public key file will look like in the GCE UI:

That rounds out our setup steps. Now we are ready to start provisioning using the knife-google plugin.

Provisioning virtual machines with the GCE

Let's warm up the engine so to speak, with a couple of knife-google plugin commands, as we have done for the previous plugins. We'll start with the server list command, which should provide us with a server list header and little else, since we haven't provisioned any servers yet. Of course, if you have pre-existing GCE instances, then you should see them listed with this command:

```
knife google server list
```

Now, let's give the image list command a shot. Issue the following command:

```
knife google image list
```

Well, that was unexpected. We have already found a common plugin command that is not available with the knife-google plugin. Using our other plugins, this command provided a list of the images available to provision from. Okay. We will figure out what our available images in the GCE are later. What we did get was a list of the knife-google commands we have available. Here is the list:

```
Available google subcommands: (for details, knife SUB-COMMAND --help)
** GOOGLE COMMANDS **
knife google disk create NAME --gce-disk-size N (options)
knife google disk delete NAME [NAME] (options)
knife google disk list
knife google project quotas
knife google zone list
knife google region quotas
knife google server create NAME -m MACHINE_TYPE -I IMAGE (options)
knife google server delete INSTANCE_NAME [INSTANCE_NAME] (options)
knife google server list
knife google server show INSTANCE_NAME (options)
knife google zone list
```

Okay, the first thing I noticed was that the help text listed the "zone list" command twice. Well, that is surely a typo in the help command output. That first zone list should probably say "region list" instead. So, let's try that command to see if there is a "region list" command:

```
knife google region list
```

Yes. It works. You should get back a list of the regions and their status and subzones. It should look something like this:

Region	Status	Zones
asia-east1	up	asia-east1-a, asia-east1-b, asia-east1-c
europe-west1	up	europe-west1-b, europe-west1-c, europe-west1-d
us-central1	up	us-central1-a, us-central1-b, us-central1-c, us-central1-f
us-east1	up	us-east1-b, us-east1-c, us-east1-d

Okay, now let's decide on an image we want to deploy. The GCE images list can be found in the UI. Log in to the Google Cloud Platform and select the Compute Engine console. From there select the "Image" views from the menu options on the left. Then, look through the available images to the right. For the examples in the rest of this section, I will select the image: `centos-7-v20160301`. So, let's build our server create command. On our Chef workstation, enter the following command:

```
knife google server create earl-gce101 \
  --gce-machine-type g1-small \
  --gce-image centos-7-v20160301 \
  --identity-file ~/.ssh/gce_rsa \
  --gce-can-ip-forward \
  --ssh-user earlwaud \
  -V
```

This command will create a new VM instance in GCE, and it will install the chef-client, registering the node with the Chef server. It will also converge the node to the desired state, but in this case, we didn't provide a run-list, so there were zero changes converged. Let's review this command in detail now. Starting with the command itself:

- `knife google server create earl-gce101`: Okay, this is the Knife command for creating our instances. We have the subcommand itself, "server create", and the first parameter, which is the name of our VM instance to be created. In this example, the VM instance name is "earl-gce101".

- `--gce-machine-type g1-small`: The value of this parameter provides the size of the instance to provision. In our example, we are creating a "g1-small" instance. This is one of the two partial vCPU flavors, with the other small one being "f1-micro". We will use a larger, nonpartial vCPU flavor in our next example, and you can read about all of the Machine Types available by visiting the relevant link provided later in the references section.

- `--gce-image centos-7-v20160301`: This parameter's value provides the name of the template image that we want to use to provision our VM instance. As mentioned already, you can discover all of the available images via the Google Compute Engine UI.

- `--identity-file ~/.ssh/gce_rsa`: The value for the identity-file parameter provides the path and filename of the private key of our key pair. The public key was uploaded to the SSH Keys section of the Google Compute Engine UI earlier.

- `--gce-can-ip-forward`: This parameter is a toggle that enables the forwarding of traffic from the public IP address to the private address. It is essentially the gate that either isolates or exposes the VM instance. The VM instance is isolated by default, and you can call that out explicitly with this parameter's opposite `--no-gce-can-ip-forward`.

- `--ssh-user earlwaud`: This parameter and value tell knife the username to use in ssh connections. This should match the username associated with the key generated and called out in our `--identity-file` parameter.

- `-V`: Once more, this is the verbose option, which can be made even more so with a second V as in `-VV`.

Okay, let's repeat our Chef server deployment, this time into GCE, to see what's different and what's same as our previous Chef server deployments.

Deploying Chef server into a GCE instance

Before we can deploy Chef server onto a GCE VM instance, we need to set up some firewall rules to allow the proper network access. To accomplish this, we are going to visit the Google Cloud Platform console. Once you've logged in, bring up the "Products & Services" menu, and choose "Networking". Then, using the navigation pane on the left, select **Firewall rules**. Now, to the right, you will see the list of firewall rules. Here is a look at what the default firewall rules look like:

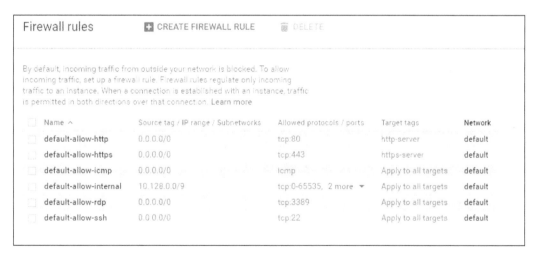

One of the key bits of information shown in the previous screenshot is the **Target tags** column. The data in that column shows the tag name we will use to enable the associated firewall rule with the instances we provision. For example, to enable SSL, we will use the tag name "https-server" in our knife server creates commands.

For Chef server, we need to open up TCP port 9683. To do this, we want to use the "Create Firewall Rule" button at the top of the window. Let's add the rule for port 9683 now. When you click on the "Create Firewall Rule" button, you are shown an input form. In that form, provide a name for the rule. I am using "chef-server". The name must be all lower case characters with no spaces. Next, we can provide an optional description. I am using "TCP port 9683 required for a Chef server". If you have created additional networks beyond the "default" provided, you can select the network to which you want to add this rule. I am using the default network, so no change is necessary for me. The next value, "Source filter" allows you to specify the systems whose traffic will be allowed though this port.

> Best practices would be to set up specific subnets to allow. If the rule will be for all possible servers, you can supply a value of "Allow from any source (0.0.0.0/0)". This is the option I am setting, knowing that this server is only a temporary test system.

The next input will provide the protocol and port that we are opening with this rule. In our example, we are entering "tcp:9683". If we were to enter just "tcp", it would open all ports, which is really not the desired state for a production system. Finally, we provide a tag name for this rule. While the form suggests that this value is optional, it is actually a requirement for us, since it is how we tell the `knife server create` command to use this rule. In the example for the Chef server rule, I am using the tag name "chef-server".

Okay, we're ready to provision our new GCE Chef server instance. With this example command, we are going to deploy the new instance, register the new node with our public Chef server, and converge the state to a Chef server with the initial chef-client run. Here's the command:

```
knife google server create earl-gce-chef \
  --node-name earl-gce-chef \
  --gce-machine-type n1-standard-1 \
  --gce-image ubuntu-1404-trusty-v20160314 \
  --bootstrap-protocol ssh \
  --ssh-user earlwaud \
  --identity-file ~/.ssh/gce_rsa \
  --user earlwaud \
  --gce-can-ip-forward \
  --gce-tags http-server,https-server,chef-server \
  --run-list="recipe['chef-server']" \
  -V
```

Let's take a closer look at the command parameters, focusing on the few parameters that are new or different from what we used in the previous command;

- `knife google server create earl-gce-chef`: This is the same command we used before; the only difference this time is the name is now "earl-gce-chef".

- `--node-name earl-gce-chef`: Again, this is the same parameter, but this time, we are using a node name of "earl-gce-chef".

- `--gce-machine-type n1-standard-1`: We need to create a VM that is a little more beefy that that provided with a "g1-small" flavor, so this time, we are using an "n1-standard-1". This will create our VM with 1 vCPU and 3.75 GB of memory (and 10 GB system drive).

- `--gce-image ubuntu-1404-trusty-v20160314`: This time, we requested an Ubuntu 14.04 server image for our Chef server provision.

- `--user earlwaud`: This parameter provides the API Client Username.

- `--gce-tags http-server,https-server,chef-server`: This parameter and its values list the firewall rules we want to put into place for the provisioned VM. The values are the tags we saw (and created) in the Google Cloud Platform Networking UI. This example is applying the http rule, the https rule, and our new chef-server rule. The resulting VM will have the TCP ports 80, 443, and 9683 open from all IP addresses.

- `--run-list="recipe['chef-server']"`: This parameter provides the now familiar run-list for our first chef-client run.

Once again, let's ssh into our new server, and issue the few commands needed to complete the Chef Server setup:

```
sudo chef-server-ctl user-create earlwaud Earl Waud earl@sandiegoearl.com
MyPassword99 --filename ~/earlwaud-gce.pem
```

```
sudo chef-server-ctl org-create sdearl "San Diego Earl" --association_
user earlwaud --filename ~/sdearl-validator-gce.pem
```

```
sudo chef-server-ctl install chef-manage
```

```
sudo chef-server-ctl reconfigure
```

```
sudo opscode-manage-ctl reconfigure
```

We now have a new Chef server ready to use, provisioned into our Google Cloud Platform. Well done! Now, let's delete it. As with the plugins we used before, we can issue a server delete command to delete the instances and unregister it from our Chef server. Here is an example command:

```
knife google server delete earl-gce-chef --purge
```

That wraps up our look into provisioning in the Google Cloud Platform. You should now have enough detail to be able to provision successfully using the GCE for whatever needs you may have. So, now we've reviewed using Knife for provisioning in the top three Cloud hosting providers. Before we switch gears a little, let's take a quick look at an honorable mention Cloud hosting provider—Linode.com.

References

- Create your account and start a free 60-day trial at `https://cloud.google.com/`.
- Chef and GCE information on Chef.io: `https://www.chef.io/solutions/google-cloud-platform/`.
- Learn about the knife-google plugin on Github at `https://github.com/chef/knife-google`.
- Learn about the GCE cookbook LWRP on Github at `https://github.com/chef/knife-google`.
- Learn about the Google Cloud Storage (GCS) cookbook LWRP on Github at `https://github.com/chef-partners/google-cloud-storage`.
- Watch some demo screencasts to learn more about Google DevOps with Chef at `http://googlecloudplatform.github.io/compute-video-demo-chef/`.
- Instructions to install the Google Cloud SDK `https://cloud.google.com/sdk/`.
- The list of Google Compute Engine Machine Types (instance sizes) is at `https://cloud.google.com/compute/docs/machine-types?hl=en_US&_ga=1.97972955.533487120.1458267295`.

Looking at an honorable mention – Linode

Here is a quick look at the Chef integration to provision to the hosting provider Linode.com. While Linode has nowhere near the market share of any of the top hosting providers we've covered so far, there is a strong user base of passionate developers (like my colleague Barry Ruffner who introduced me to Linode) and many happy companies who use the hosting service to fill their Linux-based hosts needs with distros from CentOS, Debian, Fedora, openSUSE, Ubuntu, and Slackware, to name a few. And just like with the other hosting providers we discussed, you have the ability to create and manage your servers hosted there with a knife plugin, knife-linode. You can install the plugin with the now familiar Chef command:

```
chef gem install knife-linode
```

As with our other plugins, you will want to add a linode configuration parameter to your `knife.rb` file so you don't have to provide the parameter with each command. It will contain your API key, which can be generated from the API section of your linode.com profile settings page. Here is what the `knife.rb` configuration parameter will look like:

```
#knife-linode
knife[:linode_api_key] =
'O7wCP4TVURELEDtG6uF0mp6Gxf1BVZtEc2jm6uw1V63Yc3UodwztxCuk4EU8uPvQ'
```

With that in place, you're ready to provision and manage your Linode hosts. I'm not going into any real detail on the Linode commands here because I think that with the data provided in the previous sections of this chapter, you can handle those details easily. What I will do is share a list of the subcommands available and then let you take it from there. So, without further ado, here are the knife-linode plugin subcommands:

- The knife linode server list
- The knife linode image list
- The knife linode server create
- The knife linode server delete
- The knife linode server reboot
- The knife linode data center list
- The knife linode flavor list
- The knife linode kernel list
- The knife linode stackscript list

In the references section later, you can find the links you'll need to set up your own Linode account and to learn more about the linode plugin. Note that at this time, Linode does not offer a free trial, but they do have a 7-day money-back guarantee.

References

- The Linode website: `https://www.linode.com/`
- The knife-linode plugin repo on Github: `https://github.com/chef/knife-linode`

Provisioning containers in Docker

Now you are going to learn about something a little different, Docker. Docker is a container provider, and although it is not the only container game in town, it is by far the most widely used. You will be able to leverage what you learn in this section to other container platforms as desired. Of course, you don't have to use Docker in the cloud. It is equally viable in the traditional data center, but since it is a fresh re-imagining of virtual environments, I thought it would better fit in a chapter in the clouds.

Containers offer much benefit as an alternative to "traditional" virtual machines. For example, containers are lightweight and can be deployed much more densely than traditional VMs. Containers contain fewer overhead processes, and so they can start up much faster than VMs. There are many advantages that might compel you to want to create your own containers, so let's give provisioning a try with Chef. Of course, you can use a commercial provider like dotCloud, Tutum, or Google's Container Engine. But we are going to set up or own Docker host to serve our containers.

Setting up a Docker server to host our containers

We want a Docker server to provision our containers, and since this is a book about Chef Provisioning, we're going to leverage Chef to set up our Docker server. We will download the Docker cookbook from the Chef Marketplace and then upload the cookbook to our Chef server. Once it has been uploaded, we will deploy a new server using knife and converge the server into a Docker server with the cookbook and chef-client. Let's get started. Here is the command to download the Docker cookbook:

```
knife cookbook site install docker
```

This command will download the Docker cookbook and all of its dependencies from the Chef Marketplace and then install them into the cookbooks folder of our current repo.

The docker cookbook has a dependency on the compat_resource cookbook, specifically version 12.7.1, so let's make sure that we have the desired version installed in our repo with the following command:

```
knife cookbook site install compat_resource 12.7.1
```

Now, let's upload the docker cookbook and its dependencies with the following command:

```
knife cookbook upload docker --include-dependencies
```

We need to do one more thing to finish our cookbook setup. The docker cookbook is a library-only cookbook. It does not have recipes and is intended to be used by other cookbooks. So we are going to create the most basic cookbook, named my-docker. It is going to have a default recipe that will install the docker server for us. Let's create the new cookbook structure with Chef, using this command:

```
cd ~/chef-repo
chef generate cookbook cookbooks/my-docker
```

Now, let's update the metadata for our new cookbook by editing the metadata.rb file:

```
cd ~/chef-repo
vi cookbooks/my-docker/metadata.rb
```

Update the contents of the metadata.rb file, filling in the maintainer and maintainer e-mail values, and then, most importantly, add a "depends" line for docker. The resulting file should look something like this:

```
name 'my-docker'
maintainer 'Earl Waud'
maintainer_email 'earl.waud@gmail.com'
license 'all_rights'
description 'Installs/Configures my-docker'
long_description 'Installs/Configures my-docker'
version '0.1.0'

depends 'docker', '~> 2.0'
```

Now, let's create a my-docker recipe by creating a default.rb file in the recipes folder of our new cookbook:

```
cd ~/chef-repo
vi cookbooks/my-docker/recipes/default.rb
```

Insert the following recipe code:

```
docker_service 'default' do
  action [:create, :start]
end
```

Save the file, and we can upload the cookbook to our Chef server with the following command:

```
cd ~/chef-repo
Knife cookbook upload my-docker
```

Great! We are now ready to deploy our new server and converge it into a Docker host. We have several options for where we want to deploy this new server. We can go with something in our own data center, or we can deploy it in the cloud using any of the hosting providers we've looked at in this chapter. Somewhat arbitrarily, I am going to choose the Microsoft Azure service to host our Docker server. With that decision, here is the command:

```
knife azure server create \
  --azure-dns-name earl-docker \
  --azure-vm-name earl-docker \
  --azure-vm-size Medium \
  --azure-source-image b39f27a8b8c64d52b05eac6a62ebad85__Ubuntu-14_04_1-
LTS-amd64-server-20150123-en-us-30GB \
  --azure-service-location 'Central US' \
  --ssh-user earlwaud \
  --identity-file ~/.ssh/azure_rsa \
  --bootstrap-protocol ssh \
  --node-name earl-docker \
  --run-list 'recipe['my-docker']' \
  --tcp-endpoints 80,443,3306 \
  -V
```

This command does as we desire. It provisions a new server into Azure classic, registers the node with our public Chef server, and then running the chef-client, it converges the host into the state of a Docker server. Most of this command should be very familiar, as it is nearly identical to the command we used to provision a Chef server into Azure earlier in this chapter. The only two significant differences are the run list used and the port 3306 specified in the tcp-endpoints parameter. The 3306 port is used by the Docker engine.

While this method of deploying Docker onto a server might be the long way around, it is still important because it follows our DevOps methodology and it is OS agnostic. In other words, I could have just deployed my Ubuntu server, logged in and done an appropriate `wget` command, and achieved the same state. But by using a Chef cookbook, we have achieved our infrastructure as code goal. Also, if we had used a CentOS host instead of Ubuntu, our cookbook would have still done the right thing to install the Docker engine. Likewise, if it were a Windows-based host, it would have properly installed the Docker engine.

Alright, we've got our Docker server set up and running the Docker engine. We can confirm this by using ssh to log in to the server and running a docker command. For example, we can use the following command:

```
sudo docker ps
```

This command will list the containers running on the Docker host. We are now to use Docker from our Azure instance.

Installing and using Docker on our Chef Workstation

Since we've been primarily using OS X for our Chef workstation examples, we are going to use the Docker toolbox as the local host for our Docker containers example. This is the same tool you would use for a Windows Chef Workstation.

If you are using Ubuntu or another Linux flavor, you can install docker.io and execute the remainder of the examples with a direct Docker install. Frankly, this is a much easier and better solution to create local Docker containers than the OS X option. If you can do your container work in an Ubuntu workstation, I would highly recommend it.

So, if you are still using an OS X workstation, the next step is to install the toolbox. You can download and install the toolbox for free from `www.docker.com/products/docker-toolbox`.

Once the toolbox is installed, run the "docker quickstart terminal" to open up a Terminal session with the docker environment preconfigured. This actually spins up a virtual machine that is running Docker. Fun, right?!

Now we can use the knife-docker plugin (as well as any standard docker commands, such as `docker ps`) in our Terminal window.

Now can give some Docker commands a try. Here are some commands for you:

```
docker ps
docker images
docker run -t -i ubuntu:14.04 /bin/bash
```

Using the knife-docker plugin

We are going to switch gears a little bit now. The knife-docker plugin does not successfully execute the chef client run when run on OS X. There is an unreleased version 0.0.3 that is working to address this issue, but at the time of writing this, it was not working. So, we are going to execute this example using Ubuntu for our workstation.

Let's start by installing the knife-docker plugin for working with Docker. Issue the following command:

```
chef gem install knife-docker
```

For our docker container examples, we will work with publicly downloadable docker images. Let's start by listing the docker images we have currently available on our workstation. Open up a terminal session. From within the terminal session, issue the following command:

```
sudo docker images
```

You should have an empty list of images at this point if you have just recently installed your local docker environment. Next, let's see a list of some of the publicly available images. We can do this by issuing a docker search command like this:

```
sudo docker search ubuntu
```

From that command, you should get a list of public docker images related to the search key "ubuntu". In my list, there is an image named `rastasheep/ubuntu-sshd`. I want to use that for our test of the knife-docker plugin, so I am going to download that image with the following command:

```
sudo docker pull rastasheep/ubuntu-sshd
```

Many docker images do not pre-install sshd, so we want to make sure we are working with one that does. The `rastasheep/ubuntu-sshd`, as the name suggests, is an image that runs sshd. Okay, let's issue the image command again to see if the downloaded image shows up in our list as expected:

```
sudo docker images
```

Yep, there it is. Excellent. Now we are going to use that image to deploy a docker container using the knife-docker plugin. Here is the basic command:

```
sudo knife docker create -I rastasheep/ubuntu-sshd --node-name docker01
```

This command will deploy the new container using the image rastasheep/ubuntu-sshd as the template. The container uses the credentials of username, `root`, and password, `root`, so when you are prompted for the password, enter `root`.

The command deploys the container and registers it with the Chef server as configured in our `.chef/knife.rb` file using the value in the `--node-name` parameter, in this case, `docker01`.

The other knife-docker command allows us to use the knife-docker plugin to delete our containers and clean up their artifacts from the Chef server. Here is an example command:

```
sudo knife docker delete f5e483540f3d -P
```

The two parameters used here are the container ID and the `-P` switch, which instructs knife to delete the node and client as well as the container.

> I would like to point out that using the knife-docker plugin as a container provisioning method while functional is not really the way to go. We will examine the much more favored method of deploying containers using Chef in *Chapter 8, Using Chef Provisioning*, so stay tuned.

References

- The link to the Docker home page is `https://www.docker.com/`.
- You can find the Docker repo at `https://github.com/docker/docker`.
- You can find the Chef cookbook for Docker at `https://github.com/chef-cookbooks/docker`.

- Sign up for a commercial Docker hosting service at one of these providers, Tutum (at `https://www.tutum.co/`), dotCloud (at `https://cloud.docker.com/`), or use the Container Engine system with the Google Cloud Provider (at `https://cloud.google.com/container-engine/`).

- The link to Chef.io information on using Chef for containers is `https://docs.chef.io/containers.html`.

- Find the knife-docker plugin on Github at `https://github.com/ema/knife-docker`.

- Download and install the Docker Toolbox from `https://www.docker.com/products/docker-toolbox`.

- There is an interesting Ubuntu base image for your containers at `https://github.com/phusion/baseimage-docker`.

- There is another interesting base image container at `https://github.com/phusion/passenger-docker`.

- Read through a tutorial on using Docker at `http://www.dedoimedo.com/computers/docker-networking.html` and `http://www.dedoimedo.com/computers/docker-guide.html`.

Summary

In this chapter, you learned how to turn our cloud-based servers (and containers) into code, so they can benefit from all the methodologies we are used to using for our application projects. We solidified our knowledge of using Amazon AWS EC2 instances. You learned how to leverage the next big players in the cloud provider arena, Microsoft and Google. We took a brief look at provisioning hosts on Linode. com, and you learned how to use Chef to provision our containers in Docker. Adding all this new cloud knowledge to what you learned about doing the same things in our traditional data center, we are now armed with the skills to easily create a hybrid hosting solution that lets us target our deployments in-house or in the cloud and lets us burst from one to the other depending on the needs of our business. With so many options available to provision our workloads, let's take a quick look at making sure that those workloads are as error free as possible by examining test-driven development in the next chapter. Turn the page, and I'll see you there!

7
Test-Driven Development

In this chapter, we're going to delve into the Test-driven Development model, showing how to maximize development efforts and quickly deliver highly functional and well-tested environments. The reader will learn how to transform their model for Chef from one where cookbooks are code to one, where cookbooks are artifacts, with test practices built into both models. Initially, it may seem difficult and time consuming to build the skills and habits of test-driven development. However, once the skills and habits are acquired, the development cycle becomes accelerated and the resulting infrastructure is much more stable. What's more, DevOps Engineers will have greater certainty that the infrastructure will be fully functional. It will no longer be necessary to do ad hoc tests and spot checks on infrastructure deployed into production environments. The infrastructure code will be continually tested through the development process, and the artifact deployments will be equally well-vetted before anything is ever pushed into production. The result is better deliverables and shorter development cycles.

> *"This is my advice to people: Learn how to cook, try new recipes, learn from your mistakes, be fearless, and above all have fun"* – *Julia Child*

The following topics will be covered:

- Analyzing cookbooks with RuboCop
- Analyzing cookbooks with Foodcritic
- Unit testing with ChefSpec
- Integration testing with Kitchen and ServerSpec

Analyzing cookbooks with RuboCop

We begin with a look at tools working within the cookbooks-as-code model. These tools are considered static analysis test tools, and they examine the code itself to verify syntax, structure, and alignment with desired coding practices. The first tool we'll explore is named RuboCop.

Simply put, by using RuboCop, you will produce better cookbooks. RuboCop is included as part of the ChefDK installation. It is a command-line tool used to test the syntax and style of individual cookbooks. RuboCop uses a set of rules, known as cops, to test specific considerations, such as syntax, style, and metrics for Ruby best practices. These cops deliver results as warnings, deviations from convention, and different levels of errors. The main benefits of using RuboCop are that you identify errors early in the development process and the resulting code conforms to an agreed upon style and formatting practice. So, how do we use RuboCop?
Let's take a look now.

Using RuboCop

The expectation to use RuboCop is that you provide the path and name of a cookbook to test or you execute the tool within the folder of a specific cookbook to test that cookbook. For example, two different ways to execute RuboCop to test the apache cookbook that is part of your chef-repo are as follows:

```
cd ~/chef-repo/cookbooks/apache
rubocop .
```

We also have the following:

```
cd ~/chef-repo
rubocop cookbooks/apache
```

RuboCop is a Ruby test tool, and as such, it will examine all of the Ruby files in your cookbook. By default, there are many RuboCop cops patrolling the cookbooks for violations. They are grouped into categories based on the type of rule they enforce, including lint, style, metrics, Ruby, and so on. You can see all of the cops enforced by RuboCop with the following command:

```
rubocop --show-cops
```

This command will list out all of the cops, and it includes URLs to the RuboCop documentation for the rules enforced by that cop.

With this information, you can use RuboCop to evaluate the rules of a single cop by using the parameter `--only` and the name of the cop. For example, to see if you have any lines that are longer than the standard 80 characters, you can issue the following commands:

```
cd ~/chef-repo/cookbooks/apache
rubocop --only Metrics/LineLength
```

Examining the RuboCop output

By default, RuboCop displays the results in what is known as the progress format. The available output formats include [p]rogress (default), [s]imple, [c]lang, [j]son, [h]tml, [o]ffenses, and so on. These output formats can be called upon with the `--format` (or `-f`) parameter. For example, to see the results for a RuboCop test of the NTP cookbook in the [o]ffences and [h]tml formats, issue the following commands:

```
cd ~/chef-repo
rubocop -f o -f h cookbooks/ntp > /tmp/ntp.html
```

Now you can open the output in your browser, and the output is nicely formatted and easy to review. It will look something like this:

Each Ruby file is tested for offences, and the output provides the specifics of the violations found. The first thing reported is a summary of how many files were tested and how many total violations were found. From there, the results of each file examined are provided, starting with the filename and number of violations in that file. Then, the individual violations are listed with each providing the violation details, including the type of issue. The following abbreviations are used to indicate the type of issue found:

```
'.' means the file contains no issues
'C' means there is an issue with convention
'W' means there is a warning
'E' means there is an error
'F' means there is a fatal error
```

Additional information provided in the violation details includes the line number and position within the line where the issue was found, followed by the actual line of code from the Ruby file that contains the issue. Using this information, you should be able to easily remedy the issues reported on by RuboCop.

With the multitude of cops and the extensive violation data they watch for, it can become overwhelming to keep you code in obedience with the laws. Because of this, RuboCop provides a way to customize your cops and rules so that you can focus in on the ones that are most important to you and your team. Let's look at how we can configure RuboCop to use a subset of cops without having to call them out on the command line.

Customizing RuboCop

RuboCop customization is handled via a `.rubocop.yml` file in the cookbook's folder. The easiest way to create this file is to let RuboCop help you. For example, you can issue the following commands:

```
cd ~/chef-repo/cookbooks/apache

rubocop --auto-gen-config
```

This will create a new file named .rubocop_todo.yml in the cookbook folder. Now you have a place to start. This file contains the minimum set of cop configurations that, when used by RuboCop in subsequent runs, allow your cookbook to pass all cop evaluations. For example, if the longest line of code in your cookbook is 93 characters long, the cop for line length checks will be configured to all lines to be up to 93 characters long.

With the new todo file, you can proceed in one of the three ways. You can rename your `.rubocop_todo.yml` file to `.rubocop.yml`. You can also add a parameter to your command like this:

```
rubocop --config .rubocop_todo.yml
```

Or, you can create your own `.rubocop.yml` file and add the line `inherit_from:` `.rubocop_todo.yml` to it. With any of these shortcuts, all existing violations will be ignored in your future RuboCop runs.

With any of those options in place, you can edit the configuration file and re-enable the cops that you want to address one by one. For example, if you care about maximum line lengths in your cookbooks, you can re-enable that rule check by commenting out the `Metrics/LineLength` rule in the configuration file or by adjusting the rule's setting value to the desired line length max value, that is, 80. Once this is done, violations of that rule will again be reported by the LineLength cop the next time RuboCop is executed. This will provide the data that needs to fix any violations of that rule. Using this one by one rule check and fix technique, you implement corrections to the rules that matter most to you, without being overwhelmed by the volume of violations that RuboCop can find.

One final note about RuboCop is that it offers an "auto correct" option that will fix minor violations automagically for you. Add the parameter `-a` or `--auto-correct` to your command line to use this option. While this is a very handy feature, be aware that it is not perfect, and you should review its changes for sanity. Now, let's continue our testing with the tool, Foodcritic.

References

- You can find the RuboCop home page at `http://batsov.com/rubocop`.
- Learn more about RuboCop on the Chef.io site, `https://docs.chef.io/rubocop.html`.
- There is the RuboCop repo on GitHub at `https://github.com/bbatsov/rubocop`.
- You can find the list of RuboCop cops that are enabled by default at `https://github.com/bbatsov/rubocop/blob/master/config/enabled.yml`.
- The link for the cops that are disabled by default is `https://github.com/bbatsov/rubocop/blob/master/config/disabled.yml`.

- If you want to add RuboCop support directly to your editor, visit one or more of these GitHub repos—Sublime Text at `https://github.com/pderichs/sublime_rubocop`, Atom at `https://github.com/yujinakayama/atom-lint`, or VIM at `https://github.com/ngmy/vim-rubocop`.

Analyzing cookbooks with Foodcritic

Let's take a quick look at another static analysis test tool that is included with ChefDK. That tool is named Foodcritic. Like RuboCop, Foodcritic examines the code in your cookbooks for violations to its rules. However, where RuboCop is a generic Ruby linter, Foodcritic is a Chef-specific linting tool. The difference being that using RuboCop helps you to keep your cookbooks in line with Ruby best practices, and Foodcritic helps to keep your cookbooks in line with Chef best practices. Foodcritic currently has 61 built-in rules to evaluate your cookbooks and allows the creation and use of custom rules as well. Both tools have their value, and I suggest that there is a place for each one in your DevOps workflow.

Using Foodcritic

You will find using Foodcritic to be very much like using RuboCop. It is expected that you will be testing individual cookbooks and as such will execute Foodcritic at the command line in the folder of the cookbook being tested, or you can execute Foodcritic in your chef repo with a parameter for the path to the cookbook being tested. For example, if you want to test the apache cookbook that is a part of your chef-repo, you would execute the following command:

```
cd ~/chef-repo/cookbooks/apache
foodcritic .
```

One of the optional parameters you can include will provide context data when rule violations are found. The parameter is `-C` or `--context`. I've found that using this parameter makes correcting the issues much easier. Here is an example command, which uses the context parameter with Foodcritic to test a work-in-progress apache cookbook:

```
                                            1. exit (bash)
Earls-Mac:~ earlwaud$ cd ~/chef-repo
Earls-Mac:chef-repo earlwaud$ foodcritic --context cookbooks/apache
cookbooks/apache/metadata.rb
FC008: Generated cookbook metadata needs updating
   1|name              "apache"
   2|maintainer        "YOUR_COMPANY_NAME"
FC008: Generated cookbook metadata needs updating
   3|maintainer_email "YOUR_EMAIL"
   4|license           "All rights reserved"
   5|description       "various apache server related resource provides (LWRP)"
   6|long_description IO.read(File.join(File.dirname(__FILE__), 'README.md'))
cookbooks/apache/templates/default/fast-cgi-vhost.erb
FC034: Unused template variables
   1|<VirtualHost *:<%= @params[:ssl] == false ? 80 : 443 %>>
   2|
   3|    ServerName <%= @params[:server_name] %>
   4|    <%- @params[:server_alias].each do |a| %>
cookbooks/apache/providers/fastcgi.rb
FC043: Prefer new notification syntax
  41| case node.platform # sorry for this case, but gentoo still not supported i
  42|                 # http://tickets.opscode.com/browse/COOK-817
  43| when 'gentoo'
```

Let's take a closer look at the output provided by Foodcritic.

Examining the Foodcritic output

Foodcritic has a set of rules built in that checks for specific issues in your cookbooks.
Each rule has an identifier, such as FC008 or FC043. When a rule violation is found,
Foodcritic will output the rule ID with the rule description. If you use the optional
context parameter as shown earlier, the actual code that violates the rule will also be
included in the output displayed. The nature and detail of each rule can be found on
the Foodcritic website, http://www.foodcritic.io/. Clicking on the rule ID will
take you to a description of the issue found by the rule, and it provides guidance on
how to correct that issue.

Customizing Foodcritic

Foodcritic offers a "filter" to fine tune the rules that are checked, much like RuboCop. It is applied in one of two ways. Either via a parameter on the command line or as a parameter in a special .foodcritic configuration file. To use the parameter on the command line, use a -t followed by the rule ID. For example, to check the apache cookbook for violations of only rule ID FC008, you would use a command like this:

```
cd ~/chef-repo
foodcritic -t FC008 cookbooks/apache
```

You can also check for violations of every rule except the rule specified by preceding the rule ID with a tilde. Thus, to check the apache cookbook for violations of every rule except FC008, you would use a command like this:

```
cd ~/chef-repo
foodcritic -t ~FC008 cookbooks/apache
```

Remember that you can put these parameters into a configuration file in the cookbook folder, and they will be considered in every Foodcritic run for that cookbook without needing to add them to the command line. For example, if you want to exclude the rules FC008, FC034, and FC043 every time you run Foodcritic to test the apache cookbook, you can create the configuration file using this command:

```
cd ~/chef-repo/cookbooks/apache
echo "~FC008,~FC034,~FC043" > .foodcritic
foodcritic .
```

References

- The link to the Foodcritic home page is http://www.foodcritic.io.
- You can read more about Foodcritic on the Chef.io site, https://docs.chef.io/foodcritic.html.
- The Foodcritic repo on GitHub is https://github.com/acrmp/foodcritic.
- Additional custom Foodcritic rules can be found at https://github.com/etsy/foodcritic-rules.

Unit testing with ChefSpec

Now that we have cookbooks that are adhering to the best practices of both Ruby and Chef, it is time to turn our attention away from static analysis and toward runtime testing. This is where we begin to move from a model of cookbooks-as-code to one of cookbooks-as-artifacts. Unit testing is a kind of middle ground, where we are doing a combination of code testing and artifact testing. This is also the point at which we move into a test-driven development model, where you write the tests before you write the code.

Ruby is a dynamically typed language. Ruby code is not type checked until it is executed. So in order to actually test our cookbooks, they have to be run. Before ChefSpec, this meant that you had to make the code changes to your cookbooks on your workstation, upload your modified cookbooks to your Chef server, then finally converge a node that is assigned that cookbook in order to be able to actually test your changes. This was a work- and time-intensive process that, with a complex set of cookbooks, could easily take 20 minutes or more. Not cool.

That was all before ChefSpec. ChefSpec is a unit testing tool that simulates a chef-client run to actually execute your cookbook code locally, saving you the time and effort of uploading the cookbook to your Chef server and executing a chef-client run on some node to test your changes. Using ChefSpec, you can accomplish your tests in a fraction of the time that was required before. ChefSpec is built on RSpec, which is a Ruby-specific unit test tool. ChefSpec is to RSpec what Foodcritic is to RuboCop. That is, ChefSpec takes the same unit test concepts used for Ruby in RSpec and adapts them to be Chef-specific. Both RSpec and ChefSpec are installed as part of ChefDK.

ChefSpec allows you to define what you expect the resources of your cookbooks to do. Then, you can use ChefSpec to test the cookbooks to see if they accomplish your expectations.

Using ChefSpec

Getting started doing unit testing with ChefSpec is easy. When you begin by creating your cookbooks and recipes using the generate feature of Chef, you automatically get a ChefSpec test spec template file created for you. Let's say that you want to create a new web app cookbook. Using Chef, we can create the cookbook with the following command:

```
cd ~/chef-repo/cookbooks
chef generate cookbook mywebapp
cd mywebapp
berks init
```

Allow the `berks init` command to overwrite any of the configuration files with a response of "Y" at each prompt. Now take a look at what was created:

```
Earls-Mac:mywebapp earlwaud$ tree
.
├── Berksfile
├── Gemfile
├── Policyfile.rb
├── README.md
├── Thorfile
├── Vagrantfile
├── chefignore
├── metadata.rb
├── recipes
│   └── default.rb
├── spec
│   ├── spec_helper.rb
│   └── unit
│       └── recipes
│           └── default_spec.rb
└── test
    └── integration
        ├── default
        │   └── serverspec
        │       └── default_spec.rb
        └── helpers
            └── serverspec
                └── spec_helper.rb

10 directories, 13 files
Earls-Mac:mywebapp earlwaud$
```

We have two directories that have been created for us that relate to testing. The first is named spec, and the second is named test. We will take a closer look at the folder named test in the next section of this chapter. Looking closer at the folder named spec, we can see that we have a subfolder named unit. This implies that we will be using this for our unit tests. We have a folder named recipes with a single file named `default_spec.rb` later. This file, `default_spec.rb`, is where we will create the unit tests for our corresponding `default.rb` cookbook recipe file, which as you can see in the image is found in the normal location under the cookbook's recipes folder.

In order to better understand how to use ChefSpec, let's create a very simple default recipe for our mywebapp cookbook. We will add some resources to the default recipe that installs and starts httpd, and provides a super simple `index.html` file to serve up. Start by editing the recipe file:

```
cd ~/chef-repo/cookbooks/mywebapp
vi recipe/default.rb
```

Add the following resources:

```
package 'httpd'

file '/var/www/html/index.html' do
  content '<h1>Hello MyWebApp User</h1>'
end

service 'httpd' do
  action [:enable, :start]
end
```

Now save and exit the editor. We have three resources; the first installs the httpd package, then we create an `index.html` file with the Hello Users content, and we have the service that starts httpd and makes sure that it starts on boot. It is simple, but it does enough to explore our use of ChefSpec.

At this point, we can actually run a test. Remember that ChefSpec is built upon RSpec, so we will be using RSpec to execute our test. The ChefSpec test specs are in the `spec/unit/recipes` folder, and they will have a name that matches our recipe file. That is, for a recipe file named `default.rb`, the ChefSpec test file will be named `default_spec.rb`. So, let's give it a try with the following command:

cd ~/chef-repo/cookbooks/mywebapp

chef exec rspec spec/unit/recipes/default_spec.rb

This is going to execute the unit test defined in the `default_spec.rb` file to test the cookbook default recipe found in `recipes/default.rb`. If you've been following along, and you run the command given previously, you will get results that look like this:

cd ~/chef-repo/cookbooks/mywebapp

chef exec rspec spec/unit/recipes/default_spec.rb

.

Finished in 3.84 seconds (files took 2.41 seconds to load)

1 example, 0 failures

Well, we can see that the unit test took about 4 seconds to complete, and that it had zero failures, but what did it actually test? To find out, we want to examine the contents of our `default_spec.rb` file, the one found in `cookbooks/mywebapp/spec/unit/recipes` folder:

```
cd ~/chef-repo/cookbooks/mywebapp

cat spec/unit/recipes/default_spec.rb


require 'spec_helper'

describe 'mywebapp::default' do
  context 'When all attributes are default, on an unspecified platform'
do

    let(:chef_run) do
      runner = ChefSpec::ServerRunner.new
      runner.converge(described_recipe)
    end

    it 'converges successfully' do
      expect { chef_run }.to_not raise_error
    end
  end
end
```

Okay, that is probably a bit confusing at first glance, so let's break it down. We start off with a require statement. That is your standard require gem declaration; in this case, we require the spec_helper gem. Next, we have the describe line. This is identifying the name of the cookbook and recipe that we want to test. In this case, it is the default recipe of the mywebapp cookbook. Next, we have a context block. This block is what tells ChefSpec to set up a temporary node that will be converged to the state described in the recipe. The temporary node is named runner, and it is going to converge the recipe called out in the describe line earlier. There are two types of nodes or runners that can be used, a SoloRunner or a ServerRunner. ServerRunner is the default type of runner. The next block is defining our expectation. This is the unit test we hope to see pass. In this case, it is simply saying that when we do the Chef run, we don't want to see any errors.

Expanding our tests

So far, we have created a pretty basic unit test. It just runs and checks to see whether anything had an error. What if we want to be more specific? Let's begin to expand our unit tests. This time, we want to make sure that our recipe installs the package httpd. Editing our `default_spec.rb` file, we add another expectation. Here is the resulting file content:

cd ~/chef-repo/cookbooks/mywebapp

vi spec/unit/recipes/default_spec.rb

Insert the following in the file:

```
require 'spec_helper'

describe 'mywebapp::default' do
  context 'When all attributes are default, on an unspecified
platform' do
    let(:chef_run) do
      runner = ChefSpec::ServerRunner.new
      runner.converge(described_recipe)
    end

    it 'converges successfully' do
      expect { chef_run }.to_not raise_error
    end

    it 'installs the package httpd' do
      expect(chef_run).to install_package('httpd')
    end

  end
end
```

I've highlighted the new section for easy identification. Here, we are declaring our expectation that the recipe will install the package httpd. Now, before you start to panic, wondering how in the world are you supposed to know what needs to be added to a unit test file to set the expectations, realize that the very smart people who developed ChefSpec have already thought of that. They have provided a GitHub repo that has a very well-developed set of examples. The examples provided have both the cookbook recipe resources and the corresponding unit test expectation specs. You can find these examples at `https://github.com/sethvargo/chefspec/tree/master/examples`.

So, let's run our unit test again now that we have added our new expectation:

```
cd ~/chef-repo/cookbooks/mywebapp
chef exec rspec spec/unit/recipes/default_spec.rb

..


Finished in 0.77693 seconds (files took 2.31 seconds to load)
2 examples, 0 failures
```

Now, there are zero failures. So, both of the expectations passed successfully. You may have noticed that the output from our command started off with two dots this time. There was one dot last time. The dots represent the progress of our tests. Two expectations provide two dots. This format of output is appropriately named the progress format. There are other formats in which you can have our output delivered. For example, there is a format named document format. If you add a -fd parameter to your command, it will deliver the output in the document format. Go ahead and give that a try now, as follows:

```
cd ~/chef-repo/cookbooks/mywebapp

chef exec rspec -fd spec/unit/recipes/default_spec.rb


mywebapp::default
  When all attributes are default, on an unspecified platform
    converges successfully
    installs the package httpd


Finished in 0.65813 seconds (files took 2.3 seconds to load)
2 examples, 0 failures
```

With the document format, the output is changed from a sequence of dots to a human-readable description of what is being tested. You can take it a step further and add the parameter -c to the command, and the output will be color coded for easy interpretation.

Another thing that makes this process very easy is knowing that you don't have to know how to write every expectation at the time you add them to your spec file. You can add your expectations in a "pending" form first by just inserting some it '…' lines into your spec file. For example, I could have inserted the following pending expectations into my default_spec.rb file:

```
    it 'installs a package named httpd'
    it 'makes me a cup of Earl Grey tea'
```

When you run your ChefSpec test, you will get a result that shows you have some pending expectations to complete in your spec file:

```
Earls-Mac:mywebapp earlwaud$ chef exec rspec -c -fd spec/unit/recipes/default_spec.rb

mywebapp::default
  When all attributes are default, on an unspecified platform
    converges successfully
    installs a package named httpd (PENDING: Not yet implemented)
    makes me a cup of earl grey tea (PENDING: Not yet implemented)

Pending: (Failures listed here are expected and do not affect your suite's status)

  1) mywebapp::default When all attributes are default, on an unspecified platform installs a package nam
ed httpd
     # Not yet implemented
     # ./spec/unit/recipes/default_spec.rb:24

  2) mywebapp::default When all attributes are default, on an unspecified platform makes me a cup of earl
grey tea
     # Not yet implemented
     # ./spec/unit/recipes/default_spec.rb:25


Finished in 0.40847 seconds (files took 2.23 seconds to load)
3 examples, 0 failures, 2 pending

Earls-Mac:mywebapp earlwaud$ 
```

 Remember that the best practice for test-driven development is that you create your tests first and then you create your recipe code to pass the tests you defined. With this in mind, you can create your expectations in your spec files for each recipe before you write the recipe itself.

When you initially run your ChefSpec test, all of the tests will fail, and that is okay. Then, when you create your recipe and rerun the ChefSpec test, you will see the tests passing and know that you are delivering a recipe that is converging to the state defined in your expectations.

Remember to use `chef generate` to create any additional recipes you need in your cookbooks so that the corresponding test files get created for your automatically. For example, if you want to refactor your cookbook so that it is more modular, and if you want to move the package install code into its own recipe, you can use the chef generate command to help you out. Here is the command for reference:

```
cd ~/chef-repo/cookbooks/mywebapp
chef generate recipe install
```

This command will create your `install.rb` recipe file in the recipes folder, and it will create your unit test `install_spec.rb` file in the `spec/unit/recipes` folder. From there, you can insert your expectations and begin unit testing the new recipe in the same way you did for your default recipe.

This form of unit testing is very powerful and provides a very fast method of testing your cookbook recipes. You can accomplish in seconds what it would otherwise take many minutes to achieve with full integration testing. Still, there is a place for integration testing, so let's now take a look at another testing tool, Test Kitchen, which allows us to do full integration tests with ease.

References

- There is the ChefSpec documentation on the Chef.io site at `https://docs.chef.io/chefspec.html`.

- You can find the ChefSpec repo on GitHub at `https://github.com/sethvargo/chefspec`.

- The expectation examples in the ChefSpec repo are at `https://github.com/sethvargo/chefspec/tree/master/examples`.

- There is an exceptional webinar on using ChefSpec at `https://www.chef.io/webinars/?commid=194483`.

Integration testing with Kitchen and ServerSpec

Now we are going to move to the cookbooks-as-artifacts model of testing. This is full integration testing, and we are going to look to the Test Kitchen framework as the tool for this type of test. Kitchen is another tool that is included as part of the installation of ChefDK, so there is no additional work to install it. Kitchen allows you to easily deploy a new system, install Chef, download the run-list cookbooks, and converge the node instance to fully test the functionality of our policies, roles, cookbooks, and so on.

To explore using Test Kitchen, let's imagine that we want to create a cookbook that will set up a web server to present our new application's website to users. The best way to approach this from a test-driven development aspect is to consider the desired results from the user's point of view. The user does not care that we have a web server installed and running; they only care about getting an appropriate response from our app when they visit its website. With this in mind, we will craft our tests to validate the results from our user's point of view. Does our instance deliver an appropriate response when the user visits the app's website? Realize that by testing this result in this way, we are in fact also testing the results of everything it takes to get there, that is, standing up a new instance, installing and running the web server application, setting up the web page content, and so on. This is all confirmed by a single, simple test, to make sure that the user gets the response they desire. This result-focused testing is known as behavior-driven development, or BDD. We will talk more about our BDD test shortly.

Preparing our tests

As I mentioned already, Kitchen is installed as part of ChefDK, so it should already be installed on your Chef workstation. Kitchen leverages other tools that we have talked about in earlier chapters. For example, as a default configuration, it will use the tool Vagrant to create our test nodes. Vagrant can be configured to use any number of hosting platforms as the place it launches our test nodes, but the "out-of-the-box" configuration for Kitchen is to use the open source tool VirtualBox as a local hosting platform. If you have not done so already, I would strongly suggest that you download and install both of these tools now. Once you have the tools installed, the rest of this section will be easy and make more sense as you run through the examples.

Let's take a look at a default Kitchen configuration file. To make sure that we have a "default" file, we will actually generate a new cookbook using the chef generate command (note that you may have already done this if you have been following along in this chapter):

```
cd ~/chef-repo/cookbooks
chef generate cookbook mywebapp
cd mywebapp
berks init
```

This will create a template cookbook named mywebapp in your `chef-repo/`
`cookbooks` folder. As we saw in the previous section, the files created by the chef
generate command include test input files we can build on. From these test files, we
want to begin by examining the Kitchen configuration file. It is found in the root of
the cookbook and has the name `.kitchen.yml`. Here is what that file looks like after
you've run the preceding commands (note that the `berks init` command overwrites
the `.kitchen.yml` file created by the `chef generate` command):

```
cd ~/chef-repo/cookbooks/mywebapp
cat .kitchen.yml
---
driver:
  name: vagrant
provisioner:
  name: chef_solo
platforms:
  - name: ubuntu-14.04
  - name: centos-7.1
suites:
  - name: default
    run_list:
      - recipe[mywebapp::default]
    attributes:
```

As you can see in the file contents shown earlier, we have four sections of
configuration info: driver, provisioner, platforms, and suites. Beginning with the
driver section, the default driver name is Vagrant. What this setting means is that
Kitchen will use Vagrant as the mechanism to create and manage our test instances.
Several other options for drivers are available to be installed and used, such as
Docker, EC2, Google, and OpenStack, to name a few. The Kitchen-Vagrant driver
is an excellent option for our use, as it is installed as part of ChefDK, and it is quick
and easy to integrate with an installation of VirtualBox. This option keeps all of the
provisioning local to your workstation, which allows for quick integration testing.

The next section in the configuration file calls out the type of provisioner that will
be used. There are a few choices for provisioner, with chef_solo and chef_zero as
the most common. The provisioner determines how chef-client is run, and for the
tests in this set of examples, leaving the value of chef_solo will be fine. The chef_zero
provisioner is another common option as it is more like a full Chef server, but a
Chef server in a local mode. There is another provisioner that may quickly become
common, the policyfile_zero provisioner. This is provisioner that should be used
when your run list is a policyfile.

Next, we have the platforms section. The platforms section defines the operating systems that we want to provision as test nodes. By the way, another benefit of using the Vagrant driver is that we can use abbreviated names for the platforms. For example, you can see in the configuration file contents earlier that we have the names ubuntu-14.04 and centos-7.1. This is identifying our platforms to specific versions of those OSes, without needing to fully identify the actual templates or other parameters that would be required if we were using a different driver.

Finally, we have the suites section. This defines the what-to-test configuration. In the suites section, you provide a name for each suite you wish to test and define what you want to be tested. In this case, we have just one suite named "default", and it is going to test the default recipe in the mywebapp cookbook. There is a virtually unlimited number of things that you can include in your suites configuration section, and it is way beyond the scope of this chapter to provide you with a significant sampling, so I urge you to visit the links provided in the references section later, specifically for the .kitchen.yml configuration settings and the getting started guide. For our tests, just leave this set to the default value, which is to test the mywebapp cookbook's default recipe.

There is one more comment about the platforms and suites sections of the .kitchen. yml file. The values provided in these two sections create a matrix of test scenarios. That is, if you have one platform value and one suite, those combine to create one test ($1 \times 1 = 1$). If you have two platforms and one suite, you will have two test scenarios—one suite tested in each of the two platforms ($2 \times 1 = 2$). If you have two platforms and two suites, you will have four test scenarios, with each suite tested in each platform ($2 \times 2 = 4$). Add the third platform, and you now have six test scenarios ($2 \times 3 = 6$), and so on. Make sense? To simplify the Kitchen examples that follow, I am going to comment out the Ubuntu platform line in our .kitchen.yml file so that we are focused on a single centos platform with a single suite to test. This will result in one test scenario.

If you did not create the contents for the default recipe described in the previous section of this chapter, you should add that to the default recipe file now:

```
cd ~/chef-repo/cookbooks/mywebapp
vi recipes/default.rb
```

Add the following to the file:

```
package 'httpd'

file '/var/www/html/index.html' do
  content '<h1>Hello MyWebApp User</h1>'
end
```

```
service 'httpd' do
  action [:enable, :start]
end
```

Great! That was a lot of preparation— mostly just a lot of description of what was autogenerated for us—but we are now ready to try out Test Kitchen.

Kitchen create

The first command we will try is the create command. When you execute the command, Kitchen will read the contents of the `.kitchen.yml` file:

```
cd ~/chef-repo/cookbooks/mywebapp
```

```
kitchen create
```

Based on its contents, Kitchen will use the selected driver to stand up one or more new servers as defined by the platforms configuration section. Based on our .kitchen. yml file, Kitchen will use Vagrant to deploy a new server based on the CentOS 7.1 platform. Since the default for the Vagrant driver is to use VirtualBox as the hosting provider, the server will be deployed as VirtualBox VM.

If this is the first time you have run the kitchen create command for a specified platform, the template image will be downloaded to your workstation before being deployed. Templates are cached so that when you run future kitchen create commands, they do not have to be downloaded again.

There is a fair amount of output generated from this command, but you can look for some specific bits of information. Based on the name value in the suites section (in our case "default") and the platforms listed in the platforms section (in our case "centos-7.1"), the kitchen create command will name our test server default-centos-71. In the create command output, you will see some lines that look like the following:

```
Vagrant instance <default-centos-71> created.
```

```
Finished creating <default-centos-71> (0m41.08s).
```

This is indicating that the new server instance has been deployed, and it is ready to run chef-client to prepare for the tests to follow. You should see a line like this for each of the test scenarios in the matrix defined by the `.kitchen.yml` file. Now let's use kitchen converge to run chef-client and converge our new server instance to the desired state.

At this point, if you so desire, you can log in to the instance with the command `kitchen login`. Type "exit" to log out of the instance.

Kitchen converge

To converge our server instance to the desired state, execute the following command:

```
cd ~/chef-repo/cookbooks/mywebapp
```

```
kitchen converge
```

This will instruct Kitchen to read the `.kitchen.yml` file, and then, based on the selected provisioner and the values defined in the suites section of the configuration file, Kitchen will install and run chef-client with specific settings in the deployed server instance.

By the way, you can actually skip calling the kitchen create command, and just call the kitchen converge command. This will automatically execute the kitchen create function first, if the server instances have not already been deployed with a kitchen create command.

Here is a portion of the type of output you should expect from running the kitchen converge command:

```
        Installing chef

        installing with rpm...

        warning: /tmp/install.sh.12447/chef-12.8.1-1.el7.x86_64.rpm:
Header V4 DSA/SHA1 Signature, key ID 83ef826a: NOKEY

        Preparing...                       ###########################
##### [100%]

        Updating / installing...
############################### [100%]

        Thank you for installing Chef!

        Transferring files to <default-centos-71>

        Starting Chef Client, version 12.8.1

        Creating a new client identity for default-centos-71 using the
validator key.

        resolving cookbooks for run list: ["mywebapp::default"]

        Synchronizing Cookbooks:

          - mywebapp (0.1.0)

        Installing Cookbook Gems:

        Compiling Cookbooks...

        Converging 3 resources
```

You can see in this output snippet that the kitchen converge command installs chef, synchronizes the cookbooks listed in the suite's run-list, and converges the cookbook resources. Now, let's finally do some actual testing.

Kitchen verify

Now we have a server instance running, and it's been converged to the desired state, that is, our kitchen converge completed without errors. However, this does not mean that we have actually tested anything. To test the state, we need to run kitchen verify. Kitchen verify will look at our test spec files and will validate our converged instance to verify that it passes our defined tests. So, run the verify command now:

```
cd ~/chef-repo/cookbooks/mywebapp

kitchen verify
```

This will actually test our converged instance to see if it delivers the results we desire. Kitchen will be using ServerSpec to do our tests. So, one of the first things you will see in the output from the verify command is about installing ServerSpec and its required gems. Then, you will see the ServerSpec command used to run the tests, which will be followed by the results of the tests. Here is part of what that output will look like:

```
-----> serverspec installed (version 2.31.0)
       /opt/chef/embedded/bin/ruby -I/tmp/verifier/suites/serverspec
-I/tmp/verifier/gems/gems/rspec-support-3.4.1/lib:/tmp/verifier/gems/
gems/rspec-core-3.4.4/lib /opt/chef/embedded/bin/rspec --pattern /tmp/
verifier/suites/serverspec/\*\*/\*_spec.rb --color --format documentation
--default-path /tmp/verifier/suites/serverspec


    mywebapp::default
      does something (PENDING: Replace this with meaningful tests)


    Pending: (Failures listed here are expected and do not affect your
suite's status)


      1) mywebapp::default does something
         # Replace this with meaningful tests
         # /tmp/verifier/suites/serverspec/default_spec.rb:6
```

```
Finished in 0.00052 seconds (files took 0.31508 seconds to load)
1 example, 0 failures, 1 pending


Finished verifying <default-centos-71> (0m13.90s).
-----> Kitchen is finished. (0m14.59s)
```

You can see that one test (example) was performed and that the tests took just under 15 seconds to complete. But we didn't actually perform the BDD test we discussed earlier, which was to verify that the user gets an appropriate response when they visit our new app's website. This is because we didn't write that test yet. So, let's do that now. Edit our test file:

cd ~/chef-repo/cookbooks/mywebapp

vi test/integration/default/serverspec/default_spec.rb

The file contents will look like this:

```
require 'spec_helper'

describe 'mywebapp::default' do
  # Serverspec examples can be found at
  # http://serverspec.org/resource_types.html
  it 'does something' do
    skip 'Replace this with meaningful tests'
  end
end
```

We are going to replace the inner block test it 'does something' with a new test that verifies that the user gets an appropriate response when they visit our app's website. In this oversimplified example, the appropriate response is going to be Hello MyWebApp User. To create this test, replace the inner block of test code, so the resulting file looks like this:

```
require 'spec_helper'

describe 'mywebapp::default' do
  describe command('curl http://localhost') do
    its(:stdout) { should match(/Hello MyWebApp User/) }
  end
end
```

Now save the file and run the verify command again:

cd ~/chef-repo/cookbooks/mywebapp

kitchen verify

This time, you should see that we executed our test successfully, and in fact, the results prove that the user is getting an appropriate response when they visit our new app's website:

```
-----> Running serverspec test suite
       /opt/chef/embedded/bin/ruby -I/tmp/verifier/suites/serverspec
-I/tmp/verifier/gems/gems/rspec-support-3.4.1/lib:/tmp/verifier/gems/
gems/rspec-core-3.4.4/lib /opt/chef/embedded/bin/rspec --pattern /tmp/
verifier/suites/serverspec/\*\*/\*_spec.rb --color --format documentation
--default-path /tmp/verifier/suites/serverspec


    mywebapp::default
      Command "curl http://localhost"
        stdout
          should match /Hello MyWebApp User/


    Finished in 0.20631 seconds (files took 0.31911 seconds to load)
    1 example, 0 failures


    Finished verifying <default-centos-71> (0m3.20s).
-----> Kitchen is finished. (0m3.95s)
```

If you have not previously run kitchen create or kitchen converge and you run the kitchen verify command, kitchen will execute both the create and converge steps automatically before running the verify step.

However, it is important to note that running the verify command does not automatically rerun the converge command if it has already run. If anything related to the cookbook is changed between calls to kitchen verify, it is necessary to run kitchen converge in between. Often, you'll just want to issue the commands like this:

```
cd ~/chef-repo/cookbooks/mywebapp
kitchen converge && kitchen verify
```

With that command, you can be certain that your instance is converged to the currently defined state before you try to verify your test results. Running the converge and verify commands like this is a quick way to test changes to the cookbook and ServerSpec tests. Just be aware that if a cookbook resource has already been converged, it will result in a no-op for the kitchen converge command and will just report "resource up to date" in the output. This is a valid test case for verifying instance upgrade scenarios. However, if your goal is to verify the new instance deployment scenarios, you will want to add a kitchen destroy command in between your test runs. This will shut down and delete your deployed test instance.

The command for this is as you would expect:

```
cd ~/chef-repo/cookbooks/mywebapp
kitchen destroy
```

Now when you run your kitchen verify command, a new instance will be deployed, converged, and verified. Of course, the wise people who developed Test Kitchen realize that a common test pattern is to issue the create, converge, verify, and destroy commands in sequence to do a full new deployment integration test. So, they have provided us with a single command that will do all of this for us. It actually will start with a destroy command to make sure that any existing running instances are cleaned up before we start the new tests. To execute this, you issue the command as follows:

```
cd ~/chef-repo/cookbooks/mywebapp
kitchen test
```

If the verify tests are successful, a trailing kitchen destroy command will be executed to clean up your test instance. If the verify tests result in an error, the training destroy command will not be executed. This affords you the opportunity to investigate the test image to better debug the failure. Pretty sweet, right? You bet!

So, you now have the necessary skills to do full integration testing in your test-driven development cycle. Remember that what you have shown in this chapter is just the tip of the iceberg of what is available to you for your chef testing. Visit the links provided in the references and learn how to expand on what you have already learned. Your customers will be glad you did!

References

- The link to the Chef.io information about Test Kitchen is `https://docs.chef.io/kitchen.html`.

- You can find the Test Kitchen repo on GitHub at `https://github.com/test-kitchen/test-kitchen`.

- The link to the Test Kitchen home page is `http://kitchen.ci`.

- The link to the ServerSpec site is `http://serverspec.org`.

- The link to the home page for the Vagrant tool is `https://www.vagrantup.com`.

- The VirtualBox software can be found at the link `https://www.virtualbox.org/wiki/Downloads`.

- Learn about many options that can be used in the .kitchen.yml configuration file `https://docs.chef.io/config_yml_kitchen.html`.

- An excellent Test Kitchen getting started guide is found at `http://kitchen.ci/docs/getting-started`.

- Find information about the various ServerSpec resource tests available to you at `http://serverspec.org/resource_types.html`.

Summary

In this chapter, you learned how to use several of the tools available to implement a test-driven development cycle for infrastructure code development. We looked at tools that focus on cookbooks-as-code, validating that the code is syntactically correct, that it is structurally correct, and that it follows the coding standards we want all of our source code to employ. These tools include RuboCop and Foodcritic. Then, we looked at tools that fit into the cookbooks-as-artifacts model and test the functionality and deployment aspects of our cookbooks. These tools include ChefSpec and Test Kitchen. We learned that when tests are performed on our cookbooks in both models, the result is better infrastructure delivered faster than ever before. Remember that what you learned in this chapter is only the beginning. In fact, we barely scratched the surface. It is up to you, the reader, to persist in your education and the use of these test tools. Continue to the point where your normal workflow includes using these tools as a matter of habit. Like driving a car for the first time, there seems to be too much to do, too many controls, and so much at stake. But with time and practice, it all becomes natural. Everything is executed by habit, arriving at the destination safely and efficiently, almost without thinking about it at all. So it will be with your test-driven development journey. We are now very well equipped to handle our Chef Provisioning needs and deliver solid infrastructure across a wide variety of environments, but there is one more feature provided by Chef that we can use to accelerate our provisioning. Let's wrap all of this up in a nice bow, with a look at using Chef Provisioning.

8
Using Chef Provisioning

In this chapter, you're going to learn to use Chef provisioning.

Wait… what? This is the last chapter in the book titled Chef Provisioning, and now you are going to learn to use Chef provisioning? What were we doing in Chapters 1–7?

Yes, in Chapters 1–7, we were doing Chef provisioning, but ChefDK actually comes with a feature named Chef Provisioning. In the earlier chapters, you learned how to use Chef to provision into a variety of hosting solutions, both in the data center and the cloud. However, most of the work we did to provision our environments was done in single-instance bites, creating one server instance at a time. All perfectly acceptable and very valuable. However, in the world of a DevOps Engineer, it is a rare situation when a single instance is all that is needed for an application. These days, distributed applications are built in clusters. An app will require multiple web servers, databases, app servers, networking and load balancers, and so on. Wouldn't it be great if there was way to create a cookbook to describe our application's entire cluster as code? Well, there is, and it is called Chef provisioning.

> *"The devil came to me last night and asked what I wanted in exchange for my soul. I still can't believe I said pizza. Friggin' cravings." – Marc Ostroff*

The following topics will be covered:

- What is Chef provisioning?
- How to use Chef provisioning

What is Chef provisioning?

If you have been using Chef for a while, you may have heard about a feature named Chef Metal. Chef provisioning is the rebranded and evolved tool formerly known as Chef Metal. Chef provisioning is the Chef of all things. It serves the purpose of turning your application-run books into code. Now, all the benefits of infrastructure as code that you have come to enjoy in order to manage your server instances can also be enjoyed in managing your entire application cluster. Chef provisioning lets you describe your entire app the way you currently describe a single machine, using resources. Because of this, Chef provisioning allows you to test an entire distributed application at once.

It's highly idempotent

Chef Provision is highly idempotent, meaning that you can run the same Chef provisioning command repeatedly, and only the specific resources that have changed since the previous run will be affected.

For example, when you first run the Chef Provisioning command to create a new application cluster, all the machines described will be deployed, and they will be converged to their desired state. If you're testing changes to a recipe used in the run-list of a specific role and you run the Chef Provisioning command again, Chef Provisioning will not redeploy the machines already running. It will just load the modified recipe to the instances using the modified role and reconverge only those instances to the new desired state.

This is the same idempotency behavior you have learned to depend on when using Chef for your single-instance work.

Consider the benefit of being able to rerun your Chef Provisioning commands, where they only affect changes in an application's cluster if something has diverged from the fully described cluster recipe.

A hypothetical example

Imagine that you have a new distributed web application that you need to deploy. Here is an example of how you could use Chef Provisioning to do this for you.

1. You can create a cluster recipe that, when converged, deploys your app's fully realized cluster. The recipe includes all the required web servers, DBs, load balancers, and so on.

2. You create a recipe for an "app provisioner" instance that, when converged, runs the Chef Provisioning command with the cluster recipe created in step 1.

3. You deploy your app provisioner. The app provisioner converges, and as part of that convergence, it deploys your entire app cluster. All the web servers, the DBs, the load balancers, and so on, all get stood up and configured, and they are ready to be used by your customers. And by the way, when app provisioner converges, it is configured to re-run Chef Provisioning with the app cluster's recipe every 15 minutes. Because of the idempotency of Chef Provisioning, each run is a no-op until...

4. ...Time passes with your app running and serving your happy customers, but then some unforeseen event causes a web server to crash and burn. Yikes!

   No need to worry. It's okay. Because the next time your app provisioner runs the Chef Provisioning command, it will see that one of the web servers you defined is no longer "as defined". Chef provisioning will deploy a new web server based on your cluster recipe, converging it to the desired state, and voilà, you are back to 100% functionality.

5. (Bonus step) If you really wanted to go all inception-like on this idea, you could add the ability to deploy your app provisioner to the instances in your app cluster so that they would monitor, and if necessary redeploy the provisioner. They watch the watcher. Where's my spinning top?

References

- Learn more about Chef provisioning on the chef.io site, `https://docs.chef.io/provisioning.html`.

- Review the code for Chef provisioning in the GitHub repo at `https://github.com/chef/chef-provisioning`.

How to use Chef Provisioning

Now that you have a picture of what Chef provisioning is and how you might use it to turn an application's cluster infrastructure into code, let's take a look at how to actually use it. Like other aspects of Chef, we create recipes for Chef provisioning. And like the recipes in our other cookbooks, these recipes will contain resource definitions that will describe the desired state of our application cluster.

So, let's begin by learning about the resources that we can create in our Chef provisioning recipes.

Chef Provisioning resources

A Chef Provisioning recipe can contain the definitions of the following resources:

- **with_driver**: This resource tells Chef Provisioning the name of the driver to use with subsequent machine resources. The driver name corresponds to the hosting provider, such as Vagrant, AWS, and Docker. More than one with_driver resource can be used in a recipe, providing for the ability to deploy subsets of machines to different hosting providers within the same application cluster. For example, with one recipe, you can deploy instances to both vSphere and AWS.

- **machine_image**: This resource allows you to define a template to be used when describing your machine resources.

- **machine**: This is the primary resource for your Chef Provisioning recipes. This is what you use to describe your instances.

- **machine_options**: This resource is used as a helper resource to define your machine resources.

- **machine_batch**: The machine_batch resource provides a way of describing multiple machine resources that can be deployed concurrently. When Chef Provisioning is executing recipes, it does so sequentially, in the order described. However, using the machine_batch resource tells Chef Provisioning that the resources described within can be executed concurrently.

Each of the drivers associated with specific hosting providers may support additional resource types. For example, when you are using the AWS driver, some additional resources that are available include `aws_key_pair`, `aws_launch_configuration`, and `aws_vpc`. With the Vagrant driver, you have additional resources such as `vagrant_box`. Please visit the repo associated with the driver you are using to get the full list of driver-specific resources available. Links to the most common drivers are provided in the References section later.

A Vagrant example

Let's put this information to use. Since the Vagrant driver is included in ChefDK, and we don't have to do any additional installation work to use Chef Provisioning with Vagrant and VirtualBox, we'll start there.

Here is the requirement: Deploy the new "cool-app" cluster, which needs three instances—one DB and two web servers.

Here is the solution: we will create a cluster recipe to deploy three instances — one database server and two web servers.

Let's create a new app in our chef-repo:

```
cd ~/chef-repo
chef generate app cool-app
```

Now, let's create our recipe file:

```
mkdir -p cool-app/provision/recipes
touch cool-app/provision/recipes/app-cluster.rb
```

And now, let's edit our recipe file:

```
vi cool-app/provision/recipes/app-cluster.rb
```

Enter the contents shown later in the recipe file:

```
require 'chef/provisioning/vagrant_driver'
with_driver 'vagrant'

vagrant_box 'centos-7.1' do
  url 'https://github.com/CommanderK5/packer-centos-template/releases/
download/0.7.1/vagrant-centos-7.1.box'
end

with_machine_options :vagrant_options => {
  'vm.box' => 'centos-7.1'
}

machine 'db' do
  recipe 'postgresql'
  converge true
end

num_webservers = 2
machine_batch do
  1.upto(num_webservers) do |i|
    machine "web#{i}" do
      recipe 'apache'
      converge true
    end
  end
end
```

Save the file, and we will be ready to run our Chef Provisioning command.
But before we do that, let's go over the recipe a bit.

1. We start it off with a require command that is calling out the dependency on the Vagrant driver.

2. Then, we actually describe the driver we are using in the `with_driver` resource.

3. Next, we use the `vagrant_box` resource, one that is obviously unique to the Vagrant driver, to define our centos-7.1 image.

4. In the next resource, `with_machine_options`, we are describing which image we want to use for our machine commands.

5. Next is our first `machine` resource. This one is describing our database instance. You can see that we are using the PostgreSQL recipe for our DB. Our Chef Provisioning cluster recipe will actually be using our public Chef server as defined in the `.chef/knife.rb` file, so our nodes will be registered to that Chef server as well. As such, the cookbook recipes that we use for our cool-app instances will need to have been uploaded to the Chef server before running the Chef Provisioning command.

6. The last resource block defined in our `app-cluster.rb` file is the `machine_batch` resource. This resource is describing the resources that can be deployed synchronously, in this case our two web servers, web1 and web2. These instances will have the Apache recipe applied, which, like the PostgreSQL cookbook, needs to be uploaded to the Chef server before the execution of our Chef Provisioning command.

Okay, provided we have uploaded the necessary cookbooks to the Chef server, we are ready to run the Chef Provisioning command. So, let's do so.

There are three modes you can employ when using Chef Provisioning; two modes utilize policyfiles and one does not. For this example, we will be using the non-policy mode, so the commands to run Chef Provisioning are:

```
cd ~/chef-repo
chef provision --no-policy --cookbook ./cool-app/provision -r app-cluster
```

We are telling Chef Provisioning that we are using the non-policy mode with the `--no-policy` parameter, then using the `--cookbook` parameter, we say where to find our cluster recipe, and finally using the `-r` parameter, we call out the name of our cluster recipe.

There will be a lot of output during the execution of this command, far too much to show in this space, but if everything goes as planned, your VirtualBox will have three new instances running in it. It will look something like this:

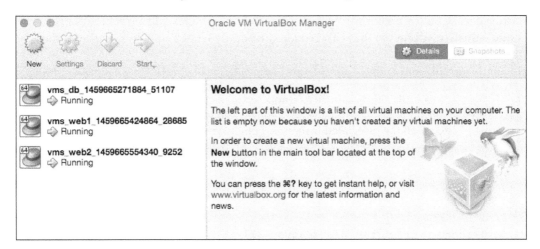

In addition, your Chef server will have three new registered nodes in the Nodes list: db, web1, and web2. It will look something like this:

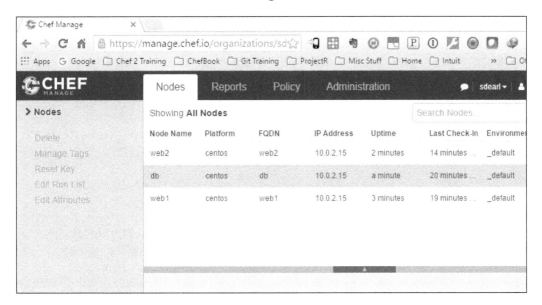

Okay, we've done a test deployment of our app cluster using Chef Provisioning, and we have these three instances and associated nodes in our Chef server that we don't really want hanging around. So what do we do?

Fortunately, Chef Provisioning has resource actions for cleanup time too. We can create a destroy-all recipe that can be called upon by Chef Provisioning that will "destroy all".

 Be careful! This is a quick example script to clean up our test environments. It will unceremoniously deregister all your nodes and delete all the associated instances. I am leaving it to you, the reader, to modify the recipe to be more focused in its clean-up actions.

With that advisory said, here is the destroy-all recipe:

```
cd ~/chef-repo
vi cool-app/provision/recipes/destroy-all.rb
```

Enter the contents as follows:

```
require 'chef/provisioning'
machine_batch do
  machines search(:node, '*:*').map { |n| n.name }
  action :destroy
end
```

Save the file and run the following command:

```
cd ~/chef-repo
chef provision --no-policy --cookbook ./cool-app/provision -r destroy-all
```

Now all of the nodes and associated instances are gone!

A cloud example with AWS

Now that we have successfully deployed our cool-app cluster onto our local workstation with Vagrant and VirtualBox, it's time to try to deploy the app to the cloud. Let's use AWS for this example, creating EC2 instances using Chef Provisioning. This time, however, we do need to install the AWS driver. To do this, enter the following commands:

```
cd ~/chef-repo
chef gem install chef-provisioning-aws
```

I've found that the AWS driver is a little finicky about a few configuration settings. Follow these three steps to make sure that your experience is a successful one.

Create a "config" file in your ~/.aws folder. The contents of the file provide a default section with the AWS region you want to work with. Here are the steps:

```
cd ~/.aws
vi ./config
```

Enter contents like the following:

```
[default]
region = us-west-2
```

It is expecting your credentials to be in the ~/.aws/credentials file. The file has to have the name credentials, and it has to be in that exact location.

Your key pair files need to be in the ~/.ssh/ folder. Even though there is a parameter available in the with_machine_options resource for key_path that you can fill with a different path for your keys, it seems that the AWS driver only looks in ~/.ssh. So, just make sure to save your key files in the ~/.ssh folder.

Okay, now let's create our new AWS cluster recipe file:

```
cd ~/chef-repo
touch cool-app/provision/recipes/aws-cluster.rb
```

Edit the new recipe file:

```
cd ~/chef-repo
vi cool-app/provision/recipes/aws-cluster.rb
```

Enter the following as the contents in the file:

```
require 'chef/provisioning/aws_driver'
with_driver 'aws'

with_machine_options ({
  bootstrap_options: {
    image_id: 'ami-8d5b11bd',
    instance_type: 't1.micro',
    key_name: 'chef-server-ec2',
    security_group_ids: 'chef-provisioning',
  },
  use_private_ip_for_ssh: false,
  transport_address_location: :public_ip,
  ssh_username: 'root',
```

```
      availability_zone: 'us-west-2a',
    })

    machine 'db' do
      recipe 'postgresql'
      converge true
    end

    num_webservers = 2
    machine_batch do
      1.upto(num_webservers) do |i|
        machine "web#{i}" do
          recipe 'apache'
          converge true
        end
      end
    end
```

Now save the file, and let's talk about some of the differences between this recipe and the previous one that we used to provision with the Vagrant driver. The first two directives, `require` and `with_driver`, are specific to our desire to provision using AWS. Then, we have a `with_machine_options` resource. This is the same type of resource we used in the Vagrant example, but this time, we have added several additional parameters that are needed for deployment to AWS, all of which should be very familiar to you if you read *Chapter 6, Provisioning in the Cloud*. After this, we have the `machine` and `machine_batch` resources, which are identical to the ones we used in the earlier example.

Okay, now let's run the Chef Provisioning command to deploy and converge our cluster:

cd ~/chef-repo

chef provision --no-policy --cookbook ./cool-app/provision -r aws-cluster

As before, our cluster recipe is used by Chef Provisioning to deploy our cool-app cluster, and we have fully realized deployment with a single command. The results on AWS should look something like this:

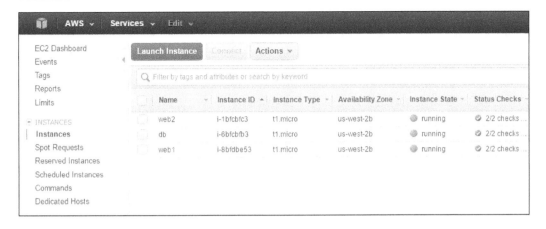

A Docker example

Okay, we are able to use Chef Provisioning to deploy our cluster to our local workstation using the Vagrant driver, and we can deploy the cluster to the cloud with the AWS driver. Let's turn our attention back to Docker and see how we can deploy our cluster as Docker containers.

We need to install the Docker driver for Chef Provisioning. To accomplish this, issue the following command:

```
cd ~/chef-repo
chef gem install chef-provisioning-docker
```

Excellent. Now let's create a new cluster recipe file:

```
cd ~/chef-repo
touch cool-app/provision/recipes/docker-cluster.rb
```

Fill the new recipe file with the following:

```
require 'chef/provisioning/docker_driver'
with_driver 'docker'

machine_image 'ubuntu' do
  machine_options :docker_options => {
    base_image: {
      name: 'ubuntu',
      repository: 'ubuntu',
      tag: '14.04'
    }
  }
```

```
  end

machine 'db' do
  from_image 'ubuntu'
  recipe 'postgresql'
  converge true
end

num_webservers = 2
machine_batch do
  1.upto(num_webservers) do |i|
    machine "web#{i}" do
      from_image 'ubuntu'
      recipe 'apache'
      converge true
    end
  end
end
```

This recipe should now seem pretty familiar. Really the only thing that is new here is that we've used a `machine_image` resource to define what our Docker image should look like, and in the machine resources, we've included the `from_image` directive. Neat, right?

Since this is a section on using Chef Provisioning with Docker, if you haven't installed your Docker environment yet, now this would be a good time to do so. Visit the Docker Toolbox site so you can download and install the toolbox.

Take a look at the URL, `https://www.docker.com/products/docker-toolbox`. Once your toolbox is installed, you'll want to launch both the "Kitematic UI" and the "Docker Quickstart Terminal". These are the tools provided by the Docker Toolbox:

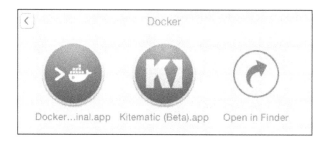

Now, within the Quickstart Terminal, you will run your Chef Provisioning commands. Let's go ahead and run the command:

```
cd ~/chef-repo
chef provision --no-policy --cookbook ./cool-app/provision -r docker-cluster
```

There will be significant output from this command, but it is interesting, so here is what you should see:

```
$ cd ~/chef-repo
$ chef provision --no-policy --cookbook ./cool-app/provision -r docker-cluster
Installing Cookbook Gems:
Compiling Cookbooks...
Recipe: provision::docker-cluster
  * machine_image[ubuntu] action create (up to date)
  * machine[db] action converge
    - create node db at https://api.chef.io/organizations/sdearl
    -   add normal.tags = nil
    -   add normal.chef_provisioning = {"from_image"=>"ubuntu",
"reference"=>{"driver_url"=>"docker:tcp://192.168.99.100:2376", "driver_
version"=>"0.9.0", "allocated_at"=>"2016-04-04 04:07:32 UTC", "host_
node"=>"https://api.chef.io/organizations/sdearl/nodes/", "container_
name"=>"db", "image_id"=>nil, "docker_options"=>nil, "container_
id"=>nil}}
    -   update run_list from [] to ["recipe[postgresql]"]
    - create container to converge db
    - start converge container chef-converge.db
    - commit and delete converged container for db
    - update node db at https://api.chef.io/organizations/sdearl
    -   update normal.chef_provisioning.reference.container_id from nil
to "43ac4f550657946e9205315d4bdddE049ca2ba0ad769854075f9bfdc74d3df23"
    - create final container for db
    - start container db
  * machine_batch[default] action converge
    - [web1] create node web1 at https://api.chef.io/organizations/sdearl
    - [web1]   add normal.tags = nil
```

```
    -  [web1]    add normal.chef_provisioning = {"from_image"=>"ubuntu",
"reference"=>{"driver_url"=>"docker:tcp://192.168.99.100:2376", "driver_
version"=>"0.9.0", "allocated_at"=>"2016-04-04 04:07:36 UTC", "host_
node"=>"https://api.chef.io/organizations/sdearl/nodes/", "container_
name"=>"web1", "image_id"=>nil, "docker_options"=>nil, "container_
id"=>nil}}
    -  [web1]    update run_list from [] to ["recipe[apache]"]
    -  [web2] create node web2 at https://api.chef.io/organizations/sdearl
    -  [web2]    add normal.tags = nil
    -  [web2]    add normal.chef_provisioning = {"from_image"=>"ubuntu",
"reference"=>{"driver_url"=>"docker:tcp://192.168.99.100:2376", "driver_
version"=>"0.9.0", "allocated_at"=>"2016-04-04 04:07:36 UTC", "host_
node"=>"https://api.chef.io/organizations/sdearl/nodes/", "container_
name"=>"web2", "image_id"=>nil, "docker_options"=>nil, "container_
id"=>nil}}
    -  [web2]    update run_list from [] to ["recipe[apache]"]
    -  [web1] create container to converge web1
    -  [web2] create container to converge web2
    -  [web1] start converge container chef-converge.web1
    -  [web2] start converge container chef-converge.web2
    -  [web1] commit and delete converged container for web1
    -  [web2] commit and delete converged container for web2
    -  [web1] update node web1 at https://api.chef.io/organizations/sdearl
    -  [web1]    update normal.chef_provisioning.
reference.container_id from nil to
"fcbdc9eb4de28474237c4ec146f3852ce796ff998af23c5bff5792a3a224d119"
    -  [web1] create final container for web1
    -  [web2] update node web2 at https://api.chef.io/organizations/sdearl
    -  [web2]    update normal.chef_provisioning.
reference.container_id from nil to
"c6c89b0c946cb76156fbaefb32a3f54bdba1e85f3a25025305ab6aa56134160d"
    -  [web2] create final container for web2
    -  [web2] start container web2
    -  [web1] start container web1
```

Some things to note in the output include the following:

1. The machine image "Ubuntu" is created first.

2. Then, we converge the DB machine. This phase ends with the starting of the DB container.

3. After this, we get to the `machine_batch` resource, which will converge two machines—web1 and web2.

Note how the output from those actions are intermixed. This is because of the synchronous nature of using the `machine_batch` resource type. Here too, this ends with the starting of our two web containers. Success!

Now we have our cool-app cluster running in Docker containers. It should look something like this:

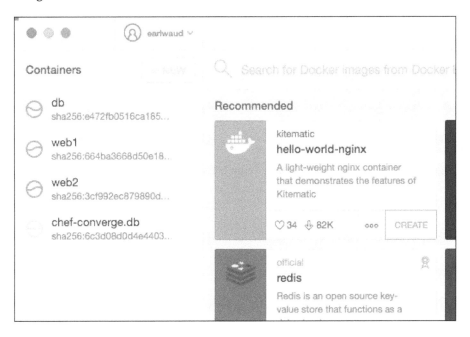

References

- Here are the GitHub repos for a few of the Chef Provisioning drivers, each of which provides examples for using Chef Provisioning as its named provider:

    ° AWS driver: `https://github.com/chef/chef-provisioning-aws`

    ° Azure driver: `https://github.com/chef/chef-provisioning-azure`

    ° Docker driver: `https://github.com/chef/chef-provisioning-docker`

    ° Vagrant driver: `https://github.com/chef/chef-provisioning-vagrant`

- ° Google driver: `https://github.com/chef/chef-provisioning-google`

- ° VSphere driver: `https://github.com/CenturyLinkCloud/chef-provisioning-vsphere`

- Here is the link to the public Vagrant boxes: `http://www.vagrantbox.es`

- Learn all of the AWS create instance options at `http://docs.aws.amazon.com/sdkforruby/api/Aws/EC2/Resource.html#create_instances-instance_method`

- You can download the Docker Toolbox at `https://www.docker.com/products/docker-toolbox`

Summary

In this chapter, we have learned how to master Chef Provisioning Finally.

Index

Symbols

.chef folder files
  using 23, 24
.kitchen.yml configuration
  URL 211

A

Amazon EC2 console
  URL 158
Atom editor
  URL 44
attribute precedence hierarchy
  about 66
  attribute precedence factors 66, 67
  resulting precedence hierarchy 68
attributes, recipes
  URL 6
AWS create instance options
  URL 228
AWS driver
  URL 227
AWS EC2 instances
  Chef Server, installing 154-158
  EC2 authentication 150
  key pairs, creating 150-152
  provisioning 150
  security groups, creating 152, 153
AWS Marketplace
  URL 159
azure-cookbook
  URL 168
Azure driver
  URL 227

Azure PublishSettings file
  URL 168

B

base image container
  URL 186
Berkshelf 13
bootstrapping data
  URL 43

C

CentOS instance image
  adding, to provision 132, 133
Certified Culinary Educator (CCE) 35
Chef
  about 2, 3
  Chef Development Kit (ChefDK) 8
  cookbooks 5
  data bags 7
  environments 7
  Ohai 5
  on-premise (private) Chef Server,
      setting up 8-12
  recipes 5
  references 3, 12
  resources 6
  roles 6
  run lists 5
  supermarket 8
  version, determining 2
chef-apply
  about 31
  advantages 31, 32
  references 32

CPSIA information can be obtained
at www.ICGtesting.com
Printed in the USA
LVHW100407131218
600301LV00014B/662/P